JUDAS

ALSO BY PETER STANFORD

How To Read a Graveyard:
Journeys in the Company of the Dead

The Death of a Child (editor)

The Extra Mile: A 21st Century Pilgrimage

C Day-Lewis: A Life

Why I Am Still A Catholic:
Essays in Faith and Perseverance (editor)

Heaven: A Travellers' Guide to the Undiscovered Country

Bronwen Astor: Her Life and Times

The She-Pope: A Quest for the Truth Behind
The Mystery of Pope Joan

The Devil: A Biography

The Outcasts' Outcast: A Life of Lord Longford

Cardinal Hume and the Changing Face of English Catholicism

Catholics and Sex (with Kate Saunders)

Believing Bishops (with Simon Lee)

JUDAS

The Most Hated Name In History

Peter Stanford

COUNTERPOINT | BERKELEY

Originally published by Hodder & Stoughton Limited,
a Hachette UK Limited company

Library of Congress Cataloging-in-Publication Data

Stanford, Peter, 1961-
Judas : the most hated name in history / Peter Stanford.
    pages cm
Includes bibliographical references and index.
ISBN 978-1-61902-709-1
1. Judas Iscariot. I. Title.
BS2460.J8S73 2016
226'.092—dc23
        2015036010

COUNTERPOINT
2560 Ninth Street, Suite 318
Berkeley, CA 94710
www.counterpointpress.com

Printed in the United States of America
Distributed by Publishers Group West

10 9 8 7 6 5 4 3 2 1

For Sue and Steve:
for your encouragement and enthusiasm

Contents

Part Three:
Judas – God's agent

The Field of Blood, Jerusalem

'Twas the body of Judas Iscariot
Lay in the Field of Blood;
'Twas the soul of Judas Iscariot
Beside the body stood.

Robert Buchanan: *The Ballad of*
Judas Iscariot (1874)

The signage in Jerusalem is, at best, intermittent. On the journey in from the airport at Tel Aviv, there are familiar, standard-issue, large roadside boards, with directions in three languages – Arabic, Hebrew and English. Once inside the Old City, with its Jewish, Muslim, Christian and Armenian quarters, it all gets much more hit and miss: odd arrows here and there, often with any wording obscured by a market vendor's display of holy pictures, pottery or pyjamas, pointing variously to the Western Wall, holy of holies for Jews, or the Church of the Holy Sepulchre, standing on what is believed to be the site where Jesus was crucified, or the Al-Aqsa mosque, high on the list of must-see sites for Muslims. But never all three at once. Perhaps – to apply the most benign standards – it is assumed that in such a small space (within its ancient walls, the Old City of Jerusalem amounts to just under a square kilometre), visitors will inevitably stumble on this extraordinary trinity if they walk around for long enough.

In my wanderings, I only spy one sign for Hakeldama

(originally the Aramaic *hagel dema*, sometimes rendered as the Greek *Akeldama*, and meaning 'Field of Blood'), the spot where Christian tradition holds that one of the twelve apostles, Judas Iscariot, ignominiously committed suicide after betraying Jesus. And, even then, it is very much a forgotten footnote, down in the corner of a weather-beaten outdoor pilgrims' map on display at the church of Saint Peter in Gallicantu, outside the Old City. Everywhere else is name-checked in big letters, with a rough drawing next to it. Hakeldama, though, floats on the margins of the map, as if halfway to oblivion.

If visitors did once seek out the scene of Judas' last moments on earth, and there is plenty of historical evidence that pilgrims did, then it has now fallen from the itineraries of the estimated 3.5 million tourists who come to Jerusalem each year. Such modern neglect has a certain logic. Encouraging hordes to seek out the spot where Christianity's most notorious traitor hanged himself would, in secular times, add a curious voyeuristic twist to 2,000 years of vilifying Judas, whom the gospels describe as partaking in the first-ever Eucharist at the Last Supper, but still managing afterwards to sell his master for a measly thirty pieces of silver.

That tawdry transaction was the first never-to-be-forgotten moment of infamy in the tale of Judas that has been handed down the centuries. In the core texts of Christianity, the second instalment comes soon afterwards when, in the Garden of Gethsemane, Judas identifies Jesus to a detachment of soldiers with the notorious 'Judas kiss'. That embrace, outwardly of friendship but in reality of betrayal, has come to sum up the reputation of the traitor within Jesus' trusted inner circle. And then, with Christianity for centuries confining Judas' biography to a three-act drama, there is the concluding spectacle of the false apostle yielding to despair and killing himself.

What is there, then, to see at the Field of Blood, other than the ugliest side of human nature – and frankly there is enough of that to witness day to day in the grating tension between holiness and darkness in the divided city of Jerusalem? Judas' place of death, moreover, offers no enticing prospect of the sort of spiritual nourishment that today draws even the most sceptical visitors to Jerusalem's array of 'holy places'. All of these sites may still cause endless, bitter disputes between the faiths. The golden-topped Dome of the Rock shrine, for example, alongside its near neighbour, the Al-Aqsa mosque, sits atop the Temple Mount, simultaneously hallowed ground in Judaism, and once commandeered by the invading Crusaders in the twelfth century for their own Christian church. Yet it still attracts crowds. We wait in long lines to pass through security points designed to filter out those fanatics with their guns and bombs who might be tempted to press by force their particular branch of religion's claim. Once inside, though, whatever its bloody, factional past and present, this sacred ground still has the capacity to inspire.

By contrast, at Hakeldama, Judas' last footprint on earth represents more of a cautionary tale, of the type once found in now-neglected children's literature such as *Struwwelpeter*,[1] and from which we adults are increasingly conditioned to recoil as too blunt, too black and white for modern sensibilities. Down the ages Judas has been singled out from innumerable other human options as absolutely the worst of the worst. In John's gospel, he is damned not just as the devil incarnate but also as 'the son of perdition'.[2] Pope Leo the Great, in the fifth century, demonised Judas as 'the wickedest man that ever lived'.[3] Nine hundred years later, in the greatest poem of the Middle Ages, Dante Alighieri's *Inferno*, he is sentenced to the ninth and final circle of hell, reserved for those who have committed the most heinous crimes of betrayal known to humankind, an eternal, icy torment shared with Brutus and Cassius, murderers of Julius Caesar, and, of course, Satan, from whose frozen mouth Judas dangles, half digested, his legs kicking in vain against his fate to the very end.[4]

And Judas Iscariot's name continues in the twenty-first century to represent a crushing rebuke, a despicable traitor, as in the controversialist Lady Gaga's 2011 single, 'Judas', about being in love with a bad 'un. 'Jesus is my virtue', she sings in a promotional video bursting with religious imagery, 'and Judas is the demon I cling to'.

Yet, even for that contemporary minority with an overactive interest in the macabre – and there are plenty, I have observed, who like nothing better than ghoulishly to travel the globe seeking out 'haunted' places where horrific deeds took place[5] – the Field of Blood scores poorly as a desirable destination. There are doubts, above all, about its authenticity.

Whose blood is it that is being remembered? That of Jesus, sacrificed on the cross on Calvary on Good Friday to save humankind, or of Judas, spilled in death following his betrayal of his master? In his gospel, Saint Matthew makes plain that it is Jesus' blood.[6] He writes bleakly and movingly (for this listener at least, when hearing the passage read aloud during mass over the years) of Judas' wretched remorse once he had sold Jesus out. He tries to salve his conscience by returning his fee – the money paid to him for Jesus' blood – but the chief priests refuse it as tainted. So, the outcast to trump all outcasts flings down the coins in the sanctuary of the Temple, takes himself off to an unnamed site and there commits suicide. The Jewish leaders thereafter pick up the sullied loot that is blood money for Jesus, and use it to purchase a plot, as a graveyard for foreigners, 'called the Field of Blood'.

This account in Matthew does not place Judas' suicide itself at Hakeldama. Indeed there is another tradition, albeit now muted, that suggests it took place within the Old City itself. So popular was it in its time that twelfth-century pilgrims would trudge along to visit the Vicus Arcus Judae (Street of the Arch of Judas), when the Christian Crusaders were running the city. One of the senior church leaders of that time, Archbishop William of Tyre, writes of Jerusalem, the city where he was born: 'By the covered street, you go through the Latin Exchange to a street called the Street of the Arch of Judas . . . because they say Judas hanged himself there upon a stone arch.'[7] On maps of the period, X marks the spot.

By contrast, in the Acts of the Apostles, coming after the gospels in the running order of the New Testament, the blood staining the Field of Blood is not that of Jesus but Judas.[8] Moreover, Acts talks not of a suicide but of Judas dying by a kind of spontaneous combustion of his body that will find no name in medical dictionaries. Saint Peter, busy stamping his authority as Jesus' anointed first leader of his fledgling church, describes, with the relish of the righteous, how Judas, his one-time fellow apostle, spent his ill-gotten silver pieces on purchasing the field himself, where 'he fell headlong and burst open, and all his entrails poured out'. It was as if Judas had been struck down by a thunderbolt that split him in two. When news spread of this gruesome death, Peter continues, 'the field came to be called the Bloody Acre, in their language Hakeldama'.

To thicken this historical mist, the precise site of Hakeldama is itself only a matter of tradition, rather than archaeological fact. It stands on a barren hillside on the south side of the valley of Hinnom, perched precariously in one of the cat's cradle of stringy ravines that intersect the peaks and troughs of Jerusalem, but this location was simply the one chosen by the early Christians. In the centuries immediately following Jesus' death, they picked out places in and around Jerusalem to associate with events described in the gospels, some on the basis of more compelling evidence than others. Their habit of praying at such sites was then taken up with gusto from the third century onwards by a new flood of pilgrims who came to the city with the specific intent of walking in the footsteps of their Lord.

On these itineraries, Hakeldama featured as the very spot where Judas lowered himself into the fires of hell with the jerk of a rope round his neck. One of the earliest references comes in *Onomasticon*, a study of place names found in Holy Scripture, compiled by Eusebius, Bishop of Caesarea in Palestine in the 330s, and one of the most hallowed of the early church historians.[9] He refers on several occasions to the pilgrim site at the Field of Blood, and places it in the valley of Hinnom, south of Mount Zion (save on one occasion, when he unaccountably moves it north of the same peak).

Eusebius' survey follows the bountiful visit to Jerusalem in 326 of Helena, mother of Constantine the Great, the Roman Emperor who in 313 had granted liberty to Christianity after centuries of persecution. A zealous Christian convert (and, by some accounts, a former barmaid who wasn't married to Constantine's father), the Empress Helena came to the city with her son's blessing, and his permission to build monuments to her faith. Principal among the works she commissioned was the Church of the Holy Sepulchre itself, where it is said she had found the remains of the 'true cross' on which Jesus had been crucified. Among her other projects, though, was a new cemetery chapel on the hillside of the Field of Blood. It marked what had, since Jesus' time, been a catacomb for the Christian dead. (This claim has some authenticity. A shroud has been found at Hakeldama still bearing clumps of human hair, dated as first century CE.)

It was not just Judas' reputation that drew these diligent, pious early church pilgrims. It was on this same spot, in the niches carved out of the rock face of Hakeldama, that the apostles were said to have hidden away once Jesus was arrested and until his resurrection. Unlike Judas' connection to Hakeldama, this claim has no basis whatsoever in the gospels, yet still became part of the tradition that developed in these first centuries of the church. Later the Crusaders, arriving at the end of the eleventh century on papal instructions to conquer Jerusalem on behalf of

Christians, were to replace Helena's cemetery chapel with a much larger structure, presumably because their arrival caused so many deaths and the foreigners' graveyard was much in demand.

So, unsignposted though it may be today, people did once head in numbers for Hakeldama – to bury and remember the dead, to follow the trail of the apostles, and to recall Judas. It was the last of these three, its link to Jesus' betrayer, that seems to have exerted the greatest pull. In the earliest surviving account of a Christian pilgrimage to Jerusalem, the *Itinerary* of the anonymous 'Pilgrim of Bordeaux' who came in 333, the author makes reference to 'returning to the city from Aceldama', having seen 'in a dark corner an iron chain with which the unhappy Judas hanged himself'.[10]

The chain seems to be his own embellishment on Matthew's gospel, which makes no mention of any such thing. It is by no means the first addition, and certainly is not the last. In the 680s, the French bishop Arculf made his own contribution. In *De locis sanctis* ('Concerning Sacred Places'), his account of a journey to the Holy Land, he reports with some excitement going to Hakeldama and seeing the very fig tree from which the traitor was found hanging.[11] The fig, by tradition the tree of life, was being crudely imported into the story of an inglorious death to amplify the significance of Judas' story in the Christian narrative. And it has been talked up ever since. There, but for the grace of God . . .

'You're very lucky,' pronounces the short, stout, balaclava'd Greek Orthodox nun who peers out round the half-opened red metal front gate of Saint Onouphrius' Monastery. Since the 1890s it has been the only lived-in structure on Hakeldama, a small, fortress-like compound, clinging to the rock face and surrounded by high walls. They are topped by barbed wire, above which peep the branches of trees. Perhaps the fig tree that Arculf saw is still in bloom? Or, better still – and now my imagination is racing away – a Judas Tree, the pink-flowering *Cercis siliquastrum*, which reputedly got its name because, in other embellished accounts, its branches once played host to Judas' rope?

'We're closed,' says the nun, with a short-sighted smile, 'but I'll let you in.' The notice board outside specifies the monastery's brief, weekly opening hours, including this particular morning and this precise time, but it feels rude to point this out as she hospitably swings the door open wide. She had been showing out some workmen who had been helping her in the monastery gardens, she explains, when she spotted me making my way up the unmarked muddy track that leads to the monastery from the main road on the valley floor. Otherwise, she implies, the bell would have gone unanswered and made my pilgrimage fruitless.

Perhaps this absence of welcome – in marked contrast to every other site I visit in Jerusalem – is another reason for the decline in numbers heading for Hakeldama. We step into a wide, glazed porch area, with large picture windows looking out northwards towards the Old City, and the white, marbled steps made up of gravestones in the Jewish cemetery as they climb up the slopes of the Mount of Olives. Around us are a couple of dusty plastic tables with cellophane-wrapped floral covers, which might once have belonged in a café, long since abandoned. In one corner stands a small, crudely constructed piety stall with sachets of dried herbs for sale, plus booklets and prayer cards about Saint Onouphrius, a fourth-century hermit monk believed to be buried here. But, curiously, not so much as a passing reference to Judas.

The nun – who doesn't tell me her name – wonders aloud what I am doing there. 'No one much comes any more,' she continues, almost to herself. Her English is perfect, and she has pulled down the flap of her balaclava sufficiently so that her words are not swallowed by the wool, but I still can't detect whether it is relief or regret in her voice. There are, she reveals guilelessly, only two sisters living in the monastery now (a third died recently) and – here she gestures to the walled garden behind her, visible through an open gate – it is all getting too much for her. A pile of pruned olive tree branches and ripped-up geranium stalks lies by the entrance, waiting to be removed.

I'm starting to wonder if I have come to the wrong place and eventually find a gap in her monologue to slip in Judas' name. There's an immediate pause, and then the nun sighs impatiently. The flap goes back up over her mouth. 'You are welcome to look round,' she says, suddenly weary, 'but the garden is private.' She turns to retreat into it. 'Is there a particular place in the monastery where Judas' death is marked?' My question is addressed to her back. I'm choosing my words as neutrally as I can, but a part of me is hoping that she will point to a tree.

Why suddenly so literal? Reason seems temporarily to have given way in me to what, with hindsight, I diagnose as a mild case of Jerusalem Syndrome, apparently a widespread affliction that sidetracks otherwise rational visitors to this city into religious fervour and a to-the-letter take on various holy books.[12] Elsewhere, for example, I have watched myself dutifully bobbing up and down to touch outcrops of otherwise unremarkable rock where various events in Jesus' life are said to have taken place. It's given me a taste for the literal. There must be some remnant of 2,000 years ago here, too, surely?

The nun turns and shakes her head pityingly, as if spotting my malady before I do. 'Our chapel is through there.' She points to an arch at the other end of the porch and then she really does disappear through the garden gate, closing it firmly behind her, leaving me all alone in this peculiar place, where visitors no longer come, and Judas is he-who-must-not-be-named.

I hadn't exactly been expecting an all-singing, all-dancing celebration of his life – the sort of dramatic re-enactment pumped out by a humming overhead projector onto a video screen that has become de rigueur in historic houses nowadays. But it had seemed reasonable, in planning this visit, and given the long

– though admittedly thinning – historical trail of pilgrims coming
to the spot, to hope for some sort of surviving discreet memorial:
a plaque, perhaps, to mark the supposed place of Judas' death,
with solemn words and an unspoken warning not to follow in the
traitor's footsteps; or else a prayer card on offer, or an invitation
to light a candle, as an opening onto a deeper reflection upon his
story, and the still-unresolved questions it poses. Whether, for
example, to abhor Judas, in line with the church's traditional and
lurid blanket condemnation of him as Satan's tool, or to be
swayed by the gentle recasting of his role as God's agent that has
gone on in recent times.

In 1963, well before he so publicly embraced Jesus, Bob Dylan
wrote a song called 'With God On Our Side' that challenged
America's claim that its actions, especially in going to war, were
somehow divinely-inspired. Dylan also included a verse that
touched on the modern re-evaluation of Judas where he asked
whether Jesus' betrayer might also be judged as having had God
on his side when he planted his traitor's kiss.

Out-and-out traitor or cog-in-the-wheel of a divine plan? The
same question, albeit without musical accompaniment, was posed
in 2006 by a senior Vatican official, Monsignor Walter Brandmuller,
head of the Pontifical Committee for Historical Science.[14]

Plain and white on the outside, save for the trademark onion
dome of Greek Orthodox churches, inside the monastery's chapel
is small, cluttered and low-ceilinged, with stalactites of hanging
lamps dividing up the space that is mostly burrowed out of the
rock face behind. Its primary purpose, it quickly becomes
apparent when I manage in the gloaming to locate the light switch,
is to honour the obscure Saint Onouphrius.

Christianity has a long track record of playing fast and loose
with its own history, covering up episodes it would rather forget
with a sugar coating of legend. So ancient pagan water shrines,

IO

for example, were, in the early church, redesignated as 'holy wells' and assigned to a suitably devout and often manufactured Christian saint. In Jerusalem, this form of victor's justice, burying the past and substituting a new one, is more marked than anywhere else I have ever come across. Layers of story, from whichever faith group was then controlling the city, are superseded by new layers, put down by new rulers, from a different faith tradition, once they wrest control. And on and on as Jerusalem has passed back and forth through the hands of Jews, Christians and Muslims to this day. Yet, probably because of all the competing claims to the ownership of the place that exist, now and apparently always, this is also a city where the surface layer of history is notoriously thin, allowing previous authorised versions to leak through.

Here at Hakeldama, the current top layer is a historically tenuous connection with a fourth-century hermit. Very little is known about Onouphrius, but even within these crumbs there is no real link to Jerusalem. No wonder so few people come to visit. So why has it happened? Why has the cult of an obscure saint been written so large as to all but obliterate the shadow that Judas' corpse, hanging on the end of a rope, casts over his 'bloody acre'?

I'm still puzzling over that one when a previous layer peeps through. As I search in the darkened corners of the chapel, I come across a single, dusty icon, dated 1912, hidden behind an Ovaltine-coloured marble plinth. It makes a crude but revealing attempt to weave Onouphrius into Judas' traitorous tale. The richly decorated panel, in greens, reds and blues against a gold background, features most obviously the risen Christ in the centre, the blood still flowing crimson from the wounds made by the crown of thorns on his head. Around this dominant figure, though, is arranged a series of small vignettes, telling in chronological order those three best-known gospel episodes in Judas' journey to this very place. Plus an extra two.

The Judas icon in the chapel of Saint
Onouphrius' Monastery at Hakeldama
in Jerusalem.

It kicks off in the top left corner with Judas being rewarded for betraying Jesus to them by the Jewish chief priests with a swag bag, marked with the number thirty in red, in case there is any room for doubt as to what it contains. Judas' countenance is monk-like behind his beard, but otherwise inscrutable, neither villainously licking his lips at the prospect of spending his ill-gotten gains, nor troubled by selling out his leader so cheaply. The conventions of icon painting, favouring flat, two-dimensional, slightly featureless faces, rule out any strong hints as to the emotional or psychological temperature, but there is one visual clue. Judas' hair has a copperish hue, the artist picking up on a long tradition in Christianity of portraying him as a red-head which, according to medieval writers, was the sure sign of a moral degenerate. Shakespeare, in *As You Like It*, likens Orlando's hair to Judas' red mop, describing it as 'the dissembling colour' and one that reveals 'a deceiver from head to toe'.

Moving over, in the top right-hand corner, is the Judas kiss by which he identified his master to the soldiers in the Garden of Gethsemane. Judas is much shorter than Jesus, as if to emphasise his moral inferiority. His upturned face now carries with it just a touch of malevolence. He purses his lips as he reaches towards the impassive, saintly face of God's Son to land his kiss, but there is no physical contact.

Back in the bottom left is the first addition – the remorseful scene from Matthew's gospel that is usually overlooked in the standard three-act account of Judas' place in Christian history.[15] Here, an emotionless Judas attempts to hand back to the Jewish authorities the thirty pieces of silver, but fails, leaving the coins scattered on the floor. Before moving on to Judas' demise in the final corner, however, the icon painter, from nowhere, conjures an image of a heavenly angel giving the bread of the Eucharist to Saint Onouphrius, immediately recognisable from the other representations around the chapel by his Rapunzel-length white beard, and simple loincloth of leaves, as befitting a hermit monk living in the wilds of the Egyptian desert.

The artist's intention seems to be to substitute an image of the monastery's patron saint receiving the communion bread instead of Judas. In three of the four gospel accounts, Judas is named as attending the Last Supper, where Jesus breaks bread and drinks wine, describes it as his body and blood, and so inaugurates what remains the central sacrament of the Christian Church.[16] Theologians have long been troubled by Jesus' willingness to allow Judas to be there at this key event for the future life of his church. This is, after all, an apostle who he knows is about to betray him. So here that unease is clumsily sidestepped by painting out Judas and inserting Onouphrius.

The story can then move seamlessly back on track for its usual conclusion: the death of Judas, hanging by a rope from a branch. His robe is now green to match the foliage – compared to the blue or yellow of earlier – and his eyes are shut. His face is suffused – I cannot help thinking – with a kind of peace; certainly not agony, though potentially a wish to be forgotten. He doesn't look like a man expecting hell, the eternal fate Christian tradition has given him,[17] in the company of his seducer, the devil.

If it is oblivion Judas is seeking, however, then here at Hakeldama his wish has been granted. The backdrop to this concluding scene is blank. There is no representation of Hakeldama; not even a hint of a hill, a garden or the Jerusalem skyline. The place of the betrayer's lonely demise has been moved to no man's land – out of sight, out of mind.

Behind the icon are various openings in the rock, their entrances secured with iron grilles. These are, according to Christian legend, the caves where the terrified apostles hid after Jesus had been arrested. The gospels recount how only Peter (and, in John's gospel, an unnamed disciple who knows the high priest[18]) follow their leader as he stands trial, and how only the women among the disciples pray at the foot of the cross as their Lord expires. The others were cowering here, scared that the soldiers would soon come for them. They only emerged after Jesus' crucifixion and resurrection.

The association is yet another piece of imprecise geography, inherited from the early church, but it offers, nevertheless, an intriguing prospect. If it is to be believed, in one part of Hakeldama, one of the twelve apostles was swinging dead at the end of a rope, while in another, his erstwhile companions were in hiding. Did they hear him cry out as the rope tightened and do nothing? Or did he die silently, such was his overwhelming sense of shame? Was it only when they summoned the courage to emerge from hiding that they discovered his body? Did they bury it? Or feel regret? Or just step over it – the bad apple getting what he 'deserved'?

I pause on leaving the chapel for a moment before deciding to brave it and give the recalcitrant nun-custodian one more try. Standing by the pile of branches and geranium stems, I call through the closed gate. 'Sister?' There's no reply for a long time, though I can hear the telltale rustling of a busy gardener. In contrast to the barren hillside all around the monastery, what I can discern through the grille is a patch of colour, shade and life that roughly equates to the *pairidaeza*, the verdant walled garden in an otherwise arid place, of the ancient kings of Persia, which gave us the word paradise.

'Sister,' I try again. And again, the note of apology less pronounced each time. Eventually the sound of leaves shaking and plants being pruned stops. I hear footsteps coming towards me. The nun reappears at the gate. 'I'm busy,' she says with little grace. Honesty being the best approach, as the benign nuns of my Catholic childhood once taught me, I explain about my interest in Judas, that I'm writing a biography of him, hence my visit to Hakeldama. And I ask about the icon in the chapel.

Her reply is a shrug, as if to say, 'It is what it is.' Then she softens a little. She steps back into the entrance porch and reaches up to put her hand on a curious D-shaped stone that is plastered into the wall of the porch. I hadn't noticed it when I first came in, but why would I? It is the same pale, sandy colour as all the others around it. The only thing that makes it stand out is its mildly irregular shape. 'Some people have said that this is the rock where he died,' she offers. 'What sort of people?' 'Archaeologists who have come here.' So there are still visitors in search of Judas. I wonder how she greeted them?

I am trying to reconcile a stone with the traditional image of a tree. Then it occurs to me that there is also Saint Peter's account in the Acts of the Apostles, where Judas' innards spill out. Onto this rock? 'I suppose so,' the nun replies. She looks sceptical. As well she might. It is not name-checked in the gospels, but then Jerusalem is full of similar rocks that I have been busy kneeling down to touch reverently. They, though, are surrounded by ornate marble frames, or found in the centre of the floor of great basilicas. Here the physical connection with the past has apparently been deliberately lost at shoulder height in a structural wall. It feels too aggressive to point that out. Instead I stretch my hand up and place it there for a few seconds. The nun looks on, unmoved.

The section in the Acts of the Apostles about Judas and his grisly end at Hakeldama is followed by a quotation from the Old Testament Book of Psalms. The whole of the New Testament is littered with references back to the Jewish Scriptures, the first Christian writers summoning up the past, its promises and prophecies, in an effort to make sense of Jesus' life, death and resurrection. 'Let his camp be reduced to ruin, let there be no one to live in it.'[19] A prophecy of Judas' death and final resting place? That is a stretch. But as a description of the rocky, barren, bare hillside of Hakeldama, and the absence of welcome that awaits contemporary visitors here, it couldn't be more accurate.

I'm shown out of the monastery. Bundled out might be more accurate. The clang of the door behind me signals how anxious my host was to put an end to the awkward questions about any traces of the traitor her monastery obscures.

It has been raining over the previous days and the track back down to the busy road below is thick with mud; the sort of reddish, viscous clay that endorses Matthew's talk of the 'Field of Blood' once having been a potter's field, its soil useless for agriculture or grazing, but a source of raw material for potters. On the way down, placing my feet carefully so as not to slip, I spot small white and blue markings, painted onto a rock, and an arrow pointing the way up another path that doubles back through the boulders to the ridge above the monastery. They are the same colour as the Greek flag I have just seen flying inside the monastery, and I decide on no basis in particular that they may therefore be a clue that Orthodox pilgrims do, contrary to all indications, actually still come here, even go in procession.

I start to follow them, picking my way over cans, plastic containers, shopping bags, even a discarded garden chair. Then the markers peter out. Hakeldama hasn't been taking new burials for over 150 years, but still I find myself in a charnel ground of modern debris. The contrast between the crowds and bustle of the Old City of Jerusalem – visible on the horizon, apparently so close I could almost reach out and touch it – and this desolate, abandoned place couldn't be plainer. It is a desert cheek-by-jowl with the city, and in all religious mythology the desert is where the evil spirits reside; where, in the gospels, the devil preys on Jesus during his forty days in the wilderness.[20]

Up on the ridge above the monastery, there is, I discover, no hoped-for peephole into its closed-off garden. Instead, what looms suddenly large, having been invisible from the road, is the ruined stone arch of the Crusader chapel, almost buried in the hillside. A steep pathway curls round and down into it, but reveals only another rubbish dump. The catacomb burial niches, cut into the rock behind, are visible, but inaccessible without clambering through the contents of Jerusalem's bins.

From the top of Hakeldama, I look out. The valley below is today called (and signposted) Hinnom, but is also known by its Old Testament name of Gehenna, the place where apostates sacrificed their children to gods by burning them alive.[21] It was regarded as cursed then, and conflated with an earthly hell. The same connotations are taken up in the New Testament, in the Talmud of Judaism, and in the Qur'an, where the word for hell – *jahannam* – is derived from Gehenna. And this is still the bleakest of all bleak places, as suitable as Dante's final layer of hell for a last, damning glimpse of the greatest of all sinners. So suitable, indeed, that Matthew, the only one of the gospel writers to describe the treacherous apostle's death, may just have been reaching back into his memory for the name of the worst location he knew and making it the site of Judas' last minutes on earth.

It's speculation, but that has long been what has happened with Judas' story because, striking as it is in the gospel accounts, it also remains frustratingly incomplete, leaving much unsaid, gaps begging to be filled. And fill them we certainly have, with 2,000 years of embellishment, straining for effect, stereotypes and symbolism tailored to the concerns of each particular age. Even here at Hakeldama, where archaeology rubs up against the detail of the gospels, there can, I realise, be no such thing as certainty.

This godforsaken landscape has highlighted, too, one of the key challenges in embarking on a biography of Judas Iscariot. Every detail of his story is capable of being looked at from a dizzying array of perspectives, through any number of historical lenses and prejudices. The questions that arise – who is telling his story, what precisely are they saying, and why are they doing it? –

are, of course, the same as arise in writing any conventional biography, but in the case of Judas, each aspect of his story has already been stretched and strained, through century after century of contexts, most recently with the much-hyped publication in 2006 of the rediscovered *Gospel of Judas*.[22]

And yet, the memory of Judas, once marked here but now all but discarded in this valley of death and debris, lives on. It is not finished with, like the rubbish on the ground around me, nor is it part of the flotsam and jetsam of religious history no longer required in our shiny new secular, scientific and sceptical age. Even those who would struggle to arrange the basic events of Jesus' life in any sort of order recognise Judas' name, and may even deploy it occasionally as a term of abuse. It is being constantly recycled as the worst of insults, 'the most hated name in human history', as Bob Dylan put it recently, returning to a character who clearly still fascinates him.[23] And while we continue so readily to scapegoat those who cross us, or take a path we disapprove of, or express an opinion that we find threatening, then the most basic story of Judas, arguably the biggest scapegoat in human history, is being repeated time and again.

Part One:

Judas – the evidence

A

Asparagus

Collecting cute things children say about God is popular on some faith-based websites, particularly in the United States. One of the most quoted in recent years features an (unnamed) child's précis of the Bible. The line that raised the warmest smile – and has become the tagline for the whole text – tells how, 'Jesus had twelve opossums. The worst one was Judas Asparagus. Judas was so evil that they named a terrible vegetable after him.'

B

Beer

Belgium is famous for its beers, many made originally by monks. Pale ales are – for reasons lost in the mists of time – produced under a variety of names linked to the bad guys of Christianity. So there are Duvel ('Devil') and 'Judas' varieties, the latter brewed by Brouwerij Alken-Maes. The Judas beer is said by connoisseurs treacherously to hide its strength when tasted by novices so as to get them drunk very quickly.

CHAPTER I

What's in a Name?

'Your son, – your dear son, – from whose sweet and open temper you have so much to expect. – Your Billy, Sir! – would you, for the world, have called him Judas?'

Laurence Sterne: *Tristram Shandy* (1759)

Iscariot has a curiously harsh ring to it in English, but to talk only of Judas risks confusing the two apostles, both with that same name, reported as being among the twelve chosen by Jesus to be his closest followers. In Luke's gospel, the third of the four in the New Testament, the list of Jesus' inner circle ends with the pairing of Judas, son of James, and Judas Iscariot.[1] And in John, the final gospel of the quartet, in his account of Jesus' 'farewell discourses', he refers to the apostle Judas, and then adds, for clarity, 'this was not Judas Iscariot'.[2]

In chronological terms, Luke and John were written after the gospels of Mark and Matthew. In the earlier two, there is just one Judas – Judas Iscariot. In place of the other Judas, the son of James, Mark lists Thaddeus,[3] and Matthew follows suit.[4] According to the conventional wisdom of biblical scholarship, though, Mark, Matthew and Luke are intimately linked, collectively known as the 'synoptic gospels' because, as the adjective suggests, they share many similarities and even a common source. So why should Luke include a second Judas, the son of James, rather than Thaddeus? In changing the line-up, is he drawing on a different source? Or is he correcting a historical inaccuracy in Mark and Matthew? Maybe they mentioned Thaddeus because they thought to have two Judases in the twelve would puzzle their readers? Or, alternatively, are Luke and John adding a second Judas to make a point that goes beyond straight history?

It's good to raise the possibility of embellishment early, because it crops up at every turn when reading the four gospels that Christianity has deemed to be the official version of Jesus' life. There are so many discrepancies between the four texts, the challenge is to know which to favour, and why. In the case of the confusion between one or two Judases, one common suggestion is that Luke and John were both keener than Mark and Matthew on posthumously heaping blame for Jesus' death on Judas Iscariot. To make their point even more forcefully, they created a 'good' Judas in Judas, son of James (worthy of receiving personal guidance from Jesus in John's gospel), and then juxtapose that 'good Judas' with the 'bad' Judas Iscariot.[5] In other words, it is a narrative device, potentially the first of many in Judas' biography.

Next, there is the name Judas Iscariot. Alone of the twelve apostles, he is identified by his town of origin, just as medieval knights were later to have their Christian names paired with that of their home turf. Judas Iscariot, it has long been held, should more properly be read as Judas, man of Qeriot, a town south of Jerusalem in Judea (*is* in Hebrew means 'man', hence Judas Is-Qeriot). That orthodoxy rests on John's version in particular, because he alone adds the clue that Judas Iscariot's father is called Simon Iscariot – or Simon, man of Qeriot.[6]

Like father, like son? Well, up to a point. There is, to this hearer at least, sufficient of a gap between Is-Qeriot and Iscariot to leave room for doubt. Moreover, according to the distinguished historian of first-century Judaism, Géza Vermes, 'qeriot' is probably closer to the word *qiryah*, 'and since *qiryah* means "town", it is of little use'.[7]

Modern biblical criticism, with its focus on probing the historical worth of details and words found in the Old and New Testaments, blossomed in the twentieth century, though it has its origins in the fifteenth and sixteenth centuries. And as the process has gathered pace, theories have multiplied, about Judas Iscariot as about every other individual named in the texts. There is a school of thought, for instance, that speculates that the anonymous *qiryah* or 'town' in question may in fact refer to a bigger town, specifically the city of Jerusalem, the largest town in the whole country.[8] So just as those in the countryside still speak of the bright lights of their capital as 'the city', in this reading of Iscariot, Judas is being labelled as the 'townie' from Jerusalem by the other eleven 'yokel' apostles.

There is certainly no sign of Qeriot on maps of the Middle East today, but the usual explanation is that it was long ago abandoned as a settlement. It is, the mainstream of biblical scholarship insists, a reference – albeit slightly garbled – to Kerioth, once a place with a proud heritage, mentioned in the Book of Joshua,[9] but now itself the subject of claim and counterclaim, with some locating its footprint at Tel Qirrioth in Israel's southern Negev Desert.

Nothing very clear there, then, and certainly no further opportunities for me to walk with any confidence in Judas' footsteps. Yet the alternative explanations for what Iscariot means are hardly more convincing. The most popular is that it is a corruption and/or mistranslation of *sicarius*, the Latin for a 'dagger-man'.[10] The same root is the origin of our word 'sickle'. The Sicarii were Jewish rebels who terrorised Judea between 40 and 50 CE. Their hallmark was to stage random murderous attacks on Jewish grandees at crowded public events (their first significant victim was reputedly a former high priest), using the short daggers that they kept concealed beneath their cloaks. As with today's suicide bombers, such a methodology had a power to terrify out of all proportion to the actual threat it posed. The Sicarii claimed a political agenda – a Jewish nationalism that sought to expel the Roman overlords who had controlled Jerusalem from 63 BCE onwards – but for some historians they were simply bandits.

Several problems arise with this explanation for Iscariot. First, there is no other suggestion in the gospels of any link between Judas and these assassins, their politics, or their practices. Second, the heyday of the Sicarii postdates the gospel versions of Judas' death in 33 CE. The attribution has, though, had the effect, as a theory, of adding marginally to the otherwise invented thread – commonly argued in more recent times by theologians and church historians – that Judas' real purpose was as a political revolutionary, intent on liberating Israel from foreign overlordship.

Another theory claims as the origin of Iscariot the Aramaic word *sheqarya*, which equates to 'fraud' or 'false one'.[11] Aramaic would have been the language Jesus and his apostles used. If true, this would mean that the gospel writers were guilty of the clumsiest over-emphasis. All of them, the first time they use the words Judas Iscariot then go on to label him the betrayer. So if Iscariot means the 'false one', they are writing 'Judas the false one' and then calling him the betrayer. Why do both?

An alternative suggestion is that Iscariot is a form of 'Issacharite', as in a member of the tribe of Issachar, one of the original twelve tribes of Israel.[12] Yet it had ceased to exist 600 years before Judas' day, during the Jews' exile in Babylon. And the list of possibilities goes on, no more convincingly. Iscariot has been linked with the Latin word *scortea*, meaning 'leather bag'. So he is Judas of the leather bag, the same bag that John's gospel has him holding as treasurer of the Jesus movement. Yet the reference in John to Iscariot is applied both to Judas and his father. So was his father 'Simon of the leather bag'? And since Mark, Matthew and Luke make no independent mention of any leather bag, or of Judas having a treasurer role, why would they call him 'Judas of the leather bag'?

A *world of Judases*

All this mulling over Iscariot is not getting much beyond the word leaving a slightly sour taste in the mouth. The name Judas, though, might offer more by way of clarity. In first-century CE Israel, it would have been about as commonplace as John, Ben or Sam are today. Quite how Judas Iscariot has changed that state of affairs can be judged by the Standesamt, or German registry of births, marriages and deaths, which provides a 'Manual of First Names' containing all those a parent can freely choose for their child. Those wanting to go off piste must apply for special approval. Among those to be avoided, the Standesamt counsels, are product names – so no babies called 'Porsche' – and those with 'evil' connotations. A lengthy legal case was fought recently in this context to get Standesamt approval for 'Jihad'. Those mums and dads tempted by 'Judas' are directed that it will only be allowed if followed by a second name that distances it from Judas Iscariot.[13]

Judas – the Greek form of the Hebrew Judah or *Yehuda* – comes from the verb to thank, or to give praise. Judah was the fourth son of the Old Testament patriarch, Jacob,[14] and as such was, along with his eleven siblings, the founding father of one of the twelve tribes of Israel, named after him, with its lands based around Jerusalem. Judah and its people were eventually to emerge – through a series of historical events in the lives of the Israelites – as the principal tribe. All the kings of the Davidic line, for example, came from it, and so Judah or *Yehuda* in Hebrew is closely linked with *Yehudi*, the Hebrew word for Jew.

As a result there are almost as many Judases liberally scattered through the Bible's Old and New Testaments, and in other histories of the period, as there are Joneses in a Welsh village. The most prominent of the Judases is Judas Maccabeus, one of a band of warrior brothers who in 164 BCE joined their father in fighting to regain control of the Temple in Jerusalem from debauched foreigners. 'He put on his breastplate like a giant', it is written of Judas Maccabeus in the Old Testament.[15] His victory is still recalled on the Jewish feast of Hanukkah, and he is celebrated in George Frederick Handel's popular 1746 oratorio *Judas Maccabeus*.

Equally rebellious was Judas the Galilean (or Judas of Gamala, as he is sometimes called), who was part of an armed uprising against Roman rule in Judea and beyond around the time of the census in 6 CE (the same census that took Joseph and Mary on their donkey to register in Bethlehem). He was part of another dynasty of nationalistic rebels, this time called the Zealots. He even gets a mention as a failed messianic leader in the Acts of the Apostles,[16] the New Testament's official history of the years immediately after Jesus' death. (Some have even tried to link 'Judas the Zealot' with Judas Iscariot, suggesting that Iscariot may – by convoluted logic – be rendered as 'the Zealot'.[17])

Bland, in comparison, is Judas Barsabbas, also name-checked in the Acts of the Apostles as a leading light in the fledgling Christian community in Jerusalem in 49 CE.[18] And positively opaque is Judas the bishop, one of thirteen to preside in Jerusalem between 106 CE and 135 CE, according to Eusebius who, in addition to his *Onomasticon*, already mentioned, produced in the fourth-century *Ecclesiastical History* the first chronologically ordered account of the early years of the church.[19]

So there is plenty of potential here for confusion, and even of conflated CVs, the attributes of the other Judases later being attached to Judas Iscariot. Judas the Galilean, for example, was someone who travelled from that northern province south to make his stand in Judea. The gospel accounts, if Iscariot really refers to Qeriot in Judah (or Judea as it became known in the Roman form of the name), turn that on its head. Judas Iscariot journeys from the southern province north to make his name in Galilee.

And the field only gets more crowded. As well as two apostles called Judas, the gospels also talk of a Jude, sometimes referred to as Judas or Judah, who is described as one of Jesus' four brothers.[20] This quartet of siblings has traditionally been down-graded by official Christianity to stepbrothers (the sons of Mary's husband, Joseph, from an earlier marriage), or to the rank of cousins, in order to maintain the notion, embraced enthusiasti-cally from the fourth century CE onwards, that Jesus' mother was a perpetual virgin. Nothing more is said specifically of this par-ticular Jude/Judas in the gospels, but there is a short, unmemorable and generally neglected Letter of Jude, included in the canon of the New Testament and sometimes attributed to him, which warns Jews who have joined the new Christian Church to beware of false teachers.

The gospels as gospel

If probing Judas Iscariot's name tends to yield only a muddle of theories and characters, then the other details about him in the four gospels of the New Testament provide the building blocks of his biography. They are in short supply, though. Despite the instant recognition that Judas continues to enjoy as a result of three infamous episodes where he looms large in Jesus' story (and a handful of others, less often highlighted), what is written by Mark, Matthew, Luke and John can hardly be said to constitute a rounded portrait.

In part, that is down to the literary style of the gospels them-selves. Christianity may be a religion of the book, yet its holiest book contains not a single physical description of Jesus, his mother or any of the apostles. Neither, in the case of Judas, is there a single word about how he sounded, or moved, or about his early years, save for that dead-end reference to his father in John. The gospel writers did not see that as their task. It never crossed their mind to sketch a convincing psychological portrait of Judas, just as they did not seek to provide a biography of Jesus. The gospels are not even strict chronological accounts. They sit broadly somewhere between history and polemics, shaped for their times, but also with an eye to previous accounts (notably the Hebrew Scriptures).

The actual style of the gospels has long been the subject of intense academic debate, but the consensus is that their often terse tone, and the occasional discrepancies between one account and another, were deliberate, the literary convention of the times being that readers should be left sufficient room to use their own imaginations. Even within such constraints, however, the gospel writers do seem to show a particular reserve when it comes to Judas. In terms of name-checks among the apostles, only Peter scores more highly in the gospel texts. Yet, compared to the many insights offered about the future pope (including that he is married[21]), and the passages where he shows very human doubts (denying Jesus three times before the cock crows[22]), there are just twenty-two specific references to Judas in all four gospels combined – a total of roughly 1,200 words.

The writers clearly felt a distaste around mentioning Judas Iscariot at all. They coped with their reluctance by dealing with him as swiftly and damningly as possible. Hence his name is always found at the very end of lists of the twelve, with his card marked as a traitor long before he does the deed, or any deed, showing scant respect for notions of an unfolding narrative. There is no 'show not tell', the basic rule of creative-writing classes. In the gospel authors' view, Judas has to be marked out as tarnished from the start, lest any reader be seduced into extending him the benefit of the doubt.

That, at least, is one way of looking at the background to the gospel texts. Others who have studied them, though, offer a different theory. They suspect the real explanation for the lack of depth in how they treat Judas reveals him as a fiction, a narrative device, invented by the four writers of the gospels simply to furnish readers with a betrayer who precipitates Jesus' death.[23] As the British literary critic, Sir Frank Kermode, wrote in a 1997 essay on Judas (one of several he penned on the subject): 'As for the historical status of Judas, there is of course no saying he didn't exist but, as we know him, he exists only in a form of fiction cultivated in the first century.'[24]

It all comes back to how you see the gospels. What exactly are they? If their writers can be accused of making up the 'character' of Judas, what else did they invent? Of all those who feature, only Jesus and the Roman governor, Pontius Pilate, are attested to in other historical sources. The Jewish historian, Flavius Josephus, in *The Antiquities of the Jews*, written around sixty years after Jesus' death, includes references to him as a notorious troublemaker. Tacitus, the Roman senator and opponent of the early Christians, gives chapter and verse in book fifteen of his *Annals*, written around 116 CE, on Jesus' death. 'Christus . . . suffered the extreme penalty during the reign of Tiberius, under one of our procurators, Pontius Pilate'. No independent report of Jesus' resurrection is offered, though, and there is no mention anywhere else in these historical sources, or any other, of Judas Iscariot.

Many contemporary Christians now question the view, handed down from pulpits for many centuries by their church, that every last sentence written in Mark, Matthew, Luke and John is the word of God and beyond contradiction, if only because the four gospel accounts contradict each other continually at the most basic level, for example over places and timings.[25] Yet they would certainly not go so far as to label the gospels a fiction. The truth, for many, lies somewhere in between.

What the gospels do uniquely convey is what Jesus said and did, setting down details and remarks that are assumed to have been circulating in the oral tradition of the first Christians between the death of Jesus, usually dated around 33 CE, and the writing of the first of the gospels, by Mark, in around 70 CE. That is a gap of getting on for four decades. Given that Mark's is also the briefest of the gospels, it is not inconceivable that he chose to leave out various stories from the oral tradition in the interests of shaping his material into a digestible whole. Subsequent gospel writers then allowed themselves a longer word count, and retrieved from the cutting-room floor those stories discarded by Mark, and integrated them into their accounts. In other words, divergence does not have to signal invention.

Indeed, many who have studied them closely – even if personally sceptical about the claims of Christianity and outside the world of biblical scholarship – conclude that the gospels incontrovertibly contain, at the very least, elements of historical truth. 'They were written at a time when fictional, that is mythological, writing simply did not have this kind of detail,' asserted the British agnostic novelist and broadcaster, Melvyn Bragg, in an essay describing his own research into the figure of Mary Magdalen. 'And further we underestimate the power of oral history, which is what the gospels were recording. We have no problem accepting the accounts of men who fought in the First World War and yet there was a shorter gap between the events the gospels depicted and their inscription than there is between 1914 and now.'[26]

There is a crucial difference, though. Most other recorders of history, in other times and places, stake a claim to objectivity (even if it can rarely be made to stand up). The gospel writers are unabashed from the start about being anything but detached. What each does is to draw on Jesus' life to convey a message to their own first- and early second-century audiences within the emerging church. Their texts aim to nourish a new religious movement. Which doesn't stop them being history, but which does mean we have to tread carefully.

There are suggestions that the four texts may have originally been written down in Aramaic, the language Jesus would have used, and then translated into Greek. This would add to their claim to historical accuracy, but if such Aramaic originals ever existed, no trace of them has ever turned up. And, for the first centuries of Christianity, the vast majority of members of the church were Greek-speaking, non-Jewish inhabitants of the Roman Empire, so it makes sense that the gospels would be written in Greek.

There are also strong Christian traditions that seek to link the four gospel authors to the original apostles in order to buttress their credibility. Mark is presented as the work of John Mark, a cousin of Barnabas, who was a close colleague of Paul (not one of the original twelve but, immediately after Jesus' death, the convert who led the missionary push of the fledgling church and whose writings, collected in the New Testament, are – as we will see later – the earliest accounts of Jesus). And the same John Mark, it is also claimed, then became the secretary or interpreter to Peter in Rome, and wrote 'his' gospel, based on the first pope's eyewitness recollections, as a means of converting Roman Christians. Hard evidence for this is, though, thin. For example, there is doubt that Peter ever even visited Rome, let alone died there.

The author of Matthew's gospel is taken to be the apostle Matthew, the tax collector among the original twelve,[27] but scholars now concur that the writer was someone close to those who were in that apostle's circle. Luke, too, is pictured as a close associate of Paul, and a physician, albeit on a similarly shaky historical basis, while John is casually interchanged with John, 'the Beloved apostle' among the twelve.[28] That would have required its author to be nigh on 100 years old when he put pen to paper, since the earliest verifiable fragments of John's gospel text date from 125 CE. And the Acts of the Apostles describes John as an 'uneducated, common man'.[29]

If authorship is unclear, then timing is also debated. Most scholars now believe John's gospel was written in the early years of the second century CE. That means it came thirty to forty years after Mark's, which is dated at 70 CE, based on clear signs in the text that it was set down shortly after the destruction by the Romans of the Second Temple in Jerusalem in that year. Matthew and Luke follow Mark from between 80 and 100 CE, and in that order. By another of those presentational quirks that now makes modern readers suspicious of the church's motives when it comes to historical accuracy, Matthew has, from the first efforts at compiling a New Testament at the end of the second century, been placed in front of Mark in the running order.

While together the four provide the main source material on Judas' biography, there were, particularly in the first four centuries of Christianity, many other 'gospels', some also claiming the names of apostles as their inspiration, including at least one 'Gospel of Judas'. All circulated among far-flung Christian communities, with widely differing viewpoints on how to interpret Jesus' message. Until Christianity was legalised as a religion in the Roman Empire by Constantine in 313, it lacked any real structure to enable the church to impose doctrinal or textual rigour on its adherents. Once it did, however, it moved to sideline these other gospels.

The displaced texts that have survived, and that are still available to us, contain evidence of a lively debate going on within the growing church as to its beliefs and its founder, and, for the purposes of this biography, about the role and significance in all of that of Judas Iscariot. But we will come to them in chronological order. The 'official' gospels are first up. From the end of the second century CE, long before the New Testament was formalised, there is plenty of evidence that the early church leaders favoured Mark, Matthew, Luke and John as the most authentic sources available. In a fragment, known as the Muratorian canon, and dated to 180 CE, the four are listed along with the other works that are now collectively known as the New Testament.

The main reason for selecting these four gospels in particular is clear. With the possible exception of the extra-canonical *Gospel of Thomas*,[30] all were written at a date considerably closer to Jesus' actual life than others that had subsequently also claimed the title gospel (which simply means 'good news'). And four, it could be argued, is better than one. While Mark, Matthew and Luke, collectively the synoptics, have a substantial degree of overlap, John is distinctive in detail, in tone, and in its presentation of Jesus. And it provides the most detailed and arguably the most influential portrait of Judas.

So, with all these caveats, let's start with the four official accounts. If they cannot be taken literally, they must still be taken seriously in what they report of Judas Iscariot.

C

Coins

The twelfth-century chronicler, Godfrey of Viterbo, was one of several to speculate on the fate of the thirty pieces of silver paid to Judas, and constructed (or repeated) an elaborate legend that had them originally made by Adam, passing through the hands of patriarchs and pharaohs, finding their way into the Jewish Temple courtesy of the Queen of Sheba, getting looted by Nebuchadnezzar and finally returning to the Jewish high priests via the three kings' gifts (they are now gold) to the infant Jesus, and Mary's subsequent carelessness in misplacing them.[1]

D

Day of Rest

In the tenth-century Voyage of Saint Brendan, an account of the Celtic monk sailing out towards the Isles of the Blessed in search of heaven, he comes upon Judas, perched on a rock, enjoying his Day of Rest. Monday to Saturday is hellish, Judas tells him – he is variously boiled in tar, flayed, frozen, and force-fed molten lead – but, thanks to God's mercy, on Sunday he can sit alone on his rock.[2] Matthew Arnold and Rudyard Kipling both produced poems on this theme, though with Judas on an iceberg.[3]

CHAPTER 2

The Twenty-Two: Judas in the Gospels

'In prison, I had the chance to read the Christ story. Over and over.
It seemed to me the greatest story I ever read. But it had one flaw.
Christ is betrayed by Judas, who is a stranger. Judas is a man he
doesn't know well. It would be artistically truer if he were betrayed
by John. Because John is the man he loves most.'

'Oscar Wilde' in David Hare: *The Judas Kiss* (1998)[4]

Mark's is both the earliest and the shortest of the four gospels.
The pace is slightly breathless, almost akin to shorthand notes,
moving quickly from detail to detail with little linguistic ornament. The Greek is rough and colloquial. One of the words used
most often is 'immediately'. Half of its length is taken up with
the events in Jerusalem in the last week leading up to Jesus'
crucifixion.

Mark makes just three of the twenty-two mentions of Judas
Iscariot in the gospels, but these represent his first appearance in
any written source. Jesus has gone 'up into the hills' where he
summons 'those he wanted'.[5] There is no explanation as to why,
or how, or even if these individuals had to travel to join his inner
circle. The assumption seems to be that they were to hand, able to
abandon whatever unmentioned things they were doing, and
answer the call. Mark simply recounts of the apostles, 'they came
to him' and that they were twelve in number. Their task is defined
as preaching, 'with power to drive out devils'.[6]

Because Judas is the only one of the twelve with two names, Judas and Iscariot, and that second name most obviously suggests he had come from afar to the Galilean hills, he is implicitly being cast from the very start as the outsider. That is further emphasised by him being the very last name on a list that is not alphabetical, as if he is the last to join, or saved to last because there is more to say about him. But there could also be something bigger going on.

In his classic study *The Scapegoat*, the cultural historian and anthropologist Professor René Girard lays down a set of common characteristics found in, or more to the point given to, society's scapegoats – those who are then unfairly blamed by the rest of us for every ill or disaster that occurs in families, communities or societies, usually as a way of avoiding a more honest distribution of culpability that may or may not include ourselves. Girard's essential point is that these characteristics are projected onto the scapegoats, to make them precisely that, rather than inherent. In the case of narratives – such as the gospels – he suggests they can be details, embroidered onto a character to turn them into a scapegoat. High on his list is that the scapegoat figure has, from the first, to be clearly identified as an outsider, as different from the others around him or her. 'In a boarding school, for example,' Girard writes, 'every individual who has difficulty adapting, someone from another country or state, an orphan, an only son, someone who is penniless, or even simply the latest arrival, is more or less interchangeable with the cripple.' And hence, he argues, with the scapegoat.[7]

It is perhaps no coincidence then that Mark adds, in the same passage, a single clause that simultaneously reveals and damns Judas. He is 'the man who was to betray him [Jesus]'.[8] Why be so specific, so early? In Girard's analysis – to set him up as a scapegoat. But for a chronological explanation, we must look at the literature that immediately preceded the writing of the gospels.

Handed over in Paul?

Though they appear after the gospels in the New Testament, the letters of Saint Paul, written between 50 and 63 CE are the earliest surviving source about Jesus (some are dated later, but are thought to be the work of his followers). They make up a quarter of the entire New Testament canon, and an influential quarter at that. Paul, like all the gospel writers, is reporting on Jesus second-hand. His arrival alongside the original apostles follows Jesus' death. His purpose, in letters written to missionary outposts, far beyond Jerusalem, to encourage them in the new faith, is not to offer a blow-by-blow account of Jesus' life, but rather to shape a narrative out of the many stories circulating, and the claims they made about Jesus and what he said and did. Paul creates the first single, clear and compelling draft of what becomes Christianity.

His work is therefore not by any standards objective, but rather evangelistic. Paul fashions what he includes about Jesus into an account of divine sacrifice, centred on the crucifixion and resurrection. The sacrifice narrative was an already well-established religious and heroic tradition, including in Greek literature, which would have been well known to Paul as a Greek-speaker.

Crucially, Paul's intended audience was both Jew and Gentile. In the years between Jesus' death and Paul's writings, two broad groupings had emerged among the new Christians: those based principally in and around Jerusalem, including some of the original apostles, but led by James, Jesus' brother, who saw Judaism as the natural first home for their new faith; and those, inspired by Paul above all, who were impatient of such a narrow approach, and who were anxious instead to proclaim Jesus as a saviour to the whole world, Jew and Gentile alike. Paul's letters reflect that second viewpoint – as do those of all the gospel writers to different degrees. They were creating a new holy book that, while drawing on the Hebrew Scriptures, would interpret them afresh in the light of Jesus' sacrifice for the whole of humankind.

Part of Paul's shaping of the Jesus story is to include the fact that he was betrayed. In his first Letter to the Church at Corinth, one of the earliest penned of his texts included in the New Testament, he writes: 'For this is what I received from the Lord, and in turn passed on to you, that on the same night that he [Jesus] was betrayed . . .'[9] Betrayal, it seems, is in Paul's eyes a necessary part of Jesus' sacrifice, a preliminary to his trial, death and rising from the dead. And that has been the argument of the Christian church ever after. Yet many scholars hold that the word betrayal should never have been used here in the first place.

In the original Greek of the letter, Paul uses the verb *para-didomi*. While most translations in the New Testament render it as 'betrayed', a highly charged word in English, there is an equally strong case for rendering it as 'gave up' or 'handed over', both of which lack that same edge and drama. Indeed, among those biblical scholars who dedicate their academic lives to such questions of translation, the consensus seems to be that both alternatives are not just possible, but perhaps preferable.[10] If so, there is potentially no betrayal, and therefore no role left for the gospel writers to fill with Judas.

Yet, is 'handing over' or 'giving up' someone to a hostile authority – as Jesus was, by Paul's account – really such a neutral act? It certainly still feels like a betrayal, even if Paul nowhere gives a detailed account of the precise consequences of the 'handing over' – namely Jesus' arrest and condemnation to death. Neither does Paul name the perpetrator of the betrayal, showing that however you translate *paradidomi*, it is perfectly possible to tell Jesus' life, death and resurrection without Judas.

Indeed, though in his subsequent writings Paul is drawn to probe further this betrayal of Jesus, he absolves the apostles. So after Jesus' resurrection from the dead, Paul writes later, in First Corinthians, he was seen by 'the twelve'.[11] No hint here that Judas had become detached, or detached himself by either handing over or betraying his master. He was as blessed and as trusted as all the others. And then, in his subsequent Letter to the Church in Rome, Paul chooses to pin the betrayal of Jesus on God the Father. 'Since God did not spare his own Son, but gave him up to the benefit of all . . .'[12]

Here, the standard translation of *paradidomi* usually opts for 'hand over' or 'give up'. Perhaps to accuse God of betrayal felt a step too far, and so the gentler option is favoured. Believers have, down the ages, found it hard to blame their gods for anything bad, especially in monotheistic faiths such as Christianity, Judaism and Islam, where in theory there is only one god, responsible for everything that happens, be it positive or negative, and in practice God is often left unsullied by anything bad, and the blame placed instead on demons, evil spirits and – mainly in Christianity – the devil.

Certainly, when the writer of Mark's gospel sat down to compose his version, much more of a blow-by-blow account of the key incidents of Jesus' public ministry than is found in Paul's letters, he felt compelled to point a finger of accusation at one person in particular when it came to that betrayal. Why? Well, if we see the gospel tellers as, in part at least, storytellers, then it makes for a better story. And, as human beings, we are prone to want to attribute guilt and it is usually simpler to lay the blame wholly on an individual rather than balance their guilt with the many factors that lie behind any crime. Black-and-white answers trump shades of grey every time. It is back to scapegoating. Mark chimes more easily with our instincts, while Paul's approach challenges them. And by encouraging scapegoating, Mark paves the way for 2,000 years of it in relation to Judas.

There may be another motivation, though, in his decision to

depart from Paul and shift the blame onto Judas. The ongoing dispute between the factions among the very early Christians meant that the advocates of building a church independent of Judaism were naturally keen to emphasise how different they were from the Jews. How tempting, then, for Mark to show that Jesus was betrayed by the Jews, and more specifically for Paul's unnamed betrayer to be Judas Iscariot, the apostle from Judea, seat of Jewish power, the apostle whose common-or-garden name was synonymous with the Jews?

That is, of course, with the benefit of hindsight. There may have been rivalry in these early decades of the Jesus movement, but the bitterness that was to fuel Christian anti-Semitism, and to cast Judas as irredeemably, was as yet a long way off.

Betrayal's human face

By beginning his account of the calling of the apostles by giving betrayal a human face in Judas Iscariot, the author of Mark may simply be repeating what was already widely circulating in the oral tradition among the first Christians. That explanation certainly fits with the way he tells it, in including the original list of twelve, as if reminding readers that this final apostle, Judas Iscariot, is the one they will have heard mention of already in their discussions as the betrayer of Jesus.

Matthew and Luke follow Mark's description of Judas as the betrayer when they introduce him as one of the twelve.[13] Both gospels are thought by scholars to be based in part on Mark's account, and in part on a now-lost source, referred to as 'Q' by scholars (from *quelle*, the German for 'source'), which contained the sayings of Jesus that are included by Matthew and Luke (but not by Mark or John). As with everything in this field, 'Q' provokes controversy. If it played such a key part in shaping the New Testament, sceptics have asked, why is it nowhere referred to in the canonical gospels and extra-canonical gospels of those first centuries of Christianity?

Standing apart, as is his habit, the author of John does not provide a list of twelve names when it comes to introducing Jesus' apostles, but instead firms up on something hinted at in the others to cast Judas, on first mention, more definitively as the outsider among the apostles. The eleven are all from Galilee, Jesus' home patch, but John labels Judas as the son of Simon Iscariot, emphasising the idea that his roots are elsewhere – if the traditional explanation of Iscariot as referring to Qeriot is accepted.[14]

Though Galilee was home to one, or even two, of the original twelve tribes of Israel (Naphtali and Dan), and hence in theory the equal of Judea, it is repeatedly scorned in traditional rabbinical writings. In Galilee, they report, Jewish religious laws are not strictly observed as they are in 'proper', more mainstream Judea. Galilee is characterised as somewhere with a penchant for a free-for-all approach to the faith, especially in its taste for miracle workers.

The silver price of blood

After naming the twelve, Mark then proceeds to treat them largely as a single entity, Judas included; as a team of bemused country lads caught up in events that they can't quite fathom. Mark's next specific reference to Judas comes totally out of the blue, just after Jesus and his followers have arrived in Jerusalem for what will turn out to be the last week of his life. 'Judas Iscariot, one of the Twelve, approached the chief priests with an offer to hand Jesus over to them. They were delighted to hear it, and promised to give him money; and he began to look for a way of betraying him when the opportunity should occur.'[15]

Typically of Mark, it is as bald as that, no explanation and no context. There has been no hint whatsoever that Judas had been harbouring doubts that might prompt him to such treachery. The only reference back, in regard to an unfolding narrative, is the remark that the chief priests were delighted. Mark has already made plain Jesus' dislike for the Jewish religious establishment. He has recounted how it, for its part, had decided not to move against Jesus until after Passover, for fear of causing 'a disturbance among the people'.[16] That may explain why they feel they need a spy in Jesus' inner circle, but it is never spelt out.

Here, the question of Judas' motive in betrayal is first raised. There is no suggestion in Mark that Judas, any more than the other eleven, is a particularly observant Jew, so it is only his possible background in Judea that might predispose him to be in league with the chief priests. And, crucially for the biography of one so often labelled the betrayer, the verb that Mark first uses of Judas' offer to the chief priests is, in the English translation, 'hand over'. Having established Judas in his first emphatic reference as the 'betrayer', Mark is now apparently softening that outright condemnation. Did Judas really expect his actions would end in Jesus' death? Did he have some naïve hope that, if Jesus and the chief priests were forced to sit down together, they might make common cause (against the Roman occupiers)? Or was he just greedy? In Mark's account, he doesn't ask for money. The fact that payment is offered by the chief priests is included almost as a throwaway line, which fails to account for such a momentous deed.

Motivation is therefore left for the other synoptic gospel writers to flesh out. That suggests, to modern ears, that they were making it up, but Matthew and Luke might have been drawing (as Mark didn't) on material in the lost 'Q' source. Or they might have been employing what academics have identified as common rabbinical practice in Judaism at the time. 'Midrash' was the addition of invented stories to illustrate or explain otherwise opaque passages in the Hebrew Scriptures, done without necessarily undermining the historical worth of the core text on which they were built.[17]

Matthew offers a few more clues about motive. In Mark, just before Judas' deal with the chief priests, there is a passage that describes a visit by Jesus to the home of Simon the leper. While they are having dinner, a woman comes into the room with an alabaster jar of 'very costly' ointment, which she proceeds to 'pour' on Jesus' head. Mark describes the indignant reaction among 'some who were there' (no names) at such indulgence by their leader. They challenge Jesus over the waste of ointment that 'could have been sold for over 300 denarii and the money given to the poor'. They are using his own teaching against him.[18] Matthew, however, sharpens the focus on these dissenters by making them specifically 'the disciples'.[19] This opens the door a crack for one of them to be Judas, and thereby, tenuously, provides him with a potential spur to seek out the chief priests.

Yet it doesn't really satisfy. For the purpose of the tale of the ointment surely lies in Jesus' response to the disciples' challenge: 'Why are you upsetting this woman? What she has done for me is one of the good works, indeed! You have the poor with you always, but you will not have me. When she poured this ointment on my body, she did it to prepare me for burial.'[20] Jesus is here prophesying his own death. That would have brought Judas, and all of the apostles, up short, but would it also have driven Judas into the arms of Jesus' opponents? No, unless he felt they might somehow protect Jesus from such a fate. And, given the hostility the chief priests are reported as having already shown, that would not have been the first conclusion for him to reach.

What Matthew does provide more forcefully, in his account of Judas' meeting with the chief priests, is a motive. 'What are you prepared to give me if I hand him over to you?' Judas asks them directly, taking the initiative to negotiate a price. 'They paid him thirty silver pieces, and from that moment he looked for an opportunity to betray him.'[21]

Matthew is the only gospel writer to mention this specific detail that has become one of the best-known aspects of Judas' story – the swag bag marked thirty in the icon at Hakeldama, and 'the silver price of blood' of Bach's *Saint Matthew Passion*. While such a sum may, at first hearing, sound large in comparison to the 300 denarii squandered on ointment in the previous passage, subsequent research suggests that it was in reality a pittance. If Judas is a rogue, willing to do anything for profit, he would surely have asked for more. The actual amount, then, even as it echoes down through history to the present day, was intended by the writer of Matthew to be of no particular importance. It was Judas' willingness to ask for and take money that counted.

The devil rides in

Luke dramatically switches track on the question of Judas' motivation, moving it out of the human sphere and placing it in the context of the eternal battle between good and evil. He links Judas' evil deed with the devil, portrayed in his gospel as the supernatural source of evil in the world. Luke features no dinner with Simon the leper. Instead he writes that the Jewish authorities 'were looking for some way of doing away with him [Jesus], because they mistrusted the people. Then Satan entered into Judas, surnamed Iscariot, who was numbered among the Twelve. He went to the chief priests and the officers of the guard to discuss a scheme for handing Jesus over to them. They were delighted and agreed to give him money. He accepted, and looked for an opportunity to betray him to them without the people knowing.'[22] One of the curiosities about traditional Christian attitudes to possession of any individual by the devil is that it can be both damning and liberating. To sup with the devil is the worst of crimes. It suggests a rejection of Jesus' promise, and therefore is often shown as the prelude to eternal damnation in hell. Yet, equally, because the devil is seen as an external force, something that possesses an individual from the outside, often literally by jumping on his or her back, or whispering in the ears, then there is also an element of reducing that individual's own guilt for what they do with the devil's prompting. Almost two decades ago, as part of research on a biography of the devil,[23] I visited a strongly evangelical Christian prayer meeting in a London church. 'I've had a terrible week,' one young woman there shared with the group. 'The devil made me spend all my money.' They comforted her, with no suggestion that she might be to blame. Was Judas then, here in Luke's account, just the hapless victim of the devil, no more blameworthy than that young woman?

The case against him is growing, though, as the number of gospel texts accumulates. Judas now has a plan, though its exact nature is not revealed. He wants to betray Jesus without the other apostles or Jesus' followers ('the people'[24]) knowing. This is starting to make him sound like a secret agent, but it sits uncomfortably with his subsequent betrayal of Jesus to the soldiers in Gethsemane with a very public kiss – hardly a way to keep his part in the plot hidden. If this is a crafted narrative, then Luke is doing a poor job here of damning Judas. The discrepancies are, arguably, better explained by him repeating facts that he has been told, facts that haven't yet been trimmed to tuck into a neat pattern.

Luke also links Judas' Satan-inspired deal with the chief priests to a promise the devil has made earlier, when he tries and fails to tempt Jesus in the wilderness with 'the kingdoms of the world'. The devil, Luke writes of that moment, 'left him, to return at the appointed time'.[25] Here, then, as the devil takes possession of Judas, Luke is making good that promise. Moreover, this fits comfortably with an overarching theme in Luke – of displaying

Jesus as the radiant beacon of goodness against the darkness and corruption to be found all around him in the world – even in his inner circle. In a fight between good and bad, Judas is just one weapon requisitioned by the devil.

John takes up this same theme with gusto. Whereas in the other three gospels, Jesus is initially ambiguous and then demanding of secrecy about his status as the Son of God, John allows him no such coyness. His Jesus is unequivocally 'the word made flesh'[26] from the very start. As the Son of God, his encounters with the devil are therefore more explicitly cosmic battles. Indeed, Christian ideas about the devil receive their fullest expression in the final, extraordinary text of the New Testament, the Book of Revelation, written around 90 CE and usually attributed to the same author as John's gospel.

This fourth gospel, having initially dispensed with the list of the twelve apostles that the other three favour, includes a wholly new exchange, in which Judas is revealed as the traitor with reference to the devil. 'Have I not chosen you, you Twelve?' Jesus replies to a question from Peter. 'Yet one of you is a devil.'[27] This must have left the apostles deeply unsettled (it comes directly after Jesus' claim to divinity has so upset some of his disciples that they 'left him and stopped going with him'[28]). It might even suggest that some of the apostles are also wavering in their loyalty to their leader. But the authorial voice of John, blessed at the very least with hindsight, then interjects forcefully to spell it out. 'He [Jesus] meant Judas son of Simon Iscariot, since this was the man, one of the Twelve, who was going to betray him.'[29]

And it is the same authorial voice, importantly not Jesus', which posits the idea that Judas is possessed. John establishes earlier than in the other gospels that the Son of God had chosen this Judas as an apostle in the full knowledge of what he will eventually do. If the traditional Christian timeline is to be accepted, it means that Jesus spent three years between the start of his public ministry and his death living and working with a man he knows will ultimately betray him (the span is slightly shorter in John).

As he goes about refashioning according to his own ends the narrative handed down by the other three gospel writers, John finds Judas a useful tool. He makes the most references to him – eight, compared to six in Luke, five in Matthew and three in Mark. And he offers new details and new clues as to Judas' true motives. So, in John, a version of the story of the expensive ointment is again told, though this time it is massaged into Jesus' body in the house of Lazarus, also in Bethany, by his sister, Mary. And it is specifically Judas who complains about the wastefulness when 300 denarii could be used to help the poor.[30]

As gospel builds on gospel, Judas' actions are revealing him ever more firmly as the fifth columnist among the twelve. It is no longer the vague 'some' or 'disciples' who take a stand against their master over the ointment in Matthew and Mark. It is Judas alone. In itself, to object to waste and luxury, and to insist on the prior claim of the poor, is surely no bad thing. A favoured line of modern Catholicism is that it is 'a poor church, for the poor'.[31] Taken in isolation, Judas' championing of the poor here in John could potentially make him the poster boy for Catholic social teaching. But the gospel writer then crudely and instantaneously dashes any such possibility. 'He said this,' he continues on the subject of Judas, 'not because he cared for the poor, but because he was a thief; he was in charge of the common fund and used to help himself to the contributions.'[32]

The treasurer's role is a curious one to allocate to Judas. After all, among the apostles is Matthew, the former tax collector. Surely he would have been the natural choice to keep the kitty. Again, Professor Girard might argue that, by giving the job to Judas, John is laying the basis for this particular apostle's future as a scapegoat. 'First,' he writes of the attributes assigned to scapegoats by their persecutors, 'there are violent crimes which choose as object those people whom it is most criminal to attack, either in the absolute sense, or in reference to the individual committing the act.'[33]

Stealing money intended for the poor fits the bill. Swindling your companions and, worse, doing it while adopting a holier-than-thou attitude, how awful is that? How hypocritical! This is the charge that down the centuries has formed the basis for so many of the stock images of Judas – as heartless, as self-seeking, as a double-dealer, as a petty thief, as insatiably greedy, as an abuser of his position, and as a moneyman. To attract such a barrage of hostility, though, he has first to be put in the dock by John, according to Professor Girard's theory. In *Judas Iscariot and the Myth of Jewish Evil*, the distinguished British academic, Hyam Maccoby, is blunt. 'This expansion of Judas' money-corruption was a most fateful development for the history of anti-Semitism.'[34]

Yet this charge-list that John provides makes no particular sense in the context. Jesus, after all, isn't paying for the ointment; he isn't dipping into community funds to allow himself a little luxury. And there is no financial gain either to be made here by the keeper of the apostles' common fund.

As well as adding detail, John also prunes back on what has gone before. So, he stands alone among the gospel writers in making no mention of Judas' meeting with the chief priests. Instead, at the start of the Passover celebrations, he echoes Luke when he writes: 'the devil had already put it into the mind of Judas Iscariot, son of Simon, to betray him'.[35] The role of the official representatives of Judaism is downplayed here, replaced by that cosmic dimension of Judas being caught up in the battle between good and evil.

The first Holy Communicants

Though all four gospel writers go out of their way to tell readers, from the outset, that Judas is not to be trusted, Mark, Matthew and Luke also have Jesus himself failing to voice any concerns at all about Judas' fidelity until right up to the Last Supper, the day before he dies. Either he's ignorant, and as surprised as the rest of the apostles when the treachery is revealed, or he knows and keeps quiet, as befits the Son of God. While neither scenario mitigates Judas' guilt for what he does, the second opens the prospect that Jesus may in some way or other be colluding with Judas, whether simply by keeping silent about what he knows lies ahead, or more actively willing Judas on. Even in John, where the Son of God speaks more freely than in the other three gospels about his divinity, it is still largely left to the author – rather than Jesus – to point the finger of accusation at Judas.

Mark's account of the Last Supper, the earliest written version, sees Jesus maintain his ignorance – or perhaps reticence – on the subject of Judas' pending betrayal. He falls short of explicitly naming him as the traitor, and confines himself to these words: 'It is one of the Twelve, one who is dipping into the same dish with me.'[36] This is a particularly disturbing image, the intimacy of sharing food mixed with the presence of an enemy, the one who is already selling you down the river. Jesus adds, coldly, of the traitor he will not name, 'Better for that man if he had never been born.'[37] '[Judas] provokes,' writes the American academic Susan Gubar in her study of Judas, 'the only instance to my knowledge of a biblical text conceivably justifying abortion'.[38]

Matthew fine-tunes Mark to put the spotlight a little more on Judas. Jesus tells the group of his closest confidants gathered around him: 'One of you is going to betray me.' They are 'greatly distressed' and reply in turn, 'Not I, Lord.' Jesus is once again quoted as saying that his betrayer would be better never born, but then Matthew adds: 'Judas, who was to betray him, asked in his turn, "Not I, Rabbi, surely?" "They are your own words," answered Jesus.'[39]

This falls short of a direct accusation, but leaves Judas a barefaced liar. There isn't a pause, or a blush, or a gulp, as Judas looks the man he has betrayed in the eye and denies all knowledge. It sends a chill up your spine.

Without hindsight, or, frankly, much insight, the other eleven do not appear, in Matthew's text, to pick up the implication of Jesus' reply to Judas. Indeed, across all four gospels the rest of the apostles are unbelievably slow to spot what is unfolding before their eyes; hence Judas' ability to stay within the inner circle for as long as he does. Again that may be a narrative device – it enables him finally and dramatically to seal the betrayal with a kiss; or it may be building on the general theme that the other apostles were a little slow-witted. It is a curious feature, nonetheless, since these gospels were being written to bolster the teaching authority of the missionary church, led by Paul and many of those original apostles. They do not emerge well from these passages. It is one of those troubling, contradictory details that again suggests the gospels are based more on fact than artifice. If it were the latter, such kinks would have been ironed out.

So no one present raises any objections when, in Mark and Matthew, talk of a betrayer in their midst gives way to the whole company of apostles joining in the first-ever Eucharist, something recalled at the alter each and every day in every church around the globe, when the priest consecrates the bread and wine. In the Upper Room in Jerusalem that evening, Jesus says, 'this is my blood', 'this is my body',[40] and then passes them around the group. All partake, including Judas.

Once more, this conforms to the typical setting-up of a scapegoat. 'There are religious crimes,' Professor Girard writes, 'such as profanation of the host. Here, too, it is the strictest taboos that are transgressed.'[41] That may explain why Mark and Matthew are content to allow Judas to participate unhindered in the first Eucharist. Since Jesus has dropped a heavy hint that he knows what Judas is soon to do, the inclusion of his betrayer must be significant. He wants it to happen. Some clerics and theologians, indeed, accept the challenge that this implies. Pope Francis, for example, writing in his first apostolic exhortation, *Evangelii Gaudium* (2013), notes that: 'The Eucharist, although it is the fullness of sacramental life, is not a prize for the perfect, but a powerful medicine and nourishment for the weak.' He may have had Judas in mind.

Others, though, have found this logic hard to accept. The author of Luke is one such. He allows no set-up for later scape-goating. His 'solution' instead is to place the first Eucharist before (rather than after) Jesus' revelation of his strong suspicion that there is a traitor in the room. It can therefore take place without an uncomfortable question mark being raised over quite what Jesus intended of Judas.[42]

It is left to John to tackle the problem head on – as ever by adding a detail or two all of his own. His version of what we know as the Last Supper includes bread, but there is no institution of the Eucharist. In an earlier episode in John's gospel, when Jesus debates with fellow Jews in the synagogue in Capernaum, he promises, 'Anyone who does eat my flesh and drink my blood has eternal life, and I shall raise him up on the last day.'[43] It shocks the apostles at the time – taken literally, it sounds like an invitation to become cannibals – but its real purpose, surely, is to bring for-ward discussion of the Eucharist and make explicit that Judas, if he were to partake of it, would be redeemed.

And that is what happens in John's not-quite-the-Last Supper. He begins his description with Jesus humbly and lovingly washing his disciples' feet, including once again Judas'. 'Love the sinner, hate the sin,' as my old Christian Brother teachers used to instruct. John accompanies this self-abasement by the Son of God – replayed each Maundy Thursday in churches (Pope Francis, before his election, did it to those suffering with AIDS[44]) – with his own commentary. 'Jesus knew the hour had come for him to pass from this world to the Father. He had always loved those who were his in the world, but now he showed how perfect his love was.'[45]

In its widest sense, these words mark a change of gear, pointing forward towards Jesus' divine sacrifice – his arrest, trial, crucifixion and resurrection. More narrowly, though, they imply that, from now on in the narrative, Jesus' relationship with the apostles he has gathered around him changes. In demonstrating his 'perfection', by washing the feet of his erstwhile companions, he also reveals himself as omniscient, and therefore as knowing, possibly before even Judas himself does, that the son of Simon Iscariot is to be the traitor.

And it is to that subject that John turns. Previously he has written: 'They were at supper, and the devil had already put it into the mind of Judas Iscariot, son of Simon, to betray him [Jesus].'[46] As yet, though, it remains just a thought, a temptation, to be acted on or not. Still Jesus himself hasn't named Judas as the traitor. 'Jesus knew the Father had put everything into his hands,' John goes on, presumably including Judas' betrayal, 'and that he had come from God and was returning to God.'[47]

After the washing of the feet, Jesus is pictured as 'troubled in spirit'. He foretells, as in the other accounts, that one around the table will betray him, but again does not name him. Then John adds a very odd and much subsequently debated bit of choreography. 'The disciples looked at one another, wondering what he meant. The disciple Jesus loved [the apostle John] was reclining next to Jesus; Simon Peter signed to him and said, "Ask who it is he means", so leaning back on Jesus' breast he said, "Who is it, Lord?"'[48]

At least, albeit by this bizarre route, they are finally exhibiting natural human curiosity. In Mark, by contrast, the bombshell of harbouring a betrayer drops, and then they calmly carry on as if nothing has happened. If I had been an apostle in that Upper Room, I would have wanted to know the identity of the traitor among my close companions, and would have either asked myself, or prompted another to do so. But I would also have noticed John cosying up to Jesus, and how Peter (elsewhere usually the asker of difficult questions) clearly feels that John is best placed to get a straight answer out of their leader. The picture painted is only partially explained by the author of this gospel wanting to create the impression that he is John the Beloved, the special apostle, or is writing on his authority.

Thus prompted, Jesus replies: 'It is the one to whom I give the piece of bread I shall dip in the dish.'[49] And then he dips the sop in the dish and hands it to Judas. No ambiguity here. Finally Jesus makes the accusation, earlier and more explicitly than in any other gospel. 'At that instant,' John writes of Judas, 'Satan entered him.'[50] He mentions no consecration of bread and wine. Instead he uses the bread as the cue for Satan to enter Judas. This is the moment when, according to John, Judas actually becomes the traitor. It is almost as if Jesus is inviting his enemy into this apostle, it having been predicted already on two previous occasions.

John continues by fashioning a new exchange. 'Jesus then said [to Judas], "What you are going to do, do quickly."'[51] This is such an important remark for the whole history of how Judas is regarded thereafter. Are the two complicit? Or do the words sound a note of resignation before the Evil One? Certainly, relationships are changing. Now Satan is inside Judas, Jesus is much more direct in conversation with the apostle – as if addressing the enemy within. Yet John continues, picking up on aspects of Judas' character he had earlier been the first to highlight: 'None of the others at table understood the reason he [Jesus] said this. Since Judas had charge of the common fund, some of them thought Jesus was telling him, "Buy what we need for the festival", or telling him to give something to the poor. As soon as Judas had taken the piece of bread, he went out. Night had fallen.'[52]

There is much ambiguity here, with John seemingly wanting to have it both ways – for Judas to be a bad person in his own right (the miserly treasurer) and, simultaneously, to be possessed by the devil and therefore not the master of his own destiny. Again the gospels, if contrived, are anything but clear. The two possible conclusions, of course, conflate in the most basic of Christian theology. The devil picks on bad people because they are more open to his blandishments. Yet on that central dilemma of whether Judas can be held responsible for his actions – and therefore damned by history – or if he was instead a pawn in a bigger battle between good and evil, God's plan and the devil's wiles, John's text remains wide open to interpretation.

The Judas kiss

In Mark's account of the Last Supper, where Jesus has not openly accused Judas, the twelve afterwards accompany their master as he adjourns to the Garden of Gethsemane, to confront in prayer the pain he is now shown as knowing will lie ahead for him. If he utters any recrimination at all, it is directed at all twelve. 'You will all lose faith,' he tells them.[53] Mark's account of what happens in the garden is characteristically sketchy. He makes no reference to Judas slipping away, while Jesus prays and the other apostles sleep. Only Judas' return is heralded, when Jesus announces, 'my betrayer is close at hand'. It is the first acknowledgement in Mark from Jesus' own lips that the role belongs to Judas. Accompanied by 'a number of men armed with swords and clubs', on the orders of the Jewish chief priests, Judas identifies his leader with a traitor's kiss. 'He went straight up to Jesus and said, "Rabbi!", and kissed him.'[54]

As a greeting, a kiss was common enough in this period for two Jewish men who were already well acquainted. Later ages were to place much more of a charge on that kiss, but here the symbolism is that a conventional gesture of friendship masks an act of betrayal. Indeed, Judas would not have suggested to the armed men a kiss as a way of singling out Jesus if it hadn't been something everyday. It was meant to be a routine gesture, perhaps also one that would go unremarked, so Judas' guilt in betraying his leader might not be immediately apparent. But the best-laid plans often go astray.

Why, though, would Judas have had to pick Jesus out of a small group of no more than twelve? It would have been blindingly obvious to the men with swords and clubs which one Jesus was, given all that had already been said about the inadequacies of the apostles. He was – and carried himself like – their leader. He had a natural charisma – as the miracle worker, and as the man whose words caused many to follow him. The apostles, by contrast, were simple fishermen. And all the gospels tell how Jesus had caused a huge stir during his brief time in Jerusalem; how he had been noted, watched and even challenged, face to face, by representatives of the Jewish establishment. This was the man who had thrown the moneylenders out of the Temple. The armed group would know which one he was without any help from Judas' kiss.

Even allowing for the gloom in the garden (other gospel writers add mentions of lanterns), the detail about the kiss reads like either unnecessary symbolism, or else as something observed, seared on memories, and passed down to subsequent generations in the oral tradition about those crucial days in Jerusalem. It is impossible to know which one it is, but without obvious reason for being included in the texts, especially in Mark's decidedly unadorned account, it is one of those curious details that has

– for this reader at least – the ring of authenticity, something that just happened.

As the Catholic novelist Graham Greene used to remark, there are certain details in the gospels that make you believe them. Notoriously prone to doubt, Greene became convinced that the gospels described real events because of one line in John, where an unnamed disciple outruns Peter to get to the empty tomb. Why include it, Greene asked, when it adds nothing in terms of propaganda or symbolism, unless it came from an eyewitness?[55]

Matthew reproduces the Gethsemane episode in almost exactly the same terms as Mark, but he gives Jesus the right of reply to the kissing traitor. 'My friend,' he says to Judas, 'do what you are here for.'[56] The line is almost the same as one that John had, at an earlier stage in the chronology, put on Jesus' lips as they dipped bread. Again it raises questions about the nature of the relationship between them. What, in particular, of that use of the word 'friend'? There is to modern ears forgiveness in it – greeting the one who has betrayed you as friend – and forgiveness remains absolutely central to the Christian message. It might, though, have been uttered with irony. Another detail largely missing from the gospels – as here – is any indication of tone of voice. Which also leaves room for it to have been said in bewilderment. Yet, there is a clear suggestion here that Jesus always knew this was going to happen, and is reassuring his 'friend' Judas that his crime will not be held against him. And there are, inevitably, countless theories as to whether the Greek word used – *hetaire* – is best rendered as friend, or comrade, colleague or even 'my man'.[57]

Matthew does try to supply a reason for an identifying kiss being required, when he writes of Jesus addressing remarks to a 'crowd' as he is taken away from the garden.[58] There might have been so many people in Gethsemane that, but for the Judas kiss, Jesus could have melted back into their ranks and escaped, had he wanted to, while the soldiers were still puzzling over which one he was. But it is pretty thin.

Luke's account follows those of Mark and Matthew, though – in line with his earlier attempt to distance Judas from the first Eucharist – he now allows Jesus to evade the proffered kiss in Gethsemane, as if having the brush of a traitor's lips on his cheek might offend more than the arrest itself. This impression is reinforced when Luke has Jesus – once he has dodged the gesture of greeting – unambiguously rebuke his apostle with, 'Judas, are you betraying the Son of Man with a kiss?'[59] It is a remark that echoes down history, even if, in this gospel, Judas does not plant the kiss.

John, as ever, adds his own unique details. The scene is no longer identified precisely as Gethsemane, but simply a garden in the Kidron Valley (where Gethsemane stands).[60] It is, he explains, a regular meeting place for the apostles. (In his gospel the adult Jesus comes to Jerusalem more than once. If the garden was so well known as a meeting place for the Jesus movement, then once again why does Judas need to be there at all?) Judas arrives but brings with him a detachment from the Roman garrison in Jerusalem rather than – as in other accounts – guards answering to the chief priests.[61] The detachment, it is said, has been sent at the request of the Jewish authorities.

In the debate that went on in the early church as these gospels were being written, John is usually seen as being toughest on the Jews, and on Judas (no coincidence, it was argued later[62]), but here he seems instead to tilt the blame for the arrest of Jesus away from the Jews and towards the Romans.

In John's account, when the guards arrive in the garden, it is the always-in-control Jesus who takes charge, rather than Judas, who is sidelined. 'Who are you looking for?' Jesus challenges the troops, going over Judas' head. When they reply, 'Jesus the Nazarene', he tells them, 'I am he.' There is absolutely no requirement for the Judas kiss. Or for Judas. 'Now Judas the traitor',

John writes, 'was standing among them [the troops]. When Jesus said, "I am he", they moved back and fell to the ground.' Judas' part in that ungainly collapse is the extent of the great betrayer's role.[63]

His treason, nevertheless, is complete. Jesus' arrest was Judas' intention, even if in John – at the crucial moment – he does little to make it happen. And an act of betrayal once more fits into the template that Professor Girard has drawn up for those who are cast as scapegoats. Their crimes, he writes, 'seem to be fundamental. They attack the very foundations of cultural order, the family and the hierarchical differences without which there would be no social order. In the sphere of individual actions, they correspond to the global consequences of an epidemic of the plague, or of any comparable danger. It is not enough for the social bond to be loosened, it must be totally destroyed.'[64] Judas has sent the Son of God to his death. And the impression of gravity is reinforced by an earlier passage, included by John alone, just before his account of the arrest, where Jesus offers a long series of 'farewell discourses' to his apostles. They feature an aside about 'the one who chose to be lost' (translated in some versions as 'the son of perdition') that is usually taken to be a sure-fire and damning reference to Judas.[65]

How, then, to reconcile the three possible strands in John – simultaneously damning Judas as bad, excusing Judas as part of God's plan, and showing him as possessed by the devil? One explanation may lie in the widespread scholarly view that John's gospel is the product of more than one author, all writing at different times. Perhaps among those different scribes there were contrasting views of Judas' crime? As there are right down to our own times.

Aftermath

If Judas betrays Jesus by handing him over to soldiers in the Garden of Gethsemane, the other eleven apostles hardly distinguish themselves in rallying to the cause of their leader. After the arrest, reports Mark, 'they all deserted him and ran away' – one of them in such a hurry that he was naked.[66] There's betrayal for you. Only Peter elects to follow his master 'at a distance',[67] joined in John's account by a disciple 'known to the high priest',[68] whose addition seems to serve little obvious purpose, and so may again be one of those authentic and inexplicable details.

In any other story of betrayal, Judas the traitor would be expected to appear as a witness against Jesus in his trial, to spill the secrets only the apostles would have heard, to have his moment of shame in court. Yet this doesn't happen in any gospel. 'Several brought false witness against him [Jesus],' Mark writes of Jesus' trial, but he makes no reference to Judas being one of them.[69] Instead, Mark falls back on the impersonal style favoured by Paul. It happened, no need to list names. And, for once, those who came after Mark did not try to fill this gap in his account.

So, with a kiss, Judas departs the narratives of Mark, Luke and John without, apparently, a backward glance, or any hint of the consequences for him of his actions. Only Matthew offers the final glimpse that took me to Hakeldama. Before examining his account of Judas' death, though, I want to attempt to make sense of what I have found in the gospels in today's Garden of Gethsemane.

E

Ear

A brown, ear-shaped fungus that grows on wood in temperate regions, the Judas Ear (more properly *Auricularia auricula-judae*) grows profusely on elder. In pagan beliefs, the elder could ward off evil spirits, but medieval Christianity – intent on suppressing paganism – turned this on its head by claiming it was the tree from which Judas had hanged himself. The fungus ear on an elder then was Judas' unquiet spirit manifesting itself on the site of his suicide. Revealing the tendency at the time to conflate Judas and Jews, the fungus was also known as Jew's Ear, but is now usually called Jelly Ear.

F

Fig

No detail, it is often said, was included in a Renaissance painting without a reason, and dotted along the table in depictions of the Last Supper from the period is a standard cast of fruit: pomegranates, their seeds a symbol of resurrection; cherries, their red the shade of Jesus' soon-to-be-spilt blood; and the Judas fig, a foretaste of the traitor's death, hanging from a fig tree, according to early Christian tradition.

CHAPTER THREE:

The Garden of Gethsemane, Jerusalem

Scarce had He spoken, suddenly appeared
A horde of slaves, a crowd of vagrants, glint
Of swords and torches, Judas at their head,
A treacherous kiss shaped ready on his lips.

'The Garden of Gethsemane'
'The Poems of Yuri Zhivago', Boris Pasternak:
Dr Zhivago (1957)

If the olive trees could talk . . . The thought takes root in my head in the Garden of Gethsemane, which owes its exotic but (thanks to Christianity) now familiar name to the Aramaic for olive presses. This, I should confess, isn't the first time I've wanted to start a conversation with an ancient tree. There was the morning I once spent sheltering from intermittent downpours under a 3,000-year-old yew in Fortingall churchyard in Perthshire. What images, I wondered then, were imprinted onto the rings of its trunk, if only I could access them?

The same thought returns to tantalise me now, though examining the gnarled, split and blackened trunks of Gethsemane's olive trees, some of them said already to have clocked up two millennia,[1] I worry that the warm sun, even on a winter's day like today, will have burnt away all traces of the past. When all else fails, writes Thomas Pakenham, in his book, *Meetings with Remarkable Trees*, he resorts to bouts of trunk-hugging to try to unlock centuries of secrets.[2] As a halfway house, where that's not possible (and there are so many other pilgrims around, I'm not sure if I would be able to risk the puzzled stares), he suggests that these witnesses to our past are akin to great cathedrals, so can be experienced by 'stepping beneath their domes and vaults to pay homage at a mysterious shrine'. I think I can manage that without blushing.

There is only one ancient olive tree here where such a pared-down ritual is physically possible. The rest are protected behind greyish-brown railings from the unwanted attention of pilgrims. A lone specimen nudges up close to the wall of the Basilica of the Agony, the modern Franciscan church that completes this cloistered garden on the spot where, 2,000 years ago, Jesus was arrested after being betrayed by the infamous Judas kiss.

Given their great age, these trees are, in theory, the next best thing to eyewitnesses to what happened that night, though the *Catholic Encyclopedia* does sound a gentle note of caution about the reliability of their evidence. 'If they were not found there in the time of Christ, they are at least the offshoots of those which witnessed his agony.'[3] Just as children do not have their parents' memories, neither will these offshoots. And there is a story, too, that in 70 CE the Emperor Titus Vespasian ordered all the olive trees in the Garden of Gethsemane cut down, to punish the Jews for their uprising against Roman rule, but it is unclear if it actually happened, or if some were spared.[4]

I pick my moment carefully. The lone accessible tree is, inevitably, popular with visitors for photographs. Next to its broad girth, a tangle of knots, lumps and periodic bursts of regeneration, some of them bolstered by stone crutches, my fellow pilgrims line up to say cheese – or olives. There is a break in the procession, my cue to step swiftly and decisively forward, and get too close for comfort. None of the trinket-sellers who hover nearby bat an eyelid. I close mine and nestle in as snugly as I can so as to hear the beating heart of this old-timer. 'Somewhere inside the ancient bark,' wrote the former Archbishop of Canterbury, Rowan Williams, in a poem about his own visit here, 'a voice has been before us'.[5]

By shuffling a few centimetres to one side, the branches seem to close in on me from above. There, that's as close as I am going to get, I figure, and wait to experience a quiet power. Or the sense of being transported back. Or anything. And I wait. The tree's embrace is certainly making me feel small, both physically and as a speck of dust in the flow of human history that it spans, but the hoped-for insights into its past are not so easily unlocked. All that I am now sensing is the presence of others – the next party of pilgrims has arrived, straight from the coaches that queue outside and all the way back along the road that runs round the foot of the Mount of Olives. As I open my eyes, they are staring back at me. One is even taking a photograph of my ad-hoc séance.

I make my excuses and leave. There is, though, and inevitably, another spot for reconnecting with Gethsemane's part in the gospel narrative. This time, it is officially sanctioned. A lump of exposed rock is contained within the Basilica of the Agony itself. The church may be a recent building – dating back only to 1924 – but, as is often the case in this city of layers, it is the latest in a line of places of worship on this site, resting on foundations that go back to the sixth century. Older still is the large slab of rock, which I find in front of the main altar. It is reputedly where Jesus momentarily faltered that night in the Garden of Gethsemane, in the face of all he knew was going to happen to him. 'He threw himself to the ground,' Mark writes, 'and prayed that, if it were possible, this hour might pass him by. "Abba, Father!" he said, "everything is possible for you. Take this cup away from me."'[6]

Unlike that other scene of despair at Hakeldama, Judas is frankly acknowledged here in Gethsemane. Acknowledged and damned. To the left of where I have just knelt to touch the rock is a large-scale fresco of the kiss – though, in line with Luke, the traitor's face hovers several inches short of Jesus', as if held at bay by the force-field of the golden halo that surrounds the latter's head, and those of the other apostles present. But not, of course, of Judas'.

The fresco is one of a pair. The other, *The Last Miracle*, is to the right of the altar. Mark and Matthew both describe how, as Jesus is arrested, one of his followers draws a sword in protest and cuts off the ear of a servant of the high priest.[7] Luke adds to this and has Jesus restoring the ear to the servant's head in the supernatural act that gives the fresco its name.[8] John's even fuller variation names the servant as Malchus, places the sword in Peter's hand but, curiously, leaves the ear detached.[9]

The artist has conflated these last two gospels – as is often the case in the telling of this episode – and has Peter brandishing the sword and Jesus reattaching the ear. Judas, though, is a notable absentee. Having pointed out Jesus (or not, according to John), he has evidently left the garden immediately, fearing quite rightly that the other disciples would rise up to defend their master. It could otherwise have been his ear that was hacked off. Would Jesus have healed it? I'd like to think he would. 'Get the traitor,' you can hear the other apostles cry out, echoing down history.

It is another symbolism in the pairing of the two frescoes, though, that stays with me. Judas and Peter are both flawed. Both do the wrong thing, left and right, but Peter's sin is redeemed. Judas' isn't. All four gospels elsewhere report Jesus predicting that Peter would either disown or deny him 'before the cock crows'.[10] And, despite his protestations at the time, all then show Peter doing precisely that. The language, of course, is different – denial and disowning on Peter's part, betrayal on Judas'. And the consequences are not the same. Judas hands Jesus over to his death. Peter fails to stand up for him through fear, but would not have been able to save him even if he had found his courage. But what

If trees could talk: the ancient olive trees of Gethsemane, potential witnesses to the 'Judas Kiss'.

'The Last Miracle', a fresco in the Basilica of the Agony in Gethsemane, Jerusalem.

really makes Peter and Judas into a contrasting pair, the good apostle and the bad apostle, in these frescoes and elsewhere in Christian art and literature, is that Peter seeks and is granted forgiveness.

Beyond the basilica and the neat, tended, cloistered garden with a handful of trees, the olive groves of Gethsemane spread further afield. Most are locked away, but below one section a rough-hewn cave-grotto can be visited via a corridor that runs down the side of a neighbouring Orthodox church. This cave is where, tradition has it, Judas arrived with the guards to find Jesus and the other apostles sheltering.

Cave-like chapels are as common in Jerusalem as men with guns, uniforms and the smell of fear. Here, as at Hakeldama, where Saint Onouphrius' memory has been elevated to push Judas' prior claim into the shadows, the memory of the Judas kiss is played down in favour of a rather loose attribution to the Virgin Mary. In the next-door church, the Orthodox watch over what they claim as Jesus' mother's tomb (though there is another grave with her name on it in Ephesus). Western Christians, in the game of musical chairs that is religious custodianship in Jerusalem, used to be in possession of that church but, since having to vacate it (reluctantly) in favour of their eastern cousins, they have been using the cave-grotto as the next best thing to recall Mary's final resting place. So, though the visitor noticeboard at the entrance claims that this is, indeed, where Judas handed Jesus over for trial, there is not a single image of the moment on display in this curious hollowed-out lair, with bare rock mixed in with concrete panels, and ugly modern storage heaters with flaking frescoes, believed to date back to the times of the twelfth-century Crusaders.

I arrive just as preparations are being made for a mass. The Franciscans have been in charge of the grotto for 600 years, and a brown-robed brother is busy sweeping the floor and tidying the altar. A coach party of Italian pilgrims is soon to arrive, with their own priest in tow, he explains, and I would be welcome to join them. I take my place in the pews.

Probing the historical claims made for sites like this in Jerusalem is not a very fruitful quest, so I banish at once the knowledge that the gospels make absolutely no mention of a cave that night in Gethsemane. Outside the Basilica of the Agony, I had spotted a notice, intended to silence the procession of tour guides who go inside: 'Please No Explanations in the Church'. Extending its remit, I decide that it is enough that people have believed in the grotto's particular place in history for so many centuries.

The 'Pilgrim of Bordeaux' describes a precise spot where Judas did the deed, but not a grotto. 'As one goes from Jerusalem, in order to ascend the Mount of Olives,' he writes of his visit here in 333, 'is the valley called that of Josaphat. Towards the left, where are vineyards, is a stone at the place where Judas Iscariot betrayed Christ.'[11] Well, there are plenty of stones here, beneath, around and above me.

By contrast, Peter the Deacon, writing in the twelfth century but purporting to translate the chronicle of another fourth-century visitor to Jerusalem, describes 'a grotto at the place where Jesus the Saviour was captured'.[12] Peter the Deacon, it should be added, though librarian of the prestigious Benedictine Abbey of Montecassino in Italy, has something of a reputation as a forger. Another monk, Theodosius the Cenobiarch, however, is held in higher regard by historians, and tells in his account of going to Jerusalem in 450 and seeing a grotto at Gethsemane where Judas betrayed his master.[13]

So, once again, I'm walking in centuries of pilgrims' footsteps, but not necessarily those of Judas'. My mind wanders, seeking something to fix onto. The frescoed ceiling above me offers little. It hangs so low over the altar that it has been blackened beyond detail by the smoke of the candles. Only a few star motifs stand out. Alone in the cave, save for the brother who has now stopped brushing and is kneeling in silent prayer, I simply wait. '*Dieci, dieci*,' he says, looking over towards me. The mass will be in ten minutes. He cups his head in his hands and resumes his devotions.

And so we remain, as if caught in a hole in time. Into the vacuum drifts the faint sound of chanting from the Orthodox neighbours. I think I am only imagining the smell of incense, but it feels real enough in my nostrils, carrying me backwards. Or is it incense? In the quiet and the semi-darkness of the first Easter, the olives would just have been harvested, giving off in this place of Gethsemane the pungent aroma of crushed fruits. There might also be a small fire burning, to take the chill out of the night air on this spring evening, using the cuttings from the pruned trees. The apostles are littered around the cave, dozing, keeping warm, utterly unaware of what is about to happen as they wait for Jesus to return from his prayers elsewhere in the garden. It has been a tumultuous day, and a tiring one. Too much to think about, they conclude, so probably better to drift off to sleep. And then suddenly they stir at the sound of heavy foot-steps approaching . . .

What I am actually hearing, though, is not a party of guards led by Judas, but a rotund, red-faced tour guide who bursts in, full of breathless apology, to inform the brother along the pew that the party of Italian pilgrims, plus priest, is not coming after all. Mass is off.

I head off to a vacant bench outside the cloistered section of the Garden of Gethsemane, to take in the view it offers of the Old City. The spirit of reverie is hard to dispel. So much for com-muning with trees, or imagining myself into the past, I decide: why not try, as a cure, a bit of old-fashioned geography? Can the gospel accounts of Judas' betrayal be reconciled with the topography of the city that stretches out ahead of me on the other bank of the valley?

The first act of the drama – where the Last Supper takes place – was in the Cenacle or Upper Room. I had been the previous day to what has long been regarded as its site, just south of the Old City walls on Mount Zion, hidden away from where I am sitting by the great platform of Mount Moriah, or the Temple Mount, crowned today by Jerusalem's main visual landmark, the giant orangey-gold bulb of the Dome of the Rock. Next, Jesus and his apostles headed from the Cenacle to the Garden of Gethsemane. They could, I suppose, have taken a wide sweep and walked round the south and east of the Old City, outside the walls, and then up the Kidron Valley, but there is no suggestion in the gospels that they ever skulked in the shadows. Quite the opposite, indeed, which is what got the authorities so worked up that they struck a deal with Judas. So, the group would have come the quickest way, through the Old City and out of the Golden Gate, now directly in my eye-line.

It requires a little imagination to picture the scene. The Temple Mount now has new tenants; the current city walls date back only to the sixteenth century, after being destroyed and rebuilt several times over; the Golden Gate is blocked up. Its twin arches, set within a buttress that juts out on the east side of the Temple Mount, were sealed in 1541 on the order of the Ottoman ruler, Suleiman the Magnificent, to dash Jewish hopes, rooted in the Hebrew Scriptures, that one day the messiah would return and enter the city via that particular gate. But it requires no great vision to be able to spot Jesus and the twelve, heading down the hillside towards me.

What are they talking about? They have just participated in the first-ever Eucharist, though they don't know that, but still they will be puzzling at what has just happened. Body and blood, bread and wine: the connection will be turning over in their minds. Jesus' words, too, have given them much to debate. In Luke's account, he promises to 'confer a kingdom' on them, that they will 'sit on thrones' to judge the twelve tribes of Israel.[14] Head-turning stuff for fishermen from Galilee. And then he has quoted a line of Scripture at them that suggests he is about to be arrested. 'If you have no sword,' he says, 'sell your cloak and buy one.'[15] Are they glancing nervously over their shoulders, preparing for a fight, wondering where to get weapons?

Worse still, Jesus has made plain at supper that there is a traitor in their midst. John gets Jesus to spell out it is Judas, but even then he gives the impression that the apostles still don't realise what has been said. They must be pondering, looking askance at each other. Matthew tells that, in between the Upper Room and Gethsemane, Jesus has spoken to Peter, the natural leader among them, predicting that 'this day, this very night, before the cock crows twice, you will have disowned me three times'.[16] He says this publicly, so all twelve will have overheard. Is Peter the one?

Only John detaches Judas from the walking party, showing him leaving the Upper Room, possessed by the devil, as Jesus instructs him, 'What you are going to do, do quickly.'[17] And John also provides sufficient time for Judas to go and find the guards because he then describes Jesus' lengthy 'farewell discourses',[18] a pep talk that is not mentioned in the other three accounts.

So where might Judas have gone? If he remained with the group I have in my mind's eye, he may have been relieved that suspicion was now directed at Peter. Soon, though, when they arrive here in Gethsemane, Jesus will take Peter (and James and John) with him as he seeks out a quiet place to pray.[19] That surely absolves Peter of the charge of being the traitor, and reopens the debate among the rest of them. Perhaps Judas waits until they have fallen into a troubled sleep, then doubles back to rouse the group of guards of the chief priests, somewhere in or around the Temple, close to the Golden Gate.

By now it will have been nightfall. The party of guards heads into the darkness of the countryside as they leave the gate, and so carry flares. It really isn't a long way down to the garden. Five minutes at the most, over exposed terrain. Had any of the apostles been awake and looking back towards the city walls, they would have seen them coming. Jesus, though, knows to look and spots the approach of Judas and the guards. 'The hour has come,' he says in Mark, '. . . My betrayer is close at hand.'[20]

Again, it is all possible, even plausible. And the walk back into Jerusalem from Gethsemane after the betrayal? From where I am sitting, once more the geography works. Jesus is surrounded by his captors – 'Take him in charge,' Judas says in Mark, 'and see he is well guarded when you lead him away.'[21] He sounds efficient, in charge and a little nervous of trouble. Matthew and Mark both say Jesus is escorted to the palace of the high priest, Caiaphas.[22] In Luke, presumably because it is so late in the evening, Jesus is taken to Caiaphas' house.[23] The site earmarked today for that high priest's residence is back on Mount Zion, where the modern church of Saint Peter in Gallicantu stands. There are 'holy steps' leading up to it, and cave-like cells in its deepest basement where, tradition holds, Jesus was chained that night before his death.

And where does Judas go? Mark, Luke and John say nothing. Yet it is human nature to be curious, so perhaps he hides away, near the route back from Gethsemane to Mount Zion, and follows the guards and their prisoner at a distance, to witness what he has precipitated. It is as impossible to know as it is for trees to speak. But a final thought occurs to me as I get up from my resting place and set off to retrace this route. What lies directly beyond the traditional site of Caiaphas' house, on the next hillside if I were to draw a direct line from where I am standing now in the Garden of Gethsemane, is Hakeldama.

G

Goat

A Judas Goat is by tradition trained to herd other animals some-where they wouldn't normally want to go, but more specifically to lead sheep into an abattoir to the slaughter. Unlike Judas Iscariot, his namesake goat is spared death having accomplished his task of betrayal.

H

Hole

A Judas Hole is found in a prison door, allowing guards to spy on the inmate without him or her being aware they are being watched. The connotation is that it enables them to watch as the prisoner betrays himself, but it might also enable the watchers to prevent a suicide.

CHAPTER FOUR:

Life After Death: How Judas Lived On

In Jerusalem, don't ask me the history of facts. Take away the fiction and there's nothing left.

Dr Nazmi al-Jubeh, historian and writer[1]

If the biography of Judas Iscariot in the gospels lacks the conventional details (date of birth, parentage, marriage, family), Matthew at least provides an ending. The passage in question sits clumsily in the flow of his narrative, an after-thought that had to be accommodated within events as they build up to Jesus' crucifixion. It is inserted, as if cutting to a parallel storyline in a film or play, once the Jewish leaders have handed Jesus over to Pontius Pilate, but before reporting any of the exchanges between the two.

'When he [Judas] found that Jesus had been condemned . . .' the author of Matthew begins.[2] It is, so far, only 'the chief priests and the elders of the people' who have ruled on Jesus' fate.[3] That may have been verdict enough for Judas, though the Roman overlord is still to have the final say. 'They had him bound and led him away to hand him over to Pilate, the governor.'[4]

News of Jesus' condemnation, according to Matthew, fills Judas with remorse. Again, there is something unsatisfactory about this remark: remorse for what? That Jesus, with whom Judas had spent the last three years, is facing a death sentence? That the chief priests and elders of the people have handed Jesus

75

over to resented Roman justice? Or that the Jewish authorities have found Jesus guilty at all? All could, potentially, prompt Judas, as Matthew reports next, to attempt the return of the thirty pieces of silver to the Jewish leaders. 'I have sinned,' he says. 'I have betrayed innocent blood.' The authorial finger of accusation is pointed at the chief priests when they turn Judas away, replying coldly: 'What is that to us? That is your concern.'[5]

In disgust, Judas flings the silver pieces down in the Temple sanctuary and makes off. It is a dramatic gesture that, reportedly, used to be re-enacted in Coptic Christian liturgies on Good Friday (I have not been able to trace anywhere it still happens). And a despairing one, since Judas then hangs himself. The details about the Field of Blood come after he is dead at the end of a rope, not to identify the location where Judas took his own life, but to explain what the chief priests subsequently did with the tainted coins.

As is the case with each new gospel expanding on those that have gone before, the Acts of the Apostles, which postdates three of the four, and which most scholars estimate was written around 90 CE by the same hand as Luke's gospel, also attempts to iron out some of the kinks in previous versions. It describes how the seat that Judas has left empty among the twelve is filled by a ballot that elects Matthias, about whom nothing else is known, even in the normally fertile field of church legend.[6] In an account that directly cuts across Paul's earlier description of the risen Christ re-engaging with the twelve original apostles, Peter explains to the rest how Judas the betrayer 'abandoned' his ministry 'to go to his proper place'[7] – presumably hell, given all the previous talk by the author in Luke of the devil. Speaking to a gathering of 120 people, including the remaining apostles, Peter goes into detail on Judas' fate.

'As you know,' he begins, 'he bought a field with the money he was paid for his crime.' Readers of the gospels do not know this, even if Peter's listeners did. Matthew has told us that the chief priests bought the field with the money Judas tried to return to them. Peter may be rewriting history. 'He fell headlong and burst open,' he continues in Acts, 'and his entrails poured out. Everyone in Jerusalem heard about it, and the field came to be called the Bloody Acre.'[8]

Again there is that insistence that this is already common knowledge. To make this point twice in as many sentences seems to be overdoing it, but the author of Acts is evidently keen to erase Matthew's earlier version, not just of the ownership of the field, but also of how Judas died. If anything can be worse than the lonely despair of suicide, then the end described in Acts is intended to be it. It also works in a devilish theme, as if Judas is possessed by an evil spirit (the prime motivation in John – written later – and to a lesser extent Luke) that exits his body by disembowelling him.

Why two different accounts? The simple explanation is that both writers want to make a point with Judas' death. If Matthew had simply wanted to tie up a loose end – i.e., Judas' fate – then he could have left his account with the betrayer trying to return the money, failing, and heading off into the wilderness. It is an eloquent enough expression of Judas' remorse and ruination, even without the suicide.

But he doesn't. Matthew's whole gospel seeks, to a greater extent than the other three, to tie Jesus into Jewish hopes of a messiah. The text begins, like the dullest of modern biographies, with a long and dizzying account of Jesus' ancestors, included with the express purpose of linking him through Joseph (bizarrely, since Mary is a virgin and Joseph therefore not what we now call his birth father) to David, the tenth-century BCE king of the Jews, and thence to Abraham, the biblical patriarch.

In the light of this agenda, what Matthew's gospel emphasises is that the chief priests and elders (and later the crowds of Jews who shout down Pilate's attempts to free Jesus) kill one of their own. Jesus is the messiah, promised by the Hebrew prophets, yet the Jews reject him and are responsible for his death. That is why Judas' remorse comes straight after the Jewish authorities have pronounced on Jesus, and before Pilate does. And Judas' treachery amplifies this same theme, since his name is almost interchangeable with the word Jew.

Yet, having cast Judas as the scapegoat, Matthew also enters a plea of mitigation for him with his account of his remorse in the run-up to his own death. It could be taken as a concession to the Jews – the author of Matthew being conscious, perhaps, of those Jewish Christians in Jerusalem, who saw the future of the 'Jesus movement' within Judaism, at variance with those, like him, who followed Paul in opening it to all as a separate church. Or it could be saying, here is the only Jew who can be absolved of the crime of killing the messiah. By Matthew's chronology, Judas dies before Jesus. (Later medieval writers would make much of this, suggesting he did so in order to position himself at the threshold of eternal life, to beg Jesus' forgiveness as he passed.)

Either way, though, here lie some of the deepest roots of Christian anti-Semitism, the notion that the Jews killed the Son of God, the crime of deicide, for which the Catholic Church continued to judge the whole Jewish people guilty until 1965.[9] Any distinction Matthew tries to make between Judas and Jews was to be lost in the early centuries of Christianity.

The backdrop to Matthew's account therefore seems likely to be that disagreement engulfing Jesus' followers over what exactly they were: a branch of Judaism, led by the faction that remained in Jerusalem, or a new church for all, outside Judaism, as pushed by Paul and his followers. This question had been thrashed out at a Council in Jerusalem around 50 CE (mentioned in the Acts of the Apostles and believed by most – but not all – historians to have been a real event[10]) as part of the debate about whether new Gentile converts had to be circumcised. The 'Jewish' group, headed by Jesus' brother, James the Just, believed that the converts were joining Judaism, albeit a form that acknowledged Jesus as the messiah, and that they therefore had to follow all other Jewish rules, including circumcision. The Pauline faction, busy converting mainly Greek-speaking non-Jewish people of the eastern Mediterranean (who objected culturally to circumcision), opposed this stance, and won the day, a further step on the road to eventual separation from the Jewish Christians.

It is worth restating that the author of Matthew, along with those of Mark, Luke, John and the Acts, is a product of the Pauline Church. All these accounts were written after the Council of Jerusalem and all appear, increasingly, to want to put clear water between themselves and all the Jews, even more so than Paul (who is believed to have died in 64 CE, before the first gospel was written). What better way of achieving this than to blame the Jews collectively for Jesus' death, and downplay the role played by the Romans – hence Pilate washing his hands, as he tells the crowd of Jews calling for Jesus to be crucified, 'I am innocent of this man's blood. It is your concern.' They reply without shame, in Matthew, 'his blood be on us and on our children!'[II]

If Matthew tries to take the edge off Judas' individual guilt, though, the other gospel writers are perfectly content to make him as much the villain of the piece as the Jewish authorities he serves. In accusing him of betrayal, they allow him no moment of regret. Here, then, is the process of establishing a scapegoat – Judas the scapegoat stands for the Jews as scapegoats, people who will carry the blame for deicide for centuries in Christian eyes, because of the connotations of his name and origins. It is a neat fit and a powerful symbolism. He is someone so close to Jesus (just like the Jews since Jesus is Jewish), belonging on the face of it to a group that stands for good, but in reality is consorting with the devil. While Jesus triumphs over death to rescue humankind, Judas hangs himself, or bursts asunder, unredeemed and unredeemable. For Jesus read Christianity. For Judas read the Jews.

This imagery was highlighted forcefully by Hyam Maccoby. 'It may seem a strange coincidence that of all Jesus' twelve disciples,' he writes, 'the one whom the gospel story singles out as a traitor bears the name of the Jewish people . . . [He] was chosen for a baleful but necessary mythological role precisely because of his name.' And having been chosen, Maccoby argues, Judas is incorporated into a 'nakedly dualistic' story by the gospel writers as the representative of evil, someone who betrays Jesus, the representative of good.[12]

Maccoby goes even further. He suggests that the character of Judas had been created deliberately, either by using one of the original apostles with a different name who was then recast as Judas, his very name an indictment of the Jews, or by imposing a wicked personality on the blank canvas of a hitherto unremarkable follower of Jesus who just happened to be called Judas, as many were at that time.[13]

And, potentially, invention begets invention, according to Sir Frank Kermode. 'We could make up more stories about his [Judas'] actions and his character, and we still can: there seems to be no end to our doing so'.[14] The Judas of the New Testament – enigmatic, sketchily and unevenly drawn, but nevertheless a decisive presence in the narrative – has proved an open invitation to project and speculate down the ages, if only because the betrayer intrigues more than the apostles who remain loyal. He is, in the language of dramatists, 'the change character' in the story.

Old Testament

The desire to create a scapegoat out of Judas is not the only thesis put forward by those who suspect he is a fiction, and who therefore want to explain him away as anything other than real. Some point to the sheer number of Old Testament references that underpin the role allotted to Judas in the gospels. This, again, is particularly true in the case of Matthew, with his keen concern for the Jewish tradition. In his telling, Judas' character and actions can at times appear like a jigsaw of pieces borrowed from the prophets of the Hebrew Scriptures, and then reassembled to make an e-fit picture of Jesus' betrayer. The main thrust may have been to hammer home the point – crucial to Matthew – that Jesus is the fulfilment of Jewish hopes of a messiah, but in the process Judas becomes regurgitated prophecy clothed as flesh and blood.

Take that curious figure of thirty pieces of silver that is so much part of Judas' cultural baggage – a detail included only in Matthew. In many bibles, there is a footnote to link this calibration with a passage in the Book of Exodus that prices the life of a slave at thirty shekels.[15] The intricacies of the shekel-to-silver-pieces exchange rate need not detain us here. It is that bare figure of thirty which carries with it an echo that is intended to be proof of prophecy coming true.

The time lapse is slightly shorter with another oft-quoted parallel to a fourth-century BCE reference in the Book of Zechariah, a minor prophet. Here, the coincidence is, arguably, greater, and it may have had more influence on the author of Matthew, since in Zechariah Israel receives 'thirty shekels of silver' for betraying its covenant with Yahweh. Later, the cash is thrown back by Zechariah into the treasury at the Temple.[16]

And finally, Matthew's account of Judas' suicide is followed by that familiar gospel phrase, 'the words of the prophet were then fulfilled'.[17] In this case the reference given by Matthew is to Jeremiah, but the words are based instead on the same passage from Zechariah as before, in this case his tale of God judging as wicked the potter who breaks unsatisfactory pots.[18] Is this why Hakeldama is described by Matthew as having once been a potter's field? It had seemed so credible when I was there, seeing the thick damp clay on the path as I walked up to the monastery's front gate.

Mark, at first glance, doesn't play the same games when he tells Judas' story, but his description of Judas kissing Jesus in Gethsemane – an unnecessary but arresting gesture – can just as easily be linked to various betrayers' kisses in the Old Testament. In the Second Book of Samuel, for example, as it chronicles the murderous battles among the relatives of King David for political power, one royal nephew, Joab, greets another, Amasa, with a kiss, but while they are embracing drives his sword into his stomach 'and spilled his entrails on the ground'.[19] Entrails feature too in Judas' end in the Acts of the Apostles.

Then, in looking for forerunners of Judas in earlier literature, the Book of Genesis offers Judah, one of the many brothers of Joseph (of the coat of many colours), who persuades his siblings to betray Joseph. After some debate, they do this by selling him for twenty pieces of silver to Midianite merchants on their way to Egypt, and then dip his coat in blood to prove he has been killed by a wild beast.[20] It is a potentially short step from Judah to Judas.

In Psalm 41, in the Old Testament, the writer bemoans the actions of one he took for a friend, who betrays him. 'Even my close friend, whom I trusted, who ate of my bread, has lifted his heel against me.'[21] It is this passage that John draws on – and which is referred to in footnotes to his gospel – when he describes Jesus for the first time talking of betrayal.[22]

Before getting carried away by such connections, though, there is an obvious health warning to issue – namely that, given the size and accumulation of detail in the Old Testament, there is most likely going to be a precedent somewhere in there for each and every thing that happens in the New Testament if you search hard enough and set the criteria wide enough.

Moreover, the Old Testament, based on the Hebrew Scriptures, is not the only source on which those creating Judas – if creation he is – might have drawn. The gospels were written in Greek, by authors whose level of education means they would most probably have been familiar with Greek epics, where the betrayer is a familiar enough figure. Dennis MacDonald, a California-based professor of New Testament studies, has made his academic reputation in this crowded field by arguing that Mark's gospel and the Acts of the Apostles are based on the Homeric epics of ancient Greece. Mark 'thoroughly, cleverly and strategically emulated' the *Odyssey*, Professor MacDonald claims, so as 'to depict Jesus as more compassionate, powerful, noble and inured to suffering than Odysseus'. That makes the earliest of the gospels 'a novel, and a prose anti-epic of sorts'.[23]

There is no independent or external evidence to back up such an assertion. Instead, Professor MacDonald is making his deductions by a very particular reading of the text. In the case of Judas, he thinks he spots a parallel between the betrayer Judas and Melanthius, the disloyal goatherd, in the *Odyssey*. When his master Odysseus is in his pursuit of Penelope, Melanthius makes a pact with his rivals, even stealing weapons to help them out in their battle with Odysseus, and at another moment coming close to unmasking a disguised Odysseus to his rivals. This, for Professor MacDonald, is the forerunner of the Judas kiss.

His betrayal of Odysseus certainly serves Melanthius ill. Like Judas, he dies a terrible death, his body mutilated and his genitals fed to the dogs. There are, though, as many divergences as potential parallels. More, indeed. Melanthius, for example, is killed by his former colleagues, Odysseus' still-loyal cowherd and swineherd, but it is not the apostles who turn on Judas. And the Judas kiss is described by Mark and Matthew as serving its purpose, rather than as a near miss.

Fact or fiction?

Trying to reach a verdict on the gospels as fact or fiction is a fool's errand. At its extreme, it is a task that demands a Dan Brown-style binge, with Robert Langdon in *The Da Vinci Code*, intrepid seeker-after-truth after centuries of church cover-up, rustling through carefully guarded Vatican archives to find the 'actual' thirty pieces of silver.[24] Yet many still construct speculative theses on the belief that the Judas of the gospels is nothing more than a creation, and therefore absolutely open to amendment, manipulation or extension. And, on the other side of the debate, a tendency to embellish is also there among those who regard the gospels as true.

If the gospels, as I have already argued, deserve to be taken seriously but not literally as historical accounts, that must logically also apply to those described in them, including Judas. If Judas is wholly manufactured, a figure custom-built to play the role of betrayer, or more subtly scapegoat, then there are surely too many jagged edges in what the four gospels tell us of him, too many slips of detail, timings and logic, too many inconsistencies, for it to be a neat package of a story designed to achieve such an end.

The Judas of the gospels, in short, seems to me too inconsistent to read as just a device. There are those flashes of recognisable humanity in his tale – his outrage at the waste of expensive ointment, that stumbling kiss, his remorse and the pitiful, despairing situation in which he ends up – that bring him to life more so than the other apostles. At times Judas feels so conflicted – above all in his motives for betrayal – that he could be one of us. Real lives, after all, don't usually fit into tidy narrative strategies or political/ religious imperatives. In the simplest of terms, we don't always do the predictable. Actions, choices, decisions defy explanation. It's part of being human. If Judas is 'just' a character, he's drawn in too much detail yet with too little clarity, certainly for this reader. Buried in there somewhere, I see glimpses of a person.

The search for a historical Jesus in the pages of the New Testament consumed forty years of Géza Vermes' career. By birth Hungarian and by descent Jewish, he was raised from the age of seven as a Catholic. His parents died in the Holocaust, after which he became a priest and an academic, specialising in the Dead Sea Scrolls, the collection of ancient manuscripts dating back to biblical times, unearthed in the Holy Land in the 1940s. He left the Church in 1957, married the following year, and returned to his Jewish roots, basing himself in the UK, and latterly Oxford, where he made his name as the doyen of scholars in the English-speaking world on the Jewish literature that was contemporary with Jesus. He died in 2013.

I met him on several occasions, during the course of which he outlined a number of basic tests he applied to texts – the gospels included – to determine their historical reliability. The first is eminently sensible, namely to attach more importance to earlier texts than later ones. In the case of Judas, then, the search for authenticity is best conducted first in the gospel of Mark, then those of Matthew and Luke and, only after these, among all those additional and sometimes confusing details included in John. 'John's narrative,' Professor Vermes made plain, 'is more fiction than history when it is compared with the Synoptics.'[25]

That means therefore that the suggestion made, above all, by John that Judas was a greedy money-grabber, and generally a thoroughly bad lot (an image that has proved so powerful in history) should carry less weight than, say, Matthew's account of the remorseful and tragic Judas, or Mark's spare, often opaque portrait.

The second Vermes point – again logical – gives greater credence to those parts of the gospels that are repeated in more than one version. Judas is there in all four, plus the Acts of the Apostles. He achieves a full house as an individual, even if the specific details of his life – Hakeldama, for instance, mentioned just in Matthew and the Acts – score less well.[26]

And Vermes' third yardstick urges caution where particular remarks or details carry with them an obvious doctrinal or theological motivation. The thirty pieces of silver, for instance, falls foul of this, because of its obvious Old Testament roots, but the Judas kiss has, as far as I have been able to discern, no ulterior motive.[27]

That said, and before I take any further encouragement from Professor Vermes' scholarship, he also provides in *The Authentic Gospel of Jesus* (2003) what might be called a traffic light system. By applying the weight of his accumulated scholarship, which started with his studies of the Dead Sea Scrolls, he ranks the sayings of Jesus in the gospels as 'authentic', 'probably authentic' and 'editorial' (i.e., made up by others later). It is the equivalent of labelling them green, amber and red. By this classification, Jesus' presence in Gethsemane gets a red – i.e. 'editorial' – ranking (though it is, of course, his words spoken there in the gospel accounts, including some addressed to Judas, that are being damned by the professor, not the fact that he may have set foot there). The same goes for Jesus' prediction, during the preparation for the Last Supper, that he would be betrayed by one of those closest to him. But his remarks about what Vermes calls 'the blessedness of the disciples' (including Judas) gets a green. Jesus saw them all as good men – and women.

All of which leaves me precisely where? Well, when hip-high in the historical currents that course in and about Jerusalem, it had been so tempting to go with the flow and be carried along towards a literal reading of Judas' biography in Mark, Matthew, Luke and John. Back on terra firma, though, that instinct has to be curbed. I need to chart my own course carefully, and at my own speed. On

which note, there is one more major item of evidence still to consider – the gospel that carries Judas' name, and which emerged
from almost two millennia in the shadows to sensational headlines and global interest in 2006.

I

Isaac

The 2011 video game, 'The Binding of Isaac', which sold two million copies worldwide, is based on the story, told in the Book of Genesis, in which God challenges the biblical patriarch Abraham to bind and sacrifice his son, Isaac. In this garbled console version, among the cast of characters is a Judas, known to gamers as 'Judas Isaac', who clutches not thirty pieces of silver but three pennies, and sports a curious fez hat, borrowed by the creators from an erstwhile friend who they claim betrayed them.

J

Jung

Carl Jung, the founder of analytical psychology, writes at length in his *Psychology of the Unconscious* (1912) about Judas, describing him as a powerful archetype, tapping into a force in the collective unconscious. Judas illustrates, he says, 'the psychological fact that envy does not allow humanity to sleep in peace, and that all of us harbour, in a hidden recess of our heart, the wish that the hero should die'.

CHAPTER FIVE:

A Good Betrayal? The Gospel of Judas

Everything connected with our ordinary conceptions of this man, of his real purposes, and of his ultimate fate, apparently is erroneous.

Thomas De Quincey: *Judas Iscariot* (1852)

Oh, to hear Judas' voice in a surviving letter or autobiographical fragment! Optimistic, of course, at 2,000 years' distance, especially when nothing that is indisputably first hand remains of any of the gospel figures. *The Gospel of Judas*, made public in April 2006, having been lost for almost two millennia, seemed briefly to be an answer to my prayers.

In our secular age, fresh discoveries in biblical scholarship tend not to make it onto the front page of newspapers, or the main television bulletins, but the reappearance of this short papyrus text, a translation into Coptic from the original Greek, carbon-dated to the end of the third century CE, proved irresistible. The combination of Judas' enduring 'bad-boy' reputation, and the promise of unearthing a buried past that the church authorities had tried to cover up, made it go global.

In part, the headlines generated can also be attributed to the careful stage-management of the whole unveiling by *National Geographic*, which funded the painstaking restoration of this lost gospel and its translation into English by a team of distinguished academics. Key to its appeal, too, was the claim, made loudly at the time, though in more muted tones since, that this rediscovered manuscript overturned 2,000 years of institutional prejudice against Judas Iscariot. The ultimate sinner was actually, in terms designed to resonate with a twenty-first-century audience, a victim of a miscarriage of justice. That was the line many reporters took. Judas was actually the good guy, someone who, this gospel said, 'exceeded' all the other apostles in Jesus' eyes, and who 'ascends to the holy generation'. His betrayal of Jesus was prompted not by malice or greed, but by friendship and admiration. He was only loyally doing what Jesus told him to do.[1]

It certainly made for a good story, but behind the headlines lies a much more nuanced picture that is closer to the New Testament accounts than might at first be thought. The original *Gospel of Judas*, on which this late third-century copy is based, postdates John's gospel by around half a century. It is known to have existed at the end of the second century CE because the early church father, Bishop Irenaeus of Lyon, mentions it in 180 CE in his tract, *Against Heresies*.[2]

On one thing, there is agreement among all the experts who have – since 2006 – examined *The Gospel of Judas*, held conferences about it and published tomes on it: this is definitively not a gospel written by Judas, a self-penned *mea culpa*. It therefore adds nothing to the details of Judas' life given in the earlier (and therefore, by the first of Géza Vermes' tests, more historically reliable) gospels of Mark, Matthew, Luke and John. Instead it is yet another account written *about* him – or, more to the point, about Jesus as seen by him. If Judas' voice is heard at all, it is only through the layers of interpretation piled on top of him by others with their own agendas.

That most of this Coptic version of *The Gospel of Judas* had survived at all is, in itself, an extraordinary tale, cloaked in mystery. At one stage in the late twentieth century the papyrus – an early form of paper, made from the pith of the papyrus plant

– had been put into a freezer in the mistaken belief that it would help preserve it. Instead it made the pages crumble into fragments, which then had to be pieced back together over five long years. Some 15 per cent had been so badly damaged that they were lost forever, and there are gaps and holes in what has been reassembled. Discovered in the 1970s in the Egyptian region of al-Minya, 150 miles south of Cairo on the western banks of the River Nile, quite how it was first found still remains unclear. One story says that local farmers or *fellahin* stumbled on it near the village of Qarara in a niche in a cave that had once been used by Coptic Christians to bury their dead. It was said to be encased, with other texts (known collectively as *Codex Tchacos*), in a white limestone box, and was lying next to a skeleton of what had presumably been its one-time owner. From Egypt, it travelled by disputed routes via Europe to America, where it was offered for sale at such an exorbitant price that it ended up sitting in a bank vault for sixteen years, waiting for a buyer with suitably deep pockets. It was only thanks to the intervention in 2001 of *National Geographic* and a dedicated Swiss antiquities expert that it was rescued and the long restoration process could begin.

The 2006 launch – accompanied by a film, which became one of the most watched items ever on the National Geographic TV Channel – was akin to firing the starting gun on a marathon for biblical scholars, each with their own theory on Judas, their own take on him, and their own agendas to expound. We'd never heard so much about Judas. It was part of a remarkable series of twentieth-century finds of religious texts from around the time of Christ – the Dead Sea Scrolls and the Nag Hammadi library, both of which surfaced from the sands of the Middle East (the West Bank in the late 1940s in the first case, and Egypt in 1945 in the second) to wreak havoc with orthodoxy. Only, in the case of *The Gospel of Judas*, the process was accelerated.

Taking a longer view, what has happened with *The Gospel of*

Judas also mirrors the early centuries of the church, once the gospels of Mark, Matthew, Luke and John became accepted as the canon. Others hurried in to draw out aspects of those core texts, including figures described in them, Judas among them, which in turn led to the development of particular theories, with those theories reflecting their broader concerns and battles within emerging Christianity.

Among modern academics, there is a broad consensus on the place of *The Gospel of Judas* within that history of the early centuries of the church. It is a polemic, produced by a dissident branch of the fast-growing but sectarian community that shared as its inspiration the life and teachings of Jesus. Many in that community didn't even call themselves Christians, and a minority remained Jews. The authority of the popes and bishops whose names are now listed on solemn tablets in basilicas and cathedrals as having served as leaders in these centuries was at that time flimsy.

The individual author of *The Gospel of Judas* is unknown, but the text was, again by common consent, intended by one of the warring factions in this divided landscape as a weapon in the doctrinal fights going on about Jesus' meaning and purpose. By the late fourth century, the victors had emerged and produced a core set of beliefs and texts. Around them, an orthodoxy was agreed, and the Christian Church flourished. The vanquished – and their beliefs and texts (including *The Gospel of Judas*) – were, as a consequence, dismissed, discredited and destroyed. Yet in the years leading up to that victory, they had enjoyed a currency. *The Gospel of Judas* reveals a great deal about how its eponymous subject was viewed in some parts of the early church of the third and fourth centuries, particularly in the parts that were not mainstream. It is back to those who, what and why questions. Who is saying what about Judas and why?

For the record

The opening section of *The Gospel of Judas* announces itself as 'the secret revelatory discourse that Jesus spoke with Judas Iscariot in the course of a week, three days before his passion'. It offers a radically new version of those key days and hours at the end of Jesus' life. Largely shapeless in chronological terms, it nevertheless carries a distilled charge to make even Mark's brief, breathless gospel sound long-winded.

It starts by skating lightly over what had gone before. 'When he [Jesus] appeared on the earth, he performed signs and great wonders for the salvation of humankind. Some [walked] on the path of justice, but others stumbled in their mistakes, and so the twelve disciples were called.' In mentioning twelve, *The Gospel of Judas* shows immediately its relationship to the canonical gospels of the New Testament. The assumption seems to be that it would be read in conjunction with them. Yet there are no equivalent miracles, and no account of Jesus' progress towards Jerusalem.

Instead it lists various incidents and discussions in no particular order. In these interactions with the apostles, the Jesus of *The Gospel of Judas* bears little resemblance to the Jesus of the New Testament; no longer earnest, charitable and charismatic, but short-tempered, mocking his inner circle's limitations and, for this reader, faintly disagreeable.

'He happened upon them as they were assembled together, seated and practising their piety. When he [drew] near to his disciples as they were assembled together, seated and giving thanks over the bread, [he] laughed. The disciples said to [him], "Master, why are you laughing at [our] prayer of thanksgiving? What is it we have done? This is what is proper." He answered and said to them, "I'm not laughing at you. You aren't doing this out of your own will, but because in this way your God [will be] praised."

93

They said, "Master you are . . . the son of our God." Jesus said to them, "How is it that you know me? [I] tell you the truth, no generation will know me among the people who are with you."[3]

'Giving thanks over bread' sounds remarkably like the celebration of the Eucharist, which by the time this gospel was written had moved centre-stage in the sacramental life practised by the mainstream of Jesus' followers. Here, though, Jesus regards this ritual as having nothing to do with him. As a detail, it points to the real motivation of the author. This gospel was not so much interested in exploring Judas' character and motivations as in distinguishing between the author's section of the fragmented Jesus movement, still a long way short of becoming a single institution, and the largest grouping, already known as the Apostolic Church, because it claimed to represent the handed-down wisdom and authority of most of the original apostles. Ridiculing the apostles – better still, having Jesus ridicule the apostles – was to challenge them. And to dismiss the Eucharist would hit at the very heart of the rival grouping, which placed great emphasis on sacraments of Baptism and Eucharist.

As well as the Apostolic Church – already recognisable as the forerunner of today's institutional Christianity – there were many other groupings. Chief among them were the Jewish Christians, mentioned already, originally based in and around Jerusalem, under the leadership of Jesus' brother James, but who had by now spread into eastern Syria, where they lived ascetic lives of poverty and were sometimes known as Ebionites (from the Hebrew word *ebyon* for 'poor'). That choice of lifestyle continues in modern Christianity in monasteries and convents, but where the Ebionites differed from what exists today is that they still clung to the hope that Jesus' legacy might be incorporated into the Jewish tradition.[4]

That was an ambition the Apostolics firmly rejected. They did not go so far (or at least not yet) as completely to reject any connection between Jesus and Judaism. That, though, was the stance of the Marcionite faction – named after Marcion, a second-century theologian, who had studied alongside Apostolic brethren in Rome but who then rejected the Hebrew Scriptures (Old Testament) and felt they should be repudiated and replaced by a stand-alone New Testament.[5]

Other factions included those of a mystical inclination, usually known as Montanists, strong in particular in the province of Phrygia, now part of modern-day Turkey, and including two women, Priscilla and Maximilla, as its leaders.[6] The Apostolics, by contrast, had moved quickly to push to the margins the women leaders of the first decades after Jesus in favour of a male, celibate elite.

And then there were the Gnostics – from whence, as Bishop Irenaeus clearly tells us, the arguments of *The Gospel of Judas* emerged. He has not an ounce of sympathy for the Gnostics, and therefore, by association, none for Judas. In *Against Heresies*, Irenaeus lumps together with Judas as Gnostic heroes the Old Testament figures of Cain (son of Adam and Eve, who murdered his brother Abel), Esau (grandson of the patriarch Abraham who tried to murder his twin, Jacob) and the Sodomites (immoral, inhospitable inhabitants of the city of Sodom in the Book of Genesis). He goes on: 'Judas the traitor, they say, had exact knowledge [a reference to the Gnostic claim to *gnosis* or 'knowledge'] of these things, and since he alone knew the truth better than the other apostles, he accomplished the mystery of betrayal.'[7]

Here, then, from Irenaeus is a new explanation of Judas' motives for betrayal. He was a Gnostic. Since he lived before Gnostics even existed, he might be regarded as the proto-type Gnostic. By laying this charge at his door, Irenaeus was using Judas as a scapegoat to attack rivals in the fractured early church.

Labelling the Gnostics as a distinct group or a faction, though, is to assign them a unity of purpose they did not possess. It might not even have been a word they used of themselves. Some would hedge their bets, joining in the rituals of the Apostolic Church, but then dissenting quietly at gatherings (or lodges) of like-minded Gnostics. Others had their own initiation ceremonies. Others still regarded themselves as independent of any other authority.

If anything united the Gnostics, it was their search for the knowledge that alone would bring salvation, for the divine within themselves, rather than looking to external authority structures, rituals and demands. They sought what might loosely be termed mystical experiences or insights, favouring, for example, an elaborate cosmology that, for modern hearers, has a tang of the New Age about it.

The Gnostics tended to take a detached, even pessimistic attitude to this world and its struggles. Because human nature was for them essentially spiritual, and the body just a shell for the eternal spirit, they wanted nothing to do with such practical matters as common wordings of prayers, shared holy books, and even the ongoing and often bloody battle with the Roman authorities for the right to practise Christian beliefs, which created so many martyrs before Constantine conceded recognition in 313. The Gnostics were particularly suspicious of the concept of sacrifice – Jesus' sacrifice of his life on Calvary for humankind, commemorated in the Eucharist, and the inspiration for martyrs who then sacrificed their lives to establish a church. So when, in *The Gospel of Judas*, Jesus scoffs at the 'piety' and propriety of the twelve apostles giving thanks over bread, his lips are moving to a Gnostic tune. And if that sacrifice was unnecessary in Gnostic eyes, then they were also going to take a fresh look at Judas because his betrayal, as told in the 'official' gospels, was redundant.

The Judas of *The Gospel of Judas* is presented as more favoured than the other eleven apostles. After the exchange where Jesus laughs at them collectively, the apostles are 'angry and hostile and blaspheming against him in their minds'. So he challenges them:

'[Let] any of you who is a [strong enough] person bring forward the perfect human being and stand before my face.' Only Judas rises to the task.

'He was able to stand before him, yet he could not look him in the eye, but he turned his face away. Judas [said] to him, "I know who you are and from what place you have come. You have come from the immortal realm of Barbelo, and I am not worthy to pronounce the name of the one who has sent you."' In Gnostic cosmology, Barbelo is the divine realm of the mother, the manifestation of the divine power in the highest God. The point being made seems to be that Judas alone knows the true God.

The exchange continues: 'Jesus understood that Judas was contemplating things that are lofty and said to him, "Move away from the others, and I shall explain to you the mysteries of the kingdom, not so that you will attain it, but you will go through a great deal of grief. For somebody else will take your place, so that the twelve [disciples] may be complete once again with their God."'

Again, this passage contains a tie-in with the New Testament, a nod to the Acts of the Apostles, where the dead and disgraced Judas is replaced as an apostle by Matthias. More significantly, though, Judas is here being singled out, not as the one who will go on to betray as in the New Testament, but apparently because of his superior understanding. Jesus is to explain mysteries to him that are beyond the other eleven. Yet there is a sting in the tail. Judas may be privy to these things, but ultimately will not 'attain' the kingdom – that is, reach the divine realm, potentially akin to what Christianity more usually calls heaven.

The Gospel of Judas then moves on to picture Jesus with the disciples. They tell him of a vision, where they have seen priests at an altar, presenting offerings – a thinly veiled reference to Eucharistic celebrations. Some of the priests 'sacrifice their own children, others their wives, while praising and acting humbly with each other', they tell Jesus. 'Some have sex with men. Some perform acts of [murder]. Some commit all sorts of sins and lawless deeds. And the men who stand [before] the altar call upon your [name].' Jesus replies damningly that their vision has been of themselves. 'That is the God you serve, and you are the men you have seen.'

Judas is implicitly included in the blanket condemnation, but this is a Gnostic attack on the hypocrisy of the Apostolic Church – the twelve representing the authority of its first leaders, the apostles, and their view of God. In line with the Gnostic tendency towards dualism – believing in equal and opposite good and bad gods, rather than embracing the monism of mainstream Christianity (which sees God as responsible for everything good and bad) – the Jesus of *The Gospel of Judas* seems to be describing here a separate bad God who allows his people to be led by corrupt, sinful, immoral men.

Judas next has a vision all of his own that he wants to share with Jesus. 'Oh thirteenth spirit, why are you so excited?' Jesus replies, here mocking Judas as he has earlier mocked the apostles, but also by the use of the number thirteen apparently detaching him from their number. 'Speak your mind, then, and I'll hear you out.' And put you right.

The use in the translation of the word 'spirit' is disputed. The team of academics who originally translated *The Gospel of Judas* for *National Geographic* opted for it, but others – notably April DeConick, Professor of Biblical Studies at Rice University in Texas, in her study of the text, *The Thirteenth Apostle* – insist that it is too neutral for the context. DeConick believes it would be much better rendered as 'demon', in line with Gnostic ideas of *daimon*, 'the supernatural host of evil spirits that populate the realms surrounding the earth'.[8] If she is right, this marks a significant shift of emphasis, and a giant step away from any notion of Judas as the good guy of this text. Professor DeConick further argues that labelling Judas as the thirteenth is significant, in that for Gnostics then, as for secular society now, that number would have been regarded as unlucky. Usually taken as a Christian legacy – and in particular linked to the idea that Judas was the thirteenth person round the table at the Last Supper – the superstition about thirteen dates back further to other faiths that existed before Christianity, including Zoroastrianism, which is believed to have had a strong influence on the Gnostics because of its dualistic view of the world.

Judas' vision is of himself being stoned and 'treated harshly' by the twelve – for which, again, read the Apostolic Church. Then he sees a large house with a thatched roof. Inside is a crowd. '"Master, let me also come in with these people," he asks. '[Jesus] answered and said, "Your star has deceived you, Judas."'

If the crowded house represents eternal afterlife, or heaven, Judas is being excluded, damned just as surely as he is in the gospels of the New Testament – as he himself realises. He now asks about his own fate. 'You will go through a great deal of grief,' Jesus tells him, 'when you see the kingdom and its entire generation.' So Judas will glimpse but, seemingly, not be part of it. Even in the gospel named after him, he is consigned to the role of the outsider, his nose pressed at the glass, peering in (though there is also a suggestion here that he will not be alone, since the 'generation' in heaven is beyond most, if not all, humans).

'"What advantage is there for me," he replies, "since you have set me apart for that generation?" Jesus answered and said, "You will be the thirteenth, and you will be cursed by the other generations, but eventually you will rule over them. In the last days they will [here a word is missing and, for once, the academics offer no suggestion] to you, that you may not ascend up to the holy [generation]."'

This is a crucial passage – and an enigmatic one. It has been much debated, with the original translation tweaked in line with objections, notably adding a 'not' initially missed out before the final 'ascend'. Despite the gaps and the arguments, though, the sense is that Judas is being set apart with unhappy eternal consequences (a form of scapegoating), even if on earth he may gain some reward.

Yet, straight afterwards, almost as if to taunt him with what he can't have, Jesus takes Judas on a tour of a strongly Gnostic-flavoured view of the divine creation. God did not create the earth but spawned an angel, who was followed by thousands of other angels. The earth, meanwhile, is brought into being by a violent, evil figure, called Nebro, and his dopey assistant, Sakla. '[Come] that I may teach you,' Jesus tells Judas, 'about the things . . . [that] no person will see. For there is a great and infinite realm, whole dimensions no angelic generation could see, [in] which is the great invisible [Spirit].' Part of this alternative creation narrative refers to Adam and Eve's son Seth and 'the incorruptible [generation]'.

In the Book of Genesis, the first book of the Hebrew Bible and the Christian Old Testament, Seth is shown as giving humankind a new beginning after one of his brothers, Abel, has been killed by the other, Cain.[9] For many Gnostics, Seth was a pre-eminent figure of *gnosis*, a heavenly figure. One group in particular saw themselves as offspring of Seth. It is specifically from the ranks of these Sethians that, it is believed, *The Gospel of Judas* emerged.

Chastened by Jesus' revelation to him of the universe (in effect a Gnostic manifesto), Judas then asks the fate of those who have been baptised in Jesus' name. Here the missing fragments of the text make the reply opaque, but Jesus concludes his answer by telling Judas that, 'you will exceed all of them. For you will sacrifice the man who bears me.' Whether 'exceeding' is a good or bad thing is open to question.[10]

The Gospel of Judas now falls back into line with the canonical gospels. It has Jesus predict Judas' betrayal, but only after Jesus' death on the cross has been radically recast. First, 'a cloud of light' appears. Jesus 'entered it', in Judas' sight, his spirit now freed of his earthly body. And it is that discarded, redundant but still-functioning earthly body which is subsequently arrested.

'[Now], their high priests murmured because [he] had stepped into the guest room for his prayer. But some scholars were there watching closely in order to lay hold of him during the prayer, for they were afraid of the people, since he was regarded by them all as a prophet.'

No Gethsemane, then, no guards, no trial (though it could be seen as implied), but still that clear indictment of the Jewish authorities, a point of convergence between these Gnostic authors and the Apostolic Church. And Judas' role? His betrayal gets curiously mixed up with the canonical gospels' account of Peter's denial of Jesus. 'And they came over to Judas and said to him, "What are you doing in this place? You are Jesus' disciple."' Another dig at the mainstream church leaders, who claimed to be the inheritors of a mandate Jesus gave Peter to lead? The gospel continues: 'He answered them in accordance with their wish. And Judas received some money and handed him over to them.'

So he does take the blood money, though an unspecified amount, and he does betray Jesus, but it is only Jesus' already discarded earthly body that he betrays, not his spirit. The context for his deed is that he plays his part in Jesus' achievement of dissolving the barriers between all things earthly and heavenly. So he may be doing Jesus a favour, doing God's work. What seems clear is that Judas is portrayed as one who has knowledge of the mysteries of the kingdom. Yet whether he emerges from the text as a tragic figure or as a demon is still disputed in academia.

The Gospel of Judas may have been heralded in 2006 as casting new light on his character, as overturning old injustices and restoring the rogue apostle to the ranks of the blessed. It held out, more widely, the prospect that Christian doctrine, as defined by the churches who claimed an exclusive right to pronounce on scripture, was more flexible and more contestable than previously believed. On closer examination, though, it has become one more piece of contested territory between those who see Judas as wicked, and those who prefer to regard him simply as doomed by the circumstances in which he found himself.

Gospels aplenty

Despite the hullabaloo that has surrounded its return from the grave, *The Gospel of Judas* isn't the only holy text from the era of the early church that substantially reimagines Judas and his act of betrayal. Other surviving documents from these contentious, argumentative first centuries of Christianity – some specifically labelled as gospels, others claiming apostolic or other legitimacy in retelling Jesus' story – also place the figure of Judas at the very centre of their argument. In the process, they add detail and colour to his legend and thereby bequeath new features to his biography, however dubious their provenance.

Their general drift, it should be noted, is against the 'doomed' argument on the question of his character, and in favour of the 'damned', leaving *The Gospel of Judas* either as the exception, or as requiring a further re-reading and re-evaluation in the context of these parallel texts. In general, the gospel-makers and sages of the early centuries took no kinder view of Judas than had Mark, Matthew, Luke and John.

Papias, Bishop of Hierapolis (in modern-day Turkey), set down in five volumes (around the turn of the second century CE) his *Expositions of the Sayings of the Lord*. He claims in his preface to have based what he wrote solely on accounts, given to him in person, by those 'elders' who had heard 'the living and surviving voice' of Jesus from the apostles or other unimpeachable sources.[11] While Papias is therefore much quoted as an authority by subsequent Christian writers, his texts are lost, and so what is left to us are fragments, taken from other sources.

In book four, he tackles the death of Judas, and attempts to square the circle of the two differing accounts of his death – by suicide in Matthew and by 'bursting asunder' in Acts. Papias ingeniously imagines a scenario that has him doing both. Judas tries to hang himself, but is cut down before he dies, and then lives on briefly in the immediate aftermath of Jesus' death and resurrection as a hideous monster, his inner evil visible in his outer shell.

'Judas went around in this world as a supreme example of impiety. He grew to be so bloated in his flesh that he could not squeeze through an opening a chariot could easily go through – not even his bulging head. They say his eyelids got so swollen that he could not see any light, and a doctor could not observe his eyes, even with an optical instrument, because they were buried so deep in the surrounding tissue.'[12]

Papias is the first writer to link Judas with sexual depravity – later to be part and parcel of the betrayer's personality, especially once Christianity had come under the influence of Saint Augustine of Hippo (354–430), often credited as the source of much of Christian pessimism over sex and sexuality. A sexually depraved Judas allowed sex itself to be damned. 'His [Judas'] genitals became more massive and repulsive than anyone else's', Papias writes, apparently quoting his sources, 'and when he relieved himself, to his perverse shame, he discharged the pus and worms that streamed all through his body'.[13]

While this account begs the question of quite what Jesus' apostles were doing spying on Judas going to the toilet instead of spreading the good news of the resurrection, it does offer a ghastly detail in Judas' outsized genitals that is surely every bit as much a mark of possession as is the account in Acts of the Apostles of Judas' innards splitting open on the soil of Hakeldama. And it is to this moment that Papias next turns.

'They say that, after suffering many torments and punishments, he died in his own piece of property, and that property has become, to the present day, desolate and uninhabited on account of the putrid smell.'[14] Other accounts, of course, tell of it as a cemetery, but the stench of rotting corpses and the equally appalling stench of Judas' corruption are here conflated. And from the stench of Judas the Jew, it became in medieval times one small step to the fantasy that there was a distinctive smell of all the Jews – *foetor iudaicus*.[15]

The *Gospel of Nicodemus* is a later text, believed to date to the early fourth century (though the version of book four of Papias quoted above comes from roughly the same time). It offers another object lesson to be drawn from Judas' death. Matthew's original account is here augmented with an exchange Judas has beforehand with his wife. 'Mrs Judas' is busy roasting a chicken when her husband, overwhelmed with remorse at betraying Jesus and fearful of the consequences of his action, asks her to help him find a rope with which to hang himself. 'In truth, you should know that I have handed my teacher Jesus over in a wicked way to the evildoers, so that Pilate might execute him,' he explains to his wife. 'But he will rise again on the third day – and woe to us!'[16]

She tells him not to be so foolish, 'for it is just as possible for this cock roasting over the charcoal fire to crow as for Jesus to rise again'.[17] This dismissal of the resurrection is followed by the chicken in the pan spreading its wings and crowing three times (with an echo, again, of Peter's betrayal), which in turns sends Judas off to his gallows.

Unlike Papias, this blatant bit of Christian propaganda at Judas' expense makes little claim to authenticity. Instead it appears to be an attempt to put words in the mouths of minor and unseen characters from the main gospel narratives to make particular points – in this case with 'Mrs Judas' substituting for those who would deny the resurrection. The chicken story, it should be added, only appears in some versions of the *Gospel of Nicodemus*, not others. As a text, though, it remained in circulation into medieval times, when it was regarded as a devotional work because it contained within its midst the 'Acts of Pilate'. These were purportedly official documents, filed on behalf of the Roman governor at the time of Jesus' crucifixion, to his master, the Emperor Tiberius, and including a blow-by-blow account of events in Jerusalem at that time. Scholars have ridiculed its claim to any sort of historical authenticity, but it certainly had an influence on the popular consciousness. Quite how Judas was regarded in the medieval mind is where we must travel next.

Part Two:

Judas – Satan's tool

K

Kiss

Judas' kiss of betrayal resonates down the centuries. In 1998, it provided the title for both David Hare's acclaimed play about Oscar Wilde's love affair with Lord Alfred Douglas, and a prize-winning crime flick starring Emma Thompson and Alan Rickman. And, in 2012, three detective novels were published, all with the title *The Judas Kiss* – one by American bestseller J.T. Ellison in her Taylor Jackson series, another by Irish writer David Butler, and a third by C.L. Batty.

L

Losing His Boots

Most languages have words and phrases to describe people, places and things by what they are said to resemble, rather than by their actual name. So in English a remote place might be referred to as 'the back of beyond'. In Portuguese, the equivalent 'placeholder name', to give the technical term, for somewhere similar is '*onde Judas perdeu as botas*', or 'where Judas lost his boots'. The origins of the phrase are obscure – and it has a cruder popular alternative. To the question, is it far away?, comes back the reply, '*Fica no cu do Judas*' – literally, 'Up Judas' arse.'

CHAPTER SIX:

The Making of the Medieval Judas

Judas heard, and was a wolf: he followed, but, clad in sheep-skin,
he was laying snares for the Shepherd.

Augustine of Hippo (354–430):
Tractates on the Epistle of John (45)

Judas' true motivation in betraying Jesus came no closer to being diagnosed in the polemical exchanges between the warring factions of the early, embattled church. That, in fairness, was scarcely their aim. Any desire to explore his story thoughtfully and prayerfully came a distant second – during a fraught period of martyrdom and persecution, external struggle and internal strife – to the impulse to deploy him as a rhetorical weapon. Talk of a 'doomed-but-special' Judas in the Gnostic gospel that carries his name was perfect for rejecting the authority of the mainstream Apostolic grouping of clerics increasingly running the church from Rome. And, in return, playing up to the idea of an evil, manipulative Judas, the tool of Satan, suited the purposes of those at the centre because he had apparently been taken up with such gusto by the Gnostics. Damn him and you could damn them too. It all comes back to scapegoating.

There is, of course, a danger of over-simplification and over-emphasis here. The Gnostics, as we have seen, weren't by any means a single unit. Some who might be given that tag also accepted much of what the bishops of the mainstream church taught. And there were plenty of shades of theological opinion and practice in between. All were struggling to define their relationship with authority, the need to agree a single set of teachings and texts around which Christianity could unite, and then to accept a cadre of bishops to impose it. Even as the challenge posed to such a structure by Gnostic ideas started to fade in the fifth century (and they were subsequently written out of Christian history for centuries by the official church), other dissenters came along to take their place. And as they did, the figure of Judas the betrayer continued to have a place in that big debate, often acrimonious, as to what was Jesus' true legacy, and who was its guardian.

There was in these disputes a particular appetite for damning opponents – real or imagined – as a way of rallying the faithful. This was done by linking them or likening them to the devil, and his supposed henchman, Judas Iscariot. In the mindset that came to dominate the medieval era, from the fifth to fifteenth centuries Judas was increasingly seen first and foremost as the representative of the devil, the human face of evil, an image based on what Luke and John had written in their gospels. Judas was presented as the one who had been given every chance of salvation by inclusion among the twelve apostles, but who had instead submitted to Satan. And, if Judas with all his privileged intimate access to Jesus could be thus corrupted by the devil, the logic of these times went, how much more precarious was the fate of the ordinary believer in a world where Satan (in the medieval imagination) lurked round every corner? Only the church, it was said, could offer any protection from the Evil One's powerful blandishments, and from the eternal damnation in hell that they inevitably led to, in the company of sinners such as Judas.

That was the message that resounded from the pulpits and was given by travelling preachers, sent out from Rome to convert the continent of Europe and beyond. They offered listeners the church's protection, but at a price – of fearfulness and obedience to a central authority, and of doing what it dictated. It was a formula that enabled the Catholic Church, as an institution, to rise and rise to control the destiny of Europe, in political and social terms as well as religious. Talking always of Judas as Satan's tool became one among many means of achieving its ambitions. Anyone who stood in the church's way was charged with being in league with the devil, as much his plaything as once Judas Iscariot had been. It was to prove a potent accusation.

Muscular Christianity

One of the first architects of this muscular style of institutional Christianity was Leo I (440–461), the first pope successfully to enforce his writ over his increasingly far-flung flock, an achievement recognised subsequently by him being referred to as Leo the Great. Until Leo, the supreme authority of the papacy, exercised by the successors of the 'chosen' apostle, Peter, might have existed in theory, but in practice most early popes were simply the bishop of Rome. Beyond the city limits, their power waned. Leo, by contrast, moved from a system of largely autonomous prelates and bishops, widely scattered about the lands of the crumbling Roman Empire, towards an ecclesiastical structure of government that owed much to ancient Rome, and which largely still operates today within Catholicism. In the process, he also asserted his importance outside the precincts of churches, famously confronting Attila the Hun in 452 (then laying waste to northern Italy and preparing to head south towards Rome) and persuading him to withdraw.

One of Leo's most effective tools for uniting his flock behind him was the distribution of his many sermons around Europe. He was crystal clear in these on the danger the devil posed to all believers. 'By the mystery of baptism you were made the temple of the Holy Ghost: do not put such a denizen to flight from you by base acts, and subject yourself once more to the devil's thralldom: because your purchase money is the blood of Christ, because He shall judge you in truth Who ransomed you in mercy, Who with the Father and the Holy Spirit reigns for ever and ever.'[1]

Mention of 'bloody money' conjures up the example of Judas. In another of his sermons, entitled *De passion Domini*, Leo spelt it out. Judas was, he stated, 'the wickedest and unhappiest man that ever lived'.[2] The remark has been much quoted down the centuries – for instance in the *Glossa ordinaria*, the standard set of scriptural commentaries used in schools and the training of priests and monks from the eighth to the fourteenth centuries.[3] Often, though, the 'unhappiest' part of the quotation was omitted, in case it somehow invited sympathy or offered a degree of mitigation. It was Judas' wickedness that made him unhappy. He was wicked on an unequalled scale.

Others followed Leo's lead, but added their own spin. One of his near successors, Gelasius I (492–496), for example, was an early papal voice who crudely but forcefully joined the outcast Judas with the entire Jewish race. 'In the Bible,' he taught, 'the whole is often named after the part: as Judas was called a devil and the devil's workman, he gives his name to the whole race.'[4] Saint Jerome (347–420), celebrated translator of the Bible into Latin (the Vulgate), and still revered by Christians to this day, labelled Judas as 'cursed, that in Judas the Jews may be accursed. [Just as] you see the Jew praying . . . nevertheless, their prayer turns into sin . . . Whom do you suppose are the sons of Judas? The Jews . . . Iscariot means money and price. Synagogue was divorced by the Saviour and became the wife of Judas the traitor.'[5] As a thorough trouncing of everything Jewish and of every Jew, this remark from Jerome is hard to match, and indeed he became thereafter a standard authority to quote from the pulpit when condemning the Jews. And Judas is at the heart of his argument, that easy, almost instinctive association of the betrayer of Jesus with a whole race, and Judas' characteristics, as listed in the gospels, attributed to all Jews.

Another outspoken and popular orator in this Judas-fuelled howl of prejudice and anti-Semitism was Saint John Chrysostom (c. 347–407), again still quoted with approval by the modern church authorities. He saw Judas' gruesome death at Hakeldama as prefiguring the fate of the whole Jewish people. 'God compelled them to call the field in Hebrew "Aceldama",' he writes in *Homilies*, as part of his commentary on Matthew's gospel. 'By this also the evils which were to come upon the Jews were declared: and Peter [in his account of Judas' death in Acts] shows the prophecy to have been so far in part fulfilled, which says, "It had been good for that man if he had not been born." We may with propriety apply this same to the Jews likewise; for if he who was guide suffered thus, much more they.'

Free will

The influential philosopher Origen was one of many at the time who took a special interest in Judas' case. His concern, though, was not so much to fuel anti-Semitism as to make his mark on another of the big debates within the early church (and indeed one that continued thereafter, up to and including the Reformation) about each individual's free will to accept or reject God. The son of a martyred Christian, Origen was a teacher in the Christian community in Alexandria in the third century, studying the Hebrew Scriptures and the gospels, and living a frugal and ascetic life (he is said to have gone so far as to castrate himself). His tract, *Against Celsus*, written around 248, is a staunch rebuttal of the ideas of a vocal critic of Christianity. Celsus was said to have been heavily influenced by the Greek philosopher Plato, and had attacked God for making Jesus' closest associates 'traitors and impious men'. To illustrate his point, Celsus had suggested that all the apostles' roles – including that of Judas – had been predetermined from on high rather than shaped by their reactions to what they saw and heard from Jesus. In other words, Celsus was claiming – as the Gnostics behind *The Gospel of Judas* had – that Judas' betrayal was not evil at all, but doing what God wanted him to do.

Origen vehemently rejects this in *Against Celsus*. God does not control our every action, he insists. Instead he gives us free will. So Judas made his own choice. He was not following a preordained plan, whereby he had to betray Jesus so that the Son of God could save humankind. To illustrate his point, Origen dwells at length on the Judas kiss, which had clearly puzzled him too. It should be read, he says, as a sign of continuing affection between the betrayer and the one he is about to hand over. 'This circumstance,' he writes, 'will satisfy all with regard to the purpose of Judas, that along with his covetous disposition, and his wicked design to betray his Master, he had still a feeling of a mixed character in his mind, produced in him by the words of Jesus, which had the appearance (so to speak) of some remnant of good.'[6]

The standard condemnations are there in Origen, but there is also that tantalising possibility of 'some remnant of good'. Which then takes Origen on to look at Judas' decision in Matthew's account to try to return the thirty pieces of silver. Here, once again, he sees evidence of free will in operation. 'If this covetous Judas, who also stole the money placed in the bag for the relief of the poor, repented, and brought back the thirty pieces of silver to the chief priests and elders, it is clear that the instructions of Jesus had been able to produce some feeling of repentance in his [Judas'] mind, and were not altogether despised and loathed by this traitor. Nay, the declaration, 'I have sinned, in that I have betrayed the innocent blood,' was a public acknowledgement of his crime. Observe, also, how exceedingly passionate was the sorrow for his sins that proceeded from that repentance, and which would not suffer him any longer to live . . . He passed sentence upon himself, showing what a power the teaching of Jesus had over this sinner Judas, this thief and traitor, who could not always treat with contempt what he had learned from Jesus . . . [These are] proofs which show that the apostasy of Judas was not a complete apostasy, even after his attempts against his master.'[7]

Origen is offering something more nuanced than a straightforward condemnation of Judas, yet he does not stray from the party line that Judas, rather than God, is solely responsible for the crimes that he, Judas, commits. Origen's argument in favour of free will may have been framed in terms of seeking out even the smallest signs of good within an otherwise wicked apostle, but its conclusion remains that Judas was evil, that he had the choice to act differently, even toyed with it, but ultimately elected of his own free will to send Jesus to his death. And so, Origen concludes, his example stands as a vivid warning to all other believers of how easy it is to go astray, even when you are in Jesus' inner circle.

Arguably even more influential than Origen on the development of Christian thought was Augustine of Hippo. A convert in 387, this former playboy became a bishop in north Africa. His texts, *Tractates on the Gospel of John* and *on the First Epistle of John*, examine the final gospel plus one of three books included towards the end of the New Testament canon and ascribed to the same author. Augustine ponders how on earth Jesus, the Son of God, could ever have welcomed Judas into the body of his chosen apostles without, by that very act, cleansing him from any inclination to evil deeds. Here again is the suggestion that Judas may be doing God's bidding in betraying Jesus. And, like Origen, Augustine totally rejects the very thought as madness.

'Was that morsel which the Lord delivered to Judas evil? [A

reference to John's account of Jesus handing Judas the piece of bread, dipped in oil.] God forbid. The physician would not give poison; it was health the physician gave; but by unworthily receiving it, he [Judas] who received it not being at peace, received it unto destruction.'[8] The blame for Judas' actions is, once again, entirely his. Does that still apply, though, if inadvertently something good came of them – that by Jesus' death and resurrection, humankind was redeemed? Drawing heavily on the unflattering portrait of Judas provided in John's gospel, Augustine dismisses this argument out of hand. 'Among all that adhered to the Master, among the twelve, to him was committed the common purse; to him was allotted the dispensing for the poor. Unthankful for so great a favour, so great an honour, he took the money, and lost righteousness: being dead, he betrayed life: Him whom he followed as a disciple, he persecuted as an enemy. All this evil was Judas'; but the Lord employed his evil for good.'[9]

Augustine is careful to decouple Judas' own evil from anything positive that came out of his deeds. Judas did not know that would be the case, and indeed did not will it.

Elsewhere, in his *City of God*, Augustine dashes the argument that Judas, by returning the thirty pieces of silver, had shown real repentance. 'Judas, by hanging himself, heightened rather than expiated that crime of dastardly betrayal – because by despairing of God's mercy he abandoned himself to an impenitent remorse and left no room in his soul for saving sorrow.'[10] To Judas' already long list of crimes is here prominently added suicide – condemned elsewhere in *City of God* as offending against the commandment 'thou shall not kill'. And despair also goes onto the list of charges against Judas, something that later was to be rated as among the most heinous of his offences in the medieval mind. To despair, when the church was there to protect you, was unforgiveable.[11]

Augustine's writings also demonstrate how frequently Judas was set up as the polar opposite of Peter, the first pope. To denigrate Judas, therefore, was to build up Peter, and thereby buttress the office of the papacy. 'Judas is not here a unit. One wicked man represents the whole body of the wicked; in the same way as Peter, the whole body of the good, yea, the body of the Church, but in respect to the good.'[12]

Too bad to forgive

Forgiveness was prominent among the teachings of the emerging Christian Church. It aspired to act in imitation of Jesus, and his words, on the cross, in Luke's gospel: 'Father, forgive them; they do not know what they are doing.'[13] If all can be forgiven, and all can be redeemed, why not extend that to Judas too?

The *Acts of Andrew and Paul*, an eighth- or ninth-century text, written in Coptic, rebuts this suggestion by the curious device of focusing in particular on the time between Jesus' death on the cross on Good Friday and his resurrection from the dead on Easter Sunday. During those 'missing' hours, according to the traditions of the church (though not spelt out explicitly in the canonical gospels), Jesus goes down to hell, to the devil's lair, and liberates all the damned – pagans as well as believers – by the sacrifice of his own life, so they can enjoy eternal life in heaven.[14] If in his 'harrowing of hell', Jesus could save pagans, then surely he could also save Judas who, according to Matthew's chronology, was already in hell when his master died on the cross?

Describing that scene in the underworld, the author of the *Acts of Andrew and Paul* places Judas among the tormented souls, 'undergoing great and grievous torment'.[15] Why hasn't he been released like the others, he is asked? 'Woe is me,' replies Judas, 'for what I have done to my Master, for I have sinned against him! I handed him over to the Jews for silver coins, which perish. To be sure, I knew he was [my] Master and the Master of the whole earth.'

This account, then, puts forward the possibility that Judas

realised that Jesus was, in fact, 'Master of the whole earth' when he handed him over, and so rapidly repented. He returned the silver coins to the high priests, and then appealed directly to Jesus – who was then in their hands awaiting trial – for forgiveness. He quotes back at Jesus his earlier words to Peter, about forgiving sins 'seven times seventy' times.[16]

Jesus' reply, according to the *Acts of Andrew and Paul*, is to send Judas 'into the desert', saying 'fear no one but God alone. If you see the devil coming, do not fear him, nor anyone except God alone.'[17] Judas is given a penance, albeit with the promise of forgiveness. But, despite Jesus' willingness to extend forgiveness at this moment to the rogue apostle, Judas is then unable to resist the devil in the desert, a place where the Evil One is often assumed to be at his most dangerous. The early hermit monks of Christianity – such as Onouphrius, today recalled so prominently at Hakeldama – went there specifically to engage in spiritual combat with Satan. Judas is not in their league, and succumbs to 'the ruler of perdition'.

Once more he repents, but this time he cannot ask Jesus for forgiveness because by now his master is being tried and crucified. So Judas hangs himself in the hope of getting to 'the realm of death' just before Jesus. Even this tiny glimmer of hope for forgiveness is snuffed out, though. In the *Acts of Andrew and Paul*, when Jesus makes his entrance into the underworld of torment, following his crucifixion, Judas reports, 'he released all the souls – except for my soul alone'.[18] Jesus chooses to leave Judas in the power of the devil, calling his erstwhile apostle a 'wretch'. If Judas had resisted the devil in the desert, Jesus tells him, he would have been forgiven again. 'But you offered a different form of service and you have done something God hates; you have brought death upon yourself.'

Judas is portrayed as doubly damned, so wicked indeed that he has put himself even beyond Jesus' promise of forgiveness. And he has done it by his own actions – by his own free will. He had the chance of forgiveness, but chose to embrace the devil in the desert. The same fate, this account of his life implicitly warns, awaits any who ignore God's demand (as articulated so loudly by the medieval church) that they too should resist the devil with all their might. It is a terrifying prospect, calibrated for the general fearfulness of the times.

A fuller biography

As far as those at the helm – practically and theologically – of the increasingly powerful Christian Church were concerned, the case against Judas was by now proven beyond any reasonable doubt. Voices might have been raised in mitigation, but all grounds for appeal had one by one been tested and rejected by the finest brains. He was damned, wicked beyond redemption and in league with the devil.

Yet the story of his betrayal continued to be replayed, in sermons, letters and lectures on the gospels, and in musings on Jesus, on morality and on the nature of evil. Why did he prove such a popular and enduring subject? Because he managed to carry with him a peculiar horror. There remained a core fascination around him, in the same way that contemporary audiences have an apparently boundless appetite for more and more speculation about society's ghouls – the brutal dictator, the savage murderer, those who prey on the innocent and vulnerable. To satisfy such curiosity, those scant twenty-two references to Judas in the gospels proved to be endlessly elastic.

The process was similar, in one way, to that with the developing cult of saints, which reached a peak in the later medieval period. It sought, with official encouragement (by the twelfth century the Vatican had taken complete charge of the whole saint-making process), to locate the seeds of their virtue in imagined early lives, or by filling in the missing details, or giving the would-be saint the 'good' death they deserved. At the opposite end of the spectrum, Judas' biography too could be substantially augmented with made-up stories in an effort to make him look not better but so much worse.

The main episodes of his life as an apostle were therefore supplemented with other material, some liberally borrowed from other sources, all casting him as an utterly bad lot from start to finish. The *Paschal Hymn* or *Carmen Paschale*, written by the Christian author, Caelius Sedulius, in the middle years of the fifth century, may contain few such new details, but it is a good example of how the authorised version of his life and death could be given a literary polish as part of a five-volume, free-flowing epic, drawing heavily in style on the poetry of Greece, on Ovid, Lucan and especially Virgil (Sedulius is sometimes called 'the Christian Virgil'). Infamy is piled on infamy in the life of Judas by choice of rancid vocabulary.

> *You bloody, savage, rash, insane, rebellious,*
> *Faithless, cruel, deceitful, bribable, unjust,*
> *Cruel betrayer, vicious traitor, merciless thief —*[19]

And, having provided a list of negative qualities for Judas that could just as easily have been attached to every one of the church's enemies, Sedulius then spells it out.

> *Do you command the sacrilegious ranks that threaten us*
> *With point and spear, as you press your face to his and mix your*
> *Poison with his honey, and betray the Lord under the pretence of*
> *affection?*[20]

Literary licence is taken much further in the *Arabic Infancy Gospel of the Saviour*. It furnishes Judas with a hitherto unmentioned childhood. Believed to have been written first in Syriac in the sixth century, and drawing in some parts on the earlier second-century *Infancy Gospel of Thomas*, this text appears in Arabic in the ninth century in a commentary by a Syrian church father on Matthew's gospel. It tells of a boy called Judas, 'tormented by Satan', who 'would bite whoever came near him, and if he found no one around him, he would bite his own hands and his other limbs'. This bloodsucking lad ends up playing with the child Jesus, who has already shown his powers when his sweat and his nappies were used to cure others and drive out demons.[21]

'Then he [Judas] was attacked by Satan in the same way as usually happened, and he wanted to bite the Lord Jesus, but he couldn't. Nevertheless, he hit Jesus on the right side, and as a result Jesus began to cry. Immediately Satan departed from that boy and fled like a mad dog.'[22]

This wholly imagined episode is linked in to the gospel accounts – tenuously but to anti-Semitic effect. 'The same side on which Judas hit him,' it tells, 'is where the Jews pierced him with a spear.' The direct parallel is with the mention in John's gospel of such a piercing of Jesus during the crucifixion, but there the one responsible is a Roman soldier.[23] Here he is a Jew.

Intriguingly, some of the tales told about the child Jesus in the *Arabic Infancy Gospel of the Saviour* are also found in the Qur'an, revealed to Muhammad, according to Islam, in the seventh century. There is, for example, in both texts the same account of Jesus – revered as a prophet by Muslims – making clay birds and then bringing them to life.[24] But the Qur'an makes no mention of Judas, or of Jesus' betrayal, stating instead that he was not killed or crucified, 'though it was made to appear like that to them'.[25]

The evidence for this rewriting of Jesus' death in the Qur'an is unknown, but it may, some scholars suggest, be drawing on an account in the *Gospel of Barnabas*. Often dated as late as the sixteenth century by those who see it as influenced by Islam (since its Jesus proclaims Muhammad to be the true messiah), there is also a school of thought that this later version incorporates a much earlier text, predating the Qur'an and therefore potentially influencing it, rather than the other way round. It gives a version of Jesus' death that fits with the description of something that looked like a crucifixion, but had been made to look that way.

'Then the marvellous God,' reports the *Gospel of Barnabas*, 'acted marvellously, for Judas was so completely transformed in his speech and appearance to resemble Jesus that we were convinced he was Jesus.'[26] Judas becomes a Jesus double, and is then taken away by the soldiers he [Judas] has treacherously summoned to Gethsemane, who mistakenly believe him to be Jesus. Despite constantly pointing out that he is not Jesus, Judas undergoes the trial and death on the cross as his body double. This fate is not a noble sacrifice by the traitor, it is emphasised by the writer, since Judas tries to escape. No, this is God's trick on him, his punishment for his attempted betrayal of the real Jesus. 'He [God] made sure that Judas would be crucified, so that he would suffer the same terrible death to which he had sold another person.'[27]

Among Gnostic-influenced texts rediscovered at Nag Hammadi, both the *Revelation of Peter* and the *Second Discourse of Seth* make the same claim as *The Gospel of Judas* that the real Jesus or his 'spirit' did not die on the cross. Meanwhile Basilides of Alexandria, another of the Gnostics condemned by Bishop Irenaeus in *Against Heresies*, proposed that it was Simon of Cyrene, described in the synoptic gospels as the man who helped Jesus carry his cross to Calvary, who actually ended up on the cross after he also took on the physical appearance of Jesus.

A Judas appears in another Nag Hammadi text, the second-century *Dialogue of the Saviour*, again Gnostic in outlook. He is one of three followers singled out by Jesus (the others are Mary Magdalen, and Matthias – Judas Iscariot's replacement in the ranks of the twelve). This Judas figure, though, is widely taken by scholars to be a different Judas, Jesus' brother, also known as Jude, but the rediscovery of the *Gospel of Judas* has raised questions about that attribution. 'Much of this presentation [in the *Dialogue of the Saviour*] of Judas coheres, in general, with the description of Judas Iscariot in the *Gospel of Judas*', writes Professor Martin Meyer.[28]

The parallels are certainly there in that, in the *Dialogue of the Saviour*, its Judas is specially favoured by Jesus in his discussions and revelations, over and above the other apostles (but then he would be if he really was Jesus' brother). Yet there is nothing in the descriptions of this pure, thoughtful but essentially blank Judas in the *Dialogue of the Saviour*, forever prompting Jesus with questions, that contains any reference to details of Judas Iscariot's story from the canonical gospels. In terms of developing either the character of Judas, or the theology around his betrayal, it brings nothing to the feast.

Family tree

Did Judas have a family? John's gospel names Simon as Judas' father, but adds nothing more. However, the *Narrative of Joseph of Arimathea*, conflated in medieval manuscripts with the *Acts of Pilate* and dated tentatively to the second century, suggests that Caiaphas, the Jewish high priest at Jesus' trial, was Judas' uncle.[29]

Joseph of Arimathea was a leading member of the Jewish establishment who had secretly become a follower of Jesus, the canonical gospels report.[30] He allowed his own tomb to be used for Jesus' body on Good Friday. Joseph has been the source of many legends ever since – including connections to the Holy Grail, to a visit to the British town of Glastonbury, and to tales of Jesus escaping death and decamping to India on one of Joseph's merchant fleet. In the *Narrative of Joseph of Arimathea*, though, that blood link to Caiaphas simply strengthens the otherwise vague connection between Judas and the Jewish authorities, and offers another reason why he might have been so easily persuaded to take their thirty pieces of silver.

'He was not personally a disciple of Jesus,' it states of Judas, directly contradicting all four canonical gospels, 'but the whole Jewish multitude urged him, in an underhanded way, to follow Jesus, not that he might be obedient to the signs done by him, or confess to him, but that he might catch him saying something false and hand him over to them.'[31] There is sufficient of the traditional picture of Judas as the outsider in the group to give it all some sort of weight, but then Judas follows these instructions and reports back to his uncle that Jesus 'has stolen the law and the prophets' – namely that he is a false messiah. Like his important Jewish relative, Judas fails, in this account, to recognise the promised messiah, and so takes 'officers' to arrest Jesus and identifies him with a kiss.

Joseph of Arimathea also features in the *Gospel of Bartholomew*'s reworking of Judas. This text may date to the second or third century and is certainly mentioned by Jerome at the end of the fourth century. It is regarded as lost by some scholars, while what others take as surviving Coptic fragments from the fifth century exist under the title *Questions of Bartholomew*. If its provenance is muddy, then the tale it tells is direct and judgemental. It gives a role once more to Judas' wife, who is presented as nurse to Joseph of Arimathea's infant son. Here there is a distinct misogyny that seeks to shift the blame for Judas' betrayal onto his spouse – the power of women to lead men astray from God being a familiar theme in early church fathers such as Augustine, Origen and John Chrysostom.

'Now [we] found that man [Judas] stealing from what was deposited in the money-bag every day, bringing it to his wife, and diminishing what was given to the poor serving among them. At times, when he went home with some of the proceeds in his hands, she expressed her pleasure with him. We also observed him when he did not bring enough to her to satisfy the evil in her eyes and her insatiable greed, and she showed her contempt for him.'[32]

Judas' wicked qualities are here transferred onto his wife. Indeed the author – unknown, but presumably a man – then likens Mrs Judas to Eve. 'He [Judas] followed her advice just as Adam listened to his wife' when he agreed a fee of 'thirty silver coins' to hand Jesus over 'to the Jews'.

An enduring portrait

The accumulation of these unflattering portraits of Judas had its effect. He was becoming as much a figure in popular culture as he was in theology or church teachings. This might have been an age of widespread illiteracy; hence the distribution of such texts – all of which had to be copied individually by hand (before Johannes Gutenberg invented printing in 1439) – was necessarily very limited. Yet many of them enjoyed an extraordinarily long shelf-life, remaining in circulation into the sixteenth and even the seventeenth centuries, latterly in printed versions, inspiring artists, playwrights, poets, and those who staged large-scale processions and public entertainments. Moreover, they became the raw material, as the centuries passed, for vernacular epics, which reached a much larger audience.

The classic example of this trickle-down effect is the *Golden Legend* or *Legenda Aurea*, compiled by Jacobus de Voragine, a Dominican prior who went on (in 1292) to became archbishop of Genoa in Italy.[33] It first appeared around 1266 and became, by the standards of the day, a bestseller. It was one of the most widely copied and read books of the later Middle Ages. Over a thousand handwritten manuscript copies in Latin survive to this day, and it was among the most popular of the first generation of printed books, translated into many languages.

As a Dominican friar, Jacobus would have had access to a good library. His work collects and popularises many of the traditions and tales that had, over the centuries, grown up around the gospels, around the lives of Jesus and his apostles, and especially around the saints. The pictures it paints in words became part of popular iconography, then and thereafter. And, in chapter 45, supposedly devoted to Saint Matthias, the substitute apostle, it quickly switches away from this enigmatic figure to give Judas Iscariot an extraordinary back-story, full of drama, twists, turns, potentially redeeming moments, but ultimately inevitable recidivism, the sort of prequel any Hollywood producer might attempt in seeking further to explain a character who had already gripped audiences.

From the outset, Jacobus makes no claim to gospel truth in his accounts. He begins his tale of Judas with a mild disclaimer. 'According to one history, which is supposedly apocryphal . . .' He then tells of a Jewish couple: Ruben (part, he says, of the tribe of Issachar 'according to Jerome', and 'otherwise known as Simon') and his wife Cyborea. One night she has a nightmare about giving birth to a son 'so wicked that he would cause the ruin of all our people'. Her husband fears 'demonic delusion', but nine months later the baby boy arrives. 'They were horrified at the thought of killing him, but determined not to raise him to bring ruin on their people; so they put him in a wicker basket and set him adrift at sea.'

The babe-in-a-basket – described as 'handsome' and a 'bonny child' in a gentler presentation than the usual medieval ghoul – washes up on the shores of an island called Scarioth, 'from where Judas subsequently took his name Iscariot'. That is a new twist on its derivation. The infant is found by a childless queen and raised as her own 'in a style befitting a prince'. Then the queen and her husband belatedly conceive their own child, a boy, who grows up playing with Judas, though the latter 'would tease and bully the king's son and frequently made him cry'. There is a clear echo here of the *Arabic Infancy Gospel of the Saviour* and its account of Judas bashing and biting the child Jesus.

His behaviour turns the queen against Judas and so she makes it known that he is not her natural son – something that she had hitherto kept to herself. In one sense, then, she betrays him. '[Judas] was utterly humiliated' – as he might be, and so a plea of mitigation of sorts – 'and he crept up on the king's son – the one he had thought was his brother – and murdered him'. Judas is thus symbolically given the 'mark of Cain', the curse placed on the son of Adam and Eve who, in the Book of Genesis, kills his brother Abel.[34] As an exercise in creating a scapegoat along the lines already set out by Professor René Girard, killing your brother scores a direct hit.

Fearing capture, the young Judas escapes the island and flees to Jerusalem, where he attaches himself to the court of the Roman governor Pontius Pilate. 'Since like attracts like, Pilate soon found that Judas and he saw eye to eye and became very fond of him.' Judas rises to be chief minister at his court. Among the tasks given to Judas by his new boss is to seize for Pilate an orchard nearby, in which the Roman governor has spotted apples that he yearns to eat (like Eve with the forbidden fruit in the Garden of Eden). That meant displacing its current owner, who turns out to be none other than Ruben, Judas' father, though neither knows it.

In his efforts to please Pilate, Judas ends up killing Ruben in a fight in the orchard. Cyborea believes her husband has died of natural causes. 'Pilate subsequently made over all Ruben's possessions to Judas, and in addition gave him Cyborea . . . to marry.' The greedy, loyal, amoral Judas has no objection to this, unaware that Cyborea is his mother. Another base is touched on the designated road to making him a scapegoat.

'One day Judas heard his wife sighing deeply and he begged her to tell him what was the matter.' She yields and mentions the son she believes drowned. Judas then shares his own story with her. 'It became clear that Judas had married his own mother and killed his own father. He was overwhelmed with remorse, and at his mother's suggestion went to our Lord Jesus Christ and begged forgiveness for his sins.'

It is an epic build-up to Judas joining the apostles, a mansion erected on the foundation of a grain of sand – namely, the only detail that the canonical gospels offer about Judas' past, that his father was called Simon. All of this back-story then allows Jesus, at very first mention of Judas in the gospels, to be seen as forgiving a notorious rogue by the very act of including him in the twelve alongside naïve fishermen from Galilee.

Having explained how Judas ended up in the inner circle, the author of the *Golden Legend* now pauses to stress, once again, that his source is found in apocryphal (non-canonical) history. 'Whether or not the tale is worth repeating', he continues, 'must be left to the reader's judgement, though it should probably be rejected as fancy rather than as fact.'

With that second disclaimer out of the way, he then plunges on, apparently unabashed, with his tale. The Judas he describes is now firmly based on the gospels of Mark, Matthew, Luke and John. Though he begins with a clean slate, having been absolved of his sins by Jesus, Judas quickly returns to the bad. It is a pessimistic view of human nature. He is variously the money keeper, the apostle appalled by the cost of the ointment, the one prepared as a result to sell Jesus for thirty pieces of silver, then the regretful sinner. The whole is hardly a hopeful tale of redemption, or even of the healing power of Jesus' forgiveness. Judas is unremittingly evil from the beginning, as his mother/wife had glimpsed in her dream.

Jacobus ends by conflating the two New Testament versions – hanging and bursting asunder – of Judas' death. 'Nothing issued from his mouth,' he writes of Judas hanging from the tree, 'because it was not fitting that a mouth that had kissed the glorious lips of Christ should be so foully defiled. However, it was perfectly fitting that the entrails which had conceived Christ's betrayal should burst apart and pour out.' The cause of Judas' betrayal, therefore, lay in his entrails.

Jacobus has still more to add on the symbolism of the death. 'He died hanging in the air, because he had offended both the angels in heaven and men on earth, so it was right that he should be kept from the regions inhabited by angels and men, and left in mid-air with the demons for company.' This is a reference to the medieval staple that demons and the devil inhabited the space between the earth and the heavens. Only at the very end, then, does the devil get a default mention.

The first half of Judas' life is presented as a mirror-image of the second. In part one, Judas murders the 'true prince' on the island of Scariot. And in part two he sends Jesus, the true messiah, to his death in Jerusalem. This shaping of the story recalls Classical literature, and points in particular to Sophocles' account of Oedipus, mythical king of Thebes, abandoned by his parents (Laius and Jocasta) because they fear he is evil, and raised by a queen. Oedipus then returns and marries his widowed mother.

It was Origen, in *Against Celsus* in the third century, who first mentioned Oedipus and Judas in the same breath, as part of his defence of the concept of free will. Was he prompted to do so by some apocryphal text, cited by Jacobus but now lost? It is impossible to know, but Origen was arguing, in the context of free will, that Judas could be held personally accountable for his sins, rather than God, just as Oedipus can be for his, rather than the gods. It might have been this reference alone that inspired the author of the *Golden Legend* to create his story, though he does effectively turn Origen's argument on its head. Jacobus' Judas is predestined from his mother's dream onwards to do evil, whatever love and forgiveness he is shown in life.

There are a number of ways of interpreting the author's purpose in so embellishing Judas' tale in the *Golden Legend*. Some see the back-story he imagines as another example of demonising Judas so as to attack the Jews. 'Judas, in every particular, echoes in his life the role of the Jews in the Christian myth and psychology,' writes Hyam Maccoby. 'Like the Jews, Judas is chosen for a great role, but he is not really the true heir when he arrives.' It is an 'allegory of the history of the Jews,' he asserts, 'who, in Christian theory, played the role for a time of God's chosen people, but turned in rage to destroy the one true Son of God when he came'.[35]

Such an emphasis, though, omits any real consideration of the particularly unflattering characterisation of Pontius Pilate, or his greedy crimes. There is a case to argue that, as presented in Jacobus de Voragine's account, the Roman governor is being used to attack the morals of chief ministers and politicians everywhere – they grab land, murder the rightful owner and use their families for their own ends.

And then there is the sex. The *Golden Legend*'s Judas could also be seen as the personification of transgressive sex, the son who marries – and presumably sleeps with – his mother. So the wickedness that Judas represents includes sexual wickedness, and thus sees him drawn in, once more, to the church's pessimism and suspicion of sexuality. If you break the plethora of rules around sex that the church has laid down, goes the moral of this particular version of Judas' story, you are no better than he is; someone who would commit incest. You will open the door to the devil and share Judas' fate.

That same warning note is sounded, too, in the thirteenth-century 'Ballad of Judas', often described as the earliest known Middle English ballad. It has several versions, and is loosely linked to other songs of the time. The tale it tells in music and words is of Judas being sent by Jesus to buy the food for the Last

Supper. He is given thirty 'plates' of silver, which he carries on his back. As he walks along a busy street, he bumps into his deceitful sister, who laughs at him for believing in Jesus, whom she labels a 'false prophet'. She then lures him to sleep by urging him, 'lay your head in my lap' – or, in alternative translations, 'on my breast' – a scene full of innuendo. She then steals his silver and makes off. Desperate only to hide his sinful, even incestuous act, Judas betrays Jesus to Pilate (not the Jewish high priests) for thirty pieces of silver. The bread and wine used at the Last Supper are therefore purchased with blood money.[36]

These were all, in their time, popular versions of Judas' life, ranging far and wide beyond the details of the New Testament, importing for a whole variety of reasons many new twists and turns, but always anchoring them in the accounts in Mark, Matthew, Luke and John.

M

Mal de Judas

In medieval presentations of Judas (on stage in mystery plays and in popular illustrations), his skin was often shown as pitted with bright red spots, as evidence of his general depravity and untrustworthiness. So when individuals developed the symptoms of what we would now diagnose as measles – including bright red spots – the disease was referred to in France as *Mal de Judas*.

N

Needle

Two British anaesthetists coined the term 'Judas Needle', in a June 2013 article, to highlight a malfunction in an air inlet needle. Instead of piercing the air seal on bottles of medicine, it had a tendency to backfire and lodge itself in the anaesthetist's hand. They likened it to the legendary 'Judas Pistol', a treacherous gun used to cheat the odds in a duel that, instead of firing a bullet forwards, had been tampered with and so backfired, killing its user.[1]

CHAPTER SEVEN

Devilish Visions in Volterra

You have both feet upon a little sphere
Whose other side Judecca occupies;
When it is morning here, there it is evening

Dante Alighieri (1265–1321): *Inferno (canto* XXXIV: 117)²

There's a flag thing going on all across the bleak landscape of the *balze* – or 'crags' – around the ancient Italian hilltop city of Volterra. Every wayside bar, shop, campsite or farmhouse I pass has put up a display of flags of the world in a none-too-subtle attempt to entice in visitors from foreign lands with the promise of a warm welcome. Fair enough, I suppose, since modern Tuscany is now so heavily dependent on the tourist trade. The French, Germans and British seem a natural enough target, as do assorted citizens of other European Union countries within a day or two's drive, hence their national symbols fluttering in the gentle breeze of a warm July morning. But how many Argentinians and Brazilians are they really expecting to happen by?

The flags continue unabated, and unabashed, once I dispense with my car and reach on foot the narrow, crowded pedestrian streets of Volterra itself, a maze of tall, thin, time-worn medieval buildings, perched behind defensive walls and gates 550 metres above sea level. A prosperous place as far back as Etruscan times in the seventh century BCE, despite being slightly out on a limb from the main trading and pilgrim routes through central Italy, it thrived then, as now, on the riches that lie beyond the walls and beneath the soil – copper, salt and, above all, alabaster. It was rare and accessible seams of this whitish, veined, chalky deposit, almost translucent and therefore prized for the skin-like quality it can give off when carved, that first elevated Volterra above its rivals. Etruscan craftsmen began to make alabaster funeral urns and caskets to accompany their own well-developed death rituals. In their hands, alabaster became the stone of the dead.

Today, Volterra flags itself up as 'the City of Alabaster', in another unsubtle effort to draw in more of the tourists who still seem to prefer nearby San Gimignano and Siena. And I'd be hard pressed to miss the message that Volterra's prized local natural resource is now also available in every conceivable shape and size, from ornamental eggs and ashtrays (complete with wading birds dipping into the cigarette ends) to elaborate table lamps, fountains and even full-sized busts. Every shop window is stuffed with examples, while down alleyways white alabaster dust drifts out of the innumerable workshops that give the city – unlike those more visited Tuscan neighbours – the air of a place that still makes something to earn its living.

Volterra has its own fiercely independent spirit, a throwback to the days pre-1361 when this was a free commune, its citizens ruling themselves without outside interference, before the mighty Florence took it under its wing. The ancient Palazzo dei Priori in the main square, where I am heading, is said to be the oldest public meeting hall in the whole of Italy, but my final destination lies opposite it.

Behind its plain brick façade, the city's Romanesque Cathedral of Santa Maria Assunta once resounded with a message that is now all but inaudible to modern ears. In medieval times, though, it was trumpeted with little more finesse than the flags or the 'buy-your-alabaster-here' shop signs. And that message was all about Judas.

The must-see gem in the dimly lit, cool sanctuary of Volterra Cathedral is not a painting or a decorated altarpiece – the layered bluey-black and white of the nave's walls was once considered sufficiently splendid not to require any more ornament – but instead the high and mighty pulpit, located in the third arch back from the altar on the left-hand side as I enter. Most of its component parts date back to the early part of the twelfth century, making them older by a few decades than this historic church itself, refashioned as it was in the middle part of that century after an earthquake. The pulpit sits proud on four tall, thin marble legs, with terrifying alabaster beasts ('*stilofori*', the explanatory plaque reads, one of those Italian words for which there is no simple alternative, but which means roughly 'column-bearers') that snap at the heels of any preacher who is so bold as to climb the steps to deliver a sermon. Some of the stone used in these *stilofori* is said to date back even further in time.

The twelfth to the fourteenth century saw a particular flourishing in and around Tuscany of the intricate art of decorating pulpits (and, on a bigger scale, church façades) with stone reliefs. It was led by a succession of acclaimed sculptors, notably Nicola Pisano, sometimes referred to as the founder of modern sculpture and responsible for two celebrated examples, in Siena's Duomo and the Baptistery in Pisa. Among others was the Dominican, Fra Guglielmo Agnelli, a pupil of Pisano, and an earlier generation of masters including Gruamonte at Pistoia and Biduino at Lucca. What they shared was a naturalistic style, influenced by Classicism, which brought a sharp realism to their depictions of the human figure.

The carvings on the Volterra pulpit belong to the century before Pisano and Guglielmo, and are simpler in their composition and execution than anything associated with these two masters. Some historians have attributed them to Biduino.[3] On the blind sides (as far as the congregation is concerned) are the Annunciation, the Visitation and the Old Testament sacrifice by Abraham of his son, Isaac, but it is the front panel, showing the Last Supper, that looms unmissably over the pews where I now take a seat. This was the image that would have inscribed itself upon the imagination of a largely illiterate congregation 750 years ago as it gathered to hear the preacher reach for the oratorical heights in his sermon (though not from the incongruous golden eagle lectern that is a much later addition to the structure). Talk of the devil was standard in such sermons, and of the danger of falling into his traps. The carving of the Last Supper was designed to amplify the theme; to add to its arresting effect in projecting a clear Christian message, it would have been illuminated, then as today, by the natural spotlight of a shaft of bright sun from a window high up on the other side of the nave.

The Last Supper, with Judas, plus devilish pursuer under the tablecloth, from the pulpit in Volterra Cathedral.

The source is clearly John's gospel – though, of course, he doesn't use the words 'Last Supper'. While Mark and Matthew have Judas as an equal participant in the first Eucharist, John describes Jesus handing Judas the sop of bread in order to identify him as the traitor with the words, 'It is the one to whom I give the piece of bread I shall dip in the dish.' At that instant, John reports, the devil takes possession of the betrayer.

This written account of the revelation of Judas as the traitor suggests that all twelve apostles were sitting around the same table as equals, but in this carving the artist has allowed himself considerable licence with the text, so as to make a wider point to those in the congregation whose eyes might wander onto the detail of the pulpit as the preacher took his time to develop his theme. Judas is here all but damned before the bread is even broken. Jesus sits on an elaborate throne at the head of the draped supper table, littered with fish and debris of the Passover meal. Only eleven of the twelve are accorded the honour of a seat behind the table. Some have beards, others don't. All are square-jawed and chiselled in their stereotypically masculine features, recognisably human as is the style, but indistinguishable one from the other, and indeed from their leader.

Placement is all, though, and the eleven have been put on the right side of the table – the good side, the upper side, the heavenly side. Meanwhile underneath, peering up and out through the folds of the cloth, as if from the depths of hell, is Judas, half kneeling, half collapsed, his face by contrast curiously feminine, and his body in its odd, distorted proportions redolent of those other-worldly creatures believed to inhabit the domain of the damned. Naturalism and realism have here been jettisoned for ghoulish effect. It is not quite a caricature – such extremes would come later in the medieval age, especially when Judas was regularly conflated by artists with Jews in an effort to dehumanise both – but here Judas certainly looks peculiar, the sort of individual one might cross the road to avoid.

This was a time where the visual was so much stronger than the written, or even the spoken. So Judas' evil had to be made very physical. In his twisted, androgynous body, he is wickedness incarnate for the viewer.

While directing his gaze unflinchingly at the eleven true apostles, including 'John the Beloved', as he is known in John's gospel (and who, here, is doing that strange cuddling up to his master that only John reports), Jesus is simultaneously handing Judas the sop of bread under the tablecloth. Multi-tasking, we might call it now, since he does it without sparing the recipient so much as a cursory glance, rather as a dog-owner might feed its pet a titbit under the tablecloth while busy attending to his guests.

Judas' vastly inferior status is unavoidable to any onlooker. Because he is under the table, it makes impossible another detail of John's gospel. In the text, as Jesus gives Judas the sop, he says, 'What you are going to do, do quickly.' It could be read as evidence of a certain collusion between the two. In the carving, though, no nod is made whatsoever to these intriguing words. It would have been regarded as muddying the essential message – that Judas was the scapegoat for the sins, perversions and temptations of all of humankind.

This archetypal image of Judas as the representative of human evil was not unique to Volterra. It had been establishing itself in religious art over the preceding centuries. The earliest known depiction of the betraying apostle is found in a long, thin, sculpted relief on an ivory chest, or reliquary, from around 370 CE, designed to hold the bones and body parts of a saint and therefore the object of popular veneration and pilgrimage. The Brescia Casket – or *Lipsanoteca di Brescia* – is now housed in the church of Santa Giulia in Brescia, in the foothills of the Italian Alps. Along with various scenes from Jesus' passion and death, as well as Old Testament episodes, Judas is shown down one side of the back panel, hanging by a noose from a tree. It is a haunting, unadorned representation.

The sixth-century Rossano Gospels, the earliest surviving depiction of Judas at the 'Last Supper'.

In terms of images of Judas' presence at the Last Supper, the sixth-century Rossano Gospels, named after a town in Calabria, southern Italy, are probably the earliest surviving example. An illuminated (illustrated) manuscript of Matthew's account, and partly of Mark's, it is one of the oldest documents of its type in the world, completed, it is thought, to celebrate the reconquest of Italy by the forces of the Christian emperor in Byzantium.[4] It is also sometimes called the 'Codex purpureus Rossanensis' because of its reddy-purple hue, and features a series of miniature, almost matchstick illustrations from the life of Christ. At the Last Supper, as in the Volterra pulpit scene, Jesus sits to one side, but in the Rossano Gospels, all twelve apostles are accommodated around the table. Judas is still one of the group, not yet cast down. He is marked out, though, because he is stretching out his spindly arm greedily towards the dish in the centre of the table, while the others are content to sit calmly beholding their leader. If it is the sop of bread he is reaching for, then John's account must also have influenced this unknown artist. And the same source may account for the devil's unmistakeable presence – as a set of three outsized blackbirds decorating the tablecloth.

Back in Volterra, the pulpit's Last Supper opts instead for a more menacing form for Satan, as chilling as the stone it is carved from. In John's account, it states that, as the sop was handed to Judas, Satan 'entered' him. So behind the cowered, contorted Judas, and stretching out all along the floor for the rest of the length of the Last Supper table, is a slithering, snarling demon, propelled by a motion that carries ever forward a body that is part lion and part scaly snake, with a dragon's knotted tail. It is as if one of the *stilofori* from the pulpit's base has climbed up and into the Last Supper scene. Biting at Judas' heels, just as in earlier literature Judas himself had been portrayed as a biter of the Christ child, this predatory lieutenant of the devil would have been immediately familiar to the medieval congregation as the fate that awaited them if, for a moment, they strayed from the church.

Judas becomes the paramount example – offered in this cathedral, in the most prominent place, where the eyes of the congregation might rest – of how not to be and not to act.

Half-digested

A great gulf existed in this era of mass illiteracy between the visual and the written, but bridging it, albeit to a limited extent, was *Inferno*, Dante Alighieri's travelogue of hell, the first of the three books of his celebrated *Divine Comedy*. It was rare in being penned in the Italian vernacular, rather than in the exclusive language of church Latin. *Inferno* comes between 100 and 150 years after the Volterra pulpit, but serves a broadly similar purpose. Dante may be in the vanguard of the new ideas of the Renaissance, but his casting of Judas is decidedly of its time.

Inferno is set in the very core of the earth, where a series of nine layers constitute hell, with the degree of eternal privation suffered by each set of damned inhabitants increasing as the narrator – Dante himself – goes further down, layer by layer, always in the company of his guide, the Roman poet, Virgil (one mark of Renaissance thinking was a renewed respect for Classical civilisations). En route, he meets individuals whose vices have landed them there. In Upper Hell, nearest the earth's surface, entered by a vestibule crowned with the doom-laden words, 'Abandon every hope, all you who enter', the population is largely non-Christian, virtuous men who are shut off from God's redeeming light only by dint of never having heard his message. Their discomforts are mild.

As the descent continues, there are the lustful, the gluttonous, the spendthrifts, the angry and the slothful, roughly in line with the Seven Deadly Sins, first codified for the Christian world by Pope Gregory the Great in the sixth century. In their midst there are obvious places where Judas might be lurking – the eerie 'Wood of Suicides' in the layer of violence, for example, with 'no green leaves, but rather black in colour/No smooth branches, but twisted and entangled/No fruit but thorns of poison bloomed instead'.[5] It could almost be a description of that bleak Jerusalem hillside at Hakeldama, outside the monastery walls.

Instead, though, Dante saves Judas for the very last circle, the domain of traitors. It contains a whole area called the Judecca, or Giudecca, named after him, emphasising once again that easy link between Judas' name and the Jews, since in the towns and cities of southern Italy and Sicily at this time the Giudecca was the Jewish ghetto. In this lowest layer of hell, 'the vast kingdom of all grief', the fate of the dead is a terrible one – to be 'fixed under ice . . . like straws worked into glass'. The sight of it makes Dante tremble.

Presiding is the devil, in the shape of a three-headed Lucifer,[6] his lower half encased in ice, tearfully chewing on three notorious sinners – Brutus and Cassius, co-conspirators against Julius Caesar, and Judas. The cold (as opposed to the more traditional flames), and the impotence rather than menace, represent Dante's fresh take on his subject, radically different from that more standard medieval fare of a beast under the table. But it is the same Judas, here again the worst of the worst.

> *'That soul up there who suffers most of all,'*
> *my guide explained, 'is Judas Iscariot:*
> *the one with head inside and legs out kicking.'*

Blood and fireworks

If I screw up my eyes, I can just about decipher above the Volterra Last Supper carving what the artist must have intended as a final touch, for that small proportion of the congregation able to read even a little. Decorating the top of the relief is a list of the names of the participants seated at the table. All the apostles from the gospels are included, but the roll of honour breaks off in the space that is high above Judas' head. There is just a crossing out. Judas has been deleted forever.

Those with time during a sermon to take in such details would then have been almost assaulted by the force of Judas' bad example, as presented here; not that it causes much more than a curious glance from my fellow visitors, who come along, take a quick photo of the pulpit, as their guides tell them they should, and then move on. There are much more obvious sights for modern, secular eyes elsewhere in the cathedral, all added after this pulpit, including a colourful, wooden, three-dimensional, thirteenth-century rendering of Christ's Deposition from the Cross. It sits in a side chapel near the altar and draws the crowds.

By contrast, the pulpit's message has been dulled by the passage of time. Religion no longer has that ability to command attention and loyalty, to control and terrify. Neither does it seek it. Sermons are now all about a God of love. In ancient churches, the preacher usually eschews the elaborate pulpit for a modest stand on the altar, and offers a gentle reflection of hope and encouragement. Not that such a switch necessarily draws much of a congregation any longer each Sunday. This cathedral is typical of many, in seeming as much a museum as a place of worship, the piped Benedictine chant making the whole place seem utterly benign.

Once, though, this pitiful picture of Judas would have reeled onlookers in and terrified them. And it was hard to avoid once inside the cathedral. All the other paintings and decorations that today grace the nave walls, including those behind and opposite the pulpit, only came along later in the sixteenth century. Prior to that, for the congregation sitting where I am, there would have been no ready distraction from the stark lesson in stone that met their eyes as they looked up at the preacher.

And Judas was just as central when, in medieval times, the gospels were carried out of the precincts of cathedrals and onto piazzas, as part of well-established religious processions and public rituals that became landmarks in local calendars. Whether Volterra had one is nowhere recorded, but variations on the theme of a 'Judas Day' were common all over Catholic and Orthodox Europe, as the betrayer took to the streets to face the public's wrath.

Czech and German towns, for instance, had their own traditions, where a wooden or straw effigy of Judas would be burnt on bonfires on Easter Saturday.[7] It was something separate from the liturgical cycle, and even from the church-organised passion plays that developed in this same period to give a more controlled dramatic expression to the gospels. Judas-burning, by contrast, represented a slightly anarchic escape valve, a mixture of high spirits and a letting-off of steam from the stifling atmosphere of fear created by so much concentration within the churches on the threat of the devil, and the danger of following in Judas' footsteps.

Judas Day usually took place on the Saturday – between Good Friday and Easter Sunday. It was a void, when the churches themselves were silent, and the altars draped in black. And so the space was filled by a mixture of religious procession and carnival. As the Judas figure was set ablaze, those watching could be casting off his shadow from their own lives or, briefly, liberating themselves from the heavy hand of the church. And then, having witnessed his death, most were ready to return to the pews the next day to welcome the risen Christ.

There were many variations in different cultures on this colourful scapegoating ritual. Some would stuff the effigy with a pig's bladder filled with blood, or blood-coloured liquid, so that Judas could first be hanged and then have his innards caused to burst asunder in imitation of the version in Acts. In other places the local butcher would supply meat to represent Judas' entrails. Often, before being set alight, his 'corpse' would be dragged through the streets – shaming the traitor, in the same way criminals might be paraded on their way to the stocks or the gallows. In Spanish towns (and later in Latin America on '*La Guema de Judas*', adopting and modifying the rituals of the Spanish conquistadors) the Judas doll would be stuffed with fireworks that exploded to capture the violence of his death – and to entertain the crowds.[8]

The practice survives in some places to this very day. On the south coast of Crete an effigy of Judas, in black hat and with a grotesque face, goes up in flames after children have pelted it with stones. In Cyprus, something similar is known as Lambratzia, and has become a tourist attraction, as has another ritual burning in the Philippines town of Baclayon. Elsewhere, it has evolved into a more general riotous farewell to Lent and its fasting – *La Quema del Año Viejo*, as it is known in Mexico: 'the burning of the old year'. That in turn has sometimes spilled into more political protests, with the Judas figure given the face of hated local politicians, bureaucrats or even drugs barons.[9]

Occasionally other interpretations of Judas' story were brought in to the festivities – with disastrous consequences. Because of that close association that grew up in medieval times between 'Judas the Jew' and the Jews in general, 'Judas Day' also became known as 'Burning of the Jew' in some cultures. As late as 1850, the British government indulged in some brutal gunboat diplomacy with recently independent Greece when a British subject, Don Pacifico, who lived in Athens and was Jewish, claimed he had been burnt out of house and home by a mob on 'Judas Day', their enthusiasm for setting light to the traitorous apostle then leading them to torch his house as the residence of a well-known Jew. Compensation was duly paid before a shot was fired in anger.[10]

But that is to race ahead. The chapter of Judas' life revealed so powerfully in medieval Volterra by its cathedral pulpit was about to give way to another, where his trademark became not so much the demonic *stilofori* that snapped at his heels, but rather his money-bag, strapped to his waist, containing the thirty pieces of silver.

O

O'Scariot

In the once strongly Catholic culture of Ireland, where the bad example of Judas was prominently held up by the church, and where the prefix O' is common before surnames, those judged to have betrayed their family, friends, community, profession or church have, on occasion, been popularly damned with the nickname Judas O'Scariot. One well-known journalist, who has suffered this fate, laments that he will carry the tag to his grave.

P

Priest

In the musical world – especially among heavy metal bands – the name Judas carries a cachet, conjuring up an audience-pleasing, dark, angry, devil-may-care approach to subverting society's norms. The most famous of them all is Britain's Judas Priest, who have sold around 50 million albums worldwide, including titles such as *Sin After Sin* and *Angel of Retribution*. They took their name, they say, from Bob Dylan's 1967 track, 'The Ballad of Frankie Lee and Judas Priest', a moral tale about an innocent seduced by a cold-eyed devilish traitor posing as his friend.

CHAPTER EIGHT:

Bags of Money: Judas and the Original Merchant-Bankers

Yet woe to the man who lost the hope of being forgiven even then – who, terror-stricken by the enormity of his crime, gave up to despair instead of returning, even then, to the Source of all mercy.

Saint Bonaventura (1221–1274): *The Tree of Life*[1]

In the wake of the global financial crash of 2007, bankers were regularly demonised by politicians and public alike because their unbridled greed was held responsible for inflicting on the rest of us an age of biting austerity, unparalleled since the 1930s. The hue and cry against bankers demonstrated, once again, the potency of the accusation of greed – usually taken to be Judas' motivation for betraying Jesus. In the case of the modern-day bankers, this was exacerbated because so few of those who had taken such fatal risks with other people's money subsequently faced either a court or loss of income themselves (their bonuses continued to be paid).

Public anger, therefore, had to seek other outlets. Incendiary anti-banker slogans were spray-painted on walls, printed on T-shirts and posted on social media; protest movements such as Occupy camped out in the financial districts of major cities to complain that a malign 1 per cent was ripping off the virtuous 99 per cent; and open season was declared on individual bankers. Among the many brickbats hurled, one in particular caught my eye, because it harked back to an earlier age when the image of Judas Iscariot, clutching his money-bag containing the thirty pieces of silver, was routinely used to articulate public disdain for bankers and moneymen. A disgruntled Russian bureaucrat and blogger, Sergey Bogdanov, trading under the name Ferrabra, dusted down the medal of the Order of Judas, set up by Tsar Peter the Great, and awarded it to 'the bankers of Wall Street'.[2] The gong he displayed online showed Judas hanging by a rope from a branch with the bulging bag prominent next to his dangling feet.

The Order of Judas had been created in anger by the tsar in 1709 to humiliate one of his closest advisors, the Ukrainian land-owner Ivan Mazepa, after he defected to the Swedish king Charles XII in the Great Northern War. When Mazepa had been a favoured figure at his court, Peter the Great had decorated him with every imperial medal going. Now, in his moment of betrayal, and unable to recapture Mazepa to make an example of him, the tsar had to content himself with stigmatising his former lieu-tenant as a Judas. To hammer home the point, he then also awarded the same medal to unlikely figures, such as his court jester. As a signal, it lodged in the collective consciousness. To this day Ukrainians refer to traitors as Mazepists.[3]

The original Order of Judas, then, had nothing to do with moneymen, but Russian blogger Ferrabra was invoking the spirit rather than the detail of Peter the Great's creation. Just as the tsar had wanted to destroy forever the good name of Mazepa, so this modern-day protestor wanted to bad-mouth bankers by tar-nishing them with the name of the ultimate traitor. And there he was, invoking something more enduring. Indeed, using Judas as a scapegoat to attack bankers and financiers goes right back to the birth of capitalism in the West in medieval northern and central Italy.

There, in ambitious city-states, thriving manufacturers started to establish a network of trade that expanded from the tenth century onwards, building on links with the Byzantine and Islamic world to the east, where the profit economy was already highly developed. As a result, Italy began to move away from a land-based, rural subsistence economy, and witnessed the rise of the first merchant-banking houses, where traders introduced paper money to oil the wheels of commerce, guaranteeing the new currency's worth with their own considerable reserves of gold and silver.

It was a development that brought extraordinary wealth to cities such as Florence, where the likes of the Bardi merchant-banking family boasted warehouses, offices and staff from London to Paris, Constantinople to Jerusalem, not to mention a stake in funding Christopher Columbus' trip to discover the New World. It also – inevitably, given human nature – prompted widespread envy and caused the merchant-bankers great unpopularity. There was fear mixed in there too, the sort of fear that comes with change. For those frightened by the disruption and dislocation caused by such a major economic shift, change can feel awfully like a betrayal of the existing order, of all that has gone before, of all that people have taken for granted, especially when only a small number of their fellow citizens are benefiting. And, once feelings of betrayal surface, the name of Judas is instantly heard.

In the case of these fast-changing medieval Italian cities, the merchant-bankers found themselves both praised for the prosperity they were bringing, and stigmatised as betrayers, especially when economic power gave them a taste for political and civic authority too, traditionally exercised by the church and its bishops and priests. The old guard responded by invoking Judas, making the connection between the merchant-bankers and Jesus' betrayer stick by a variety of devices – principal among them, Judas' bag of thirty silver pieces. Paper money may have begun to appear, but these coins remained a readily understood symbol of the rise of the buying-and-selling economy, of making money out of money, and therefore of greedy bankers.

The Collegiata Church of San Gimignano in Tuscany contains celebrated fresco cycles from the Old and New Testaments. This twelfth-century Romanesque masterpiece is part of a UNESCO World Heritage Site and was originally built out of the riches the town accumulated in the medieval period, as both a trading centre and a stopping-off point on the Via Francigena, the main pilgrim route that led through it southwards to Rome.

Among the New Testament scenes painted by Taddeo di Bartolo in the Collegiata Church in the 1330s is 'Judas selling Jesus to the Jewish high priests'. The rogue apostle is clustered with two priests, with their scarf-like head-coverings and long heavy beards. Judas sports only a modest goatee, but he is darkly, almost menacingly, intent to the point of obsession on those thirty coins as they emerge from the bag and are passed from hand to hand. His love of money, above everything else, is clearly signalled, as is the evil that it represents.

What roused particular popular resentment was the merchant-bankers' habit of charging interest on any money that they lent, and thereby, in the popular mind, amassing fortunes at the expense of their clients. The church had long loudly decried the practice of usury from the pulpit. It was, they pointed out, condemned in the gospels[4] (as well as in the Hebrew Scriptures[5] and the Qur'an[6]). In 1179, responding to the concerns of the time that had been prompted by the rise of a new economic order, the Third Lateran Council took this one step further when it ruled that anyone engaged in usury was to be excommunicated, a crushing verdict on the new financial and mercantile class. It was reached despite the fact that in medieval Italy most of the members of this class were devout Catholics, such as the Bardi, Medici and Peruzzi.

In 1311, Pope Clement V even went so far as to rule that usury was a heresy. He insisted, moreover, on the primacy of church law in financial matters, over and above the civil law codes that covered money transactions in most of the self-governing cities and regions of Italy. These did allow the charging of interest, within reason. Clement was therefore setting the church's rulebook – and public face – against the civic authorities and their support for merchant-bankers. And that dispute had a larger dimension. Who was really in control in medieval Italy: bishops or local politicians or moneymen?

This was a major theological, political, social and economic battle of the thirteenth and fourteenth centuries. The church hierarchy claimed the moral high ground – apparently standing up for ordinary citizens against the merchant-bankers by bemoaning the sinfulness of usury. Yet its populist posturing should be treated with caution. Much of the cost of papal initiatives to send Crusaders to Jerusalem to recapture the 'holy sites', for example, was covered by loans from the self-same merchant-bankers the church was so extravagantly accusing of heresy. If usury was so bad, why take the usurers' money? And how very convenient, when it came to the requirement to pay the money back with interest, for churchmen to launch into a frenzy of condemnation of merchant-bankers. If they could be demonised by accusing them of greed to rival that of Judas, the arch-betrayer of the gospels, then these financial titans might feel forced to waive or reduce their fees to escape further public moral censure. The net result would then be a financial saving for popes and bishops. Not for the first time, Judas was part of a propaganda war.

Money as the root of Judas' evil

If bankers' reputations are today regarded as being at a low ebb, reading Dante's *Inferno* suggests there is further they could fall. Despite being the son of a banker, and the brother-in-law of a moneylender, he captures the widespread antagonism to the new rich in booming Italian cities when he consigns merchant-bankers to the seventh circle of hell, reserved for those who have committed crimes of violence and 'other practisers of unnatural vice', such as blasphemers and 'sodomites'. That leaves them just two levels above Judas in the worst category of all: that restricted to traitors. It is, furthermore, a ranking that also damned them as worse sinners than inhabitants of higher levels that contain the lusty, the gluttons, the greedy popes and the angry politicians. Among those moneymen Dante specifically names and shames is Cavalcante de'Cavalcanti, the thirteenth-century Florentine who had lent money to the papacy on allegedly extortionate terms.

This wasn't just Dante currying favour with the church, playing on the public's prejudices, or creating scapegoats to make a point for his times to soothe his own disappointments in Florentine politics. In the internal debates of Catholicism, usury was very much a live issue. Thomas Aquinas, the thirteenth-century Italian Dominican theologian, still highly influential in contemporary Christian thought, was one of many to reflect deeply on the morality of usury as the rise of capitalism challenged traditional church teaching. And he did so by quoting the example of Judas. 'It was from love that the Father delivered Christ, and Christ gave himself up to death; it is for reason that both are praised', he wrote in his *Summa Theologica*. 'Judas however delivered him out of avarice ... which is why [he] has such a bad name'. Lending money might, in some cases, be licit, Aquinas conceded. What tipped the practice into usury and hence into sinfulness was when it was done with the same greed that Judas had demonstrated in betraying Jesus.

Judas' central place in this whole debate about usury may explain why he is seen so much in Italian art of the period. In Assisi, in the Basilica of Saint Francis, the three-part cycle of frescoes on Jesus' passion, death and resurrection, completed in the early fourteenth century, includes Judas in all five scenes of act one, the build-up to Jesus' trial. As well as the episodes where he would have been hard to overlook (the betrayal and the Last Supper), he is also allotted a new and unwarranted (by the gospels) prominence, for example, among the followers of Jesus on his triumphant entry into Jerusalem on Palm Sunday. Judas stands at the front, next to Peter, as if both are the leaders of the apostles, though Judas, of course, has no halo.

That same juxtaposing of Peter and Judas is seen again in the depiction of the Last Supper, as Jesus gives Judas the sop of bread that marks him out as the traitor. Here Judas is no longer relegated to under the tablecloth, assailed by demons, but instead he and Peter carefully balance each other at either end of the supper table, both prominent and in the foreground. And, once again, the Peter-versus-Judas configuration of virtue-versus-treachery is there in the depictions of Jesus washing the apostles' feet, *and* the arrest in Gethsemane. Setting off these two apostles carries a symbolic message on a variety of levels. Among them is the suggestion that the church – in the person of Peter, its first leader, sign of its continuing authority – is head to head with usurious merchants and bankers, as conjured up by Judas, the apostle who was obsessed with money. Only the church, this cycle seems to argue, can protect the faithful against both the devil and the stresses and strains of the new capitalist economy.

There is a total of eleven depictions of Judas in Assisi's Basilica of Saint Francis, dating from the twelfth through to the thirteenth century. It is an unusually high number, but part of a marked increase of images of Judas in prosperous Italy in this later medieval period. 'My study of the iconography', writes distinguished British art historian Janet Robson, who has made a special study of the subject, 'has revealed 37 images [of Judas] from the twelfth century, 65 from the thirteenth century, then a mighty leap to 201 from the fourteenth century.'[7]

With the flood of new money into their civic coffers, towns and cities wanted to build bigger, better and more richly decorated churches to celebrate their success and promote local pride (*campanilismo*). This instinct to endow and commission seemingly overrode any antagonism over usury between the new capitalists and the church, and has been labelled by Robson as 'competitive *campanilismo*'.[8]

The impetus, though, was not only rich citizens, wanting to show off their prosperity and enhance their town's status. 'The adage that devotion could be aroused "more by what is seen than what is heard",' writes Robson, 'was coined in the thirteenth century by both Saint Thomas Aquinas and Saint Bonaventura to justify images in churches.'[9] Ever more elaborate church decoration was seen as a vital tool of evangelisation, pictures often having more power than words. But what particular effect was the ever-present Judas intended to have?

It was largely still that traditional element of wanting to induce fear that stretches back through the Volterra pulpit into earlier centuries. Yet, the extent to which Judas' fate was now resonating ever more loudly in the popular imagination in this new capitalist world can be seen by the fact that the punitive, vengeful Psalm 109 – quoted by Peter in the Acts of the Apostles when he tells the disciples of Judas' terrible death,[10] and today usually blandly entitled 'An appeal against enemies' – was known in this period as the 'Judas' Psalm', though it contains no mention of the false apostle (because it long predates him).

> *In return for my friendship, they denounce me, though all I had done was pray for them;*
> *They pay me back evil for kindness, and hatred for friendship.*
> *'Give him a venal judge, find someone to frame the charge;*
> *Let him be tried and found guilty, let his prayer be construed as a crime!*
> *'Let his life be cut short, let someone else take his office;*

May his children be orphaned and his wife widowed!
'May his children be homeless vagabonds, beggared and hounded
from the hovels;
May the creditor seize his possessions and foreigners swallow his
profits!

As well as a 'Judas Psalm', there was also a 'Judas curse', recorded as in use from the eighth through to the fourteenth century, sometimes in official documents, and in quasi-legal settings. Anyone swearing an oath would pledge only to break it at the risk of 'having his part with Judas'. In wordier versions, those who stepped beyond their publicly made promises were 'placed with Judas the traitor in the fires of hell'.[11] And a version of the Judas curse is even found on tombstones, according to the American academic, Kim Paffenroth. He identifies a grave from around the third century that is inscribed: 'The tomb of Andrew and Athenais and their child Maria, those who finished life virtuously. And if anyone should dare to open [the tomb] also to sun, he will share the lot of Judas, all things will become darkness to him, and God will destroy him on that day.'[12]

Saint Francis' own personal Judas

The rise of a culture of wealth and excess in medieval Italy increasingly swept up the church and eventually provoked a reaction within Catholicism itself in the form of a new enthusiasm for embracing poverty. Religious orders were founded, known as mendicant because they begged in order to survive rather than relying on endowments from bankers and merchants. They threw their lot in with the needy and oppressed and turned their back on the world of the privileged. That, famously, was the inspiration of Francis of Assisi, founder of the Friars Minor, the son of a wealthy merchant draper, who as a young man had lived a frivolous, carefree life of indulgence typical of his nouveau-riche class. After hearing the voice of God telling him to 'repair my falling house',[13] he disowned his family and fortune 'to wed Lady Poverty', and shed his fine robes in favour of a simple tunic, tied with a cord, and bare feet. In 1210 he founded his order.

The Franciscans were in the vanguard of the anti-capitalist movement in the church in Italy (and later beyond), and so it comes as no surprise that they too were drawn to make use of the figure of Judas. They even had their own personal Judas.

In the hagiography that grew up around Francis after his death, he was portrayed not simply as a champion of the poor, or a man of exceptional saintly goodness, but as a Christ-like figure – 'alter Christus' was the phrase used. His life story was then reshaped – as the biographies of saints had been for centuries – to fit that particular perspective. So Francis' founding group of followers was said to number twelve, like the apostles (in reality there were more), and one of the twelve, by the same logic, had to be a traitor. In the *Fioretti*, a widely circulated fourteenth-century vernacular book of stories about Francis and his early companions, the following tale is told:

'We must first consider how the glorious Sir Saint Francis was conformed to the blessed Christ in all the acts of his life; as Christ at the beginning of his preaching chose twelve Apostles to despise all worldly things and to follow him in poverty and in the other virtues; in the same way Saint Francis chose at the beginning of the foundation of the Order twelve companions who possessed the highest poverty. And just as one of the twelve Apostles, the one called Judas Iscariot, became an apostate from the apostolate, betraying Christ, and hanging himself by the neck; so one of the twelve companions of Saint Francis, who was named Brother John Cappella, became an apostate and finally hanged himself by the neck.'[14]

Other earlier, and probably more measured, historical records of the founding of the Order of Friars Minor do indeed mention John Cappella. Some even paint him as an agitator in the ranks, a potential rival to Francis, wanting to set up his own group. Yet over time his character evolved into the Judas-like figure found in the *Fioretti*. Judas/John is the one who stands in the way of Jesus/Francis. To hammer home the likeness, extra details were then added. Later accounts, for example, describe John Cappella as becoming a leper, with physical deformities, or going insane in that period between splitting away from Francis and his core group and hanging himself.

More than money

This prominence of Judas in medieval Italy cannot, however, be explained only by the connection made between him and the perceived greed of the nouveau riche. His story touched on other aspects of the age. In the magnificent mosaic ceiling of the cupola of the twelfth-century octagonal Florence Baptistery (where Dante was christened), Judas features in the Last Judgement. On Christ's left hand are the sinners in hell, being roasted on spits, bitten by snakes or attacked by wild beasts. And there, too, is Judas, hanging by a tree from a rope.

The location of his suicide has been transferred from the earthly desolation of Hakeldama to the subterranean furnace of the devil's lair. Though this contradicts the official teaching of Catholicism (which has always refused to confirm or deny that any named individual is in hell, the whole question being left to God), it does capture the spirit of what was routinely said about Judas' fate in the church. What is unusual, though, is the demon shown pulling on the rope that goes around Judas' neck. Judas is being executed, rather than committing suicide. Having the demon as hangman may simply have been another way of showing that Judas was completely taken over by the devil in those last

Judas dies in hell, part of the mosaic of *The Last Judgement*, in
Florence's twelfth-century Baptistery.

days of his life – in line with Luke and John's gospel, but might
there also have been a question mark here about the morality of
capital punishment, common in these centuries? Was it the devil's
work? Or is that projecting twenty-first-century values onto an
earlier epoch?

Certainly showing Judas executed lessens the possibility of
seeing his suicide as a demonstration of remorse for what he has
done. The hangman also takes away any element of Judas making
a choice about the manner of his death, and points instead at his
malice. He is no better than a common murderer.

In the medieval mind, among the greatest of offences against
God was malice. 'Some sins', wrote the thirteenth-century
Franciscan Saint Bonaventura, a theologian closely associated
with Thomas Aquinas, 'are due to impotence, others to ignorance, and others again to malice.'[15] Malice, he taught, was the

worst of the three – and Judas, he noted, was malicious. He may have been the tool of Satan but, for Bonaventura, he also possessed an innate wickedness and treachery that could not all be blamed on the devil. He represented the sort of motiveless, treacherous villain who, out of choice, was at heart evil for its own sake. Such a malicious character might logically end up with the hangman.

Another common accusation levelled against Judas was that, by killing himself, he succumbed to despair rather than throw himself on God's mercy and forgiveness. Those who despair end up in hell – as the Judas of the Florence Baptistery illustrates. 'Despair consists', wrote Thomas Aquinas, 'in a man ceasing to hope for a share in God's goodness.' And so 'Judas desperatus' was a readily understood figure, seen, for example, in Nicholas of Bologna's celebrated illustrations for a 1354 manuscript version of Pope Gregory IX's *Decretals*, which is today in Milan's Biblioteca Ambrosiana.[16] A row of virtuous figures stands with those who have demonstrated the equivalent vice humbled at their feet. The noble embodiment of hope towers over 'Judas desperatus', the noose still around his neck.

As ever, images were not just to delight the eye but to make a practical point. If hope was the believer's antidote to Judas' despair, how to achieve it? The medieval church had a ready answer in the sacrament of confession. Heinous crimes could be confessed to a priest, who had the authority to intercede with God on the sinner's behalf to grant absolution. Some crimes, though, were beyond absolution. There was no depiction of Judas seeking it in confession. Instead his role in the imagery of the time was to show the despair that existed without recourse to the sacrament.

In 1215 the Fourth Lateran Council had formalised requirements that every baptised Catholic should seek absolution for their sins through the sacrament of confession at least once a year.

This increasing emphasis on confession was accompanied by a taste for calibrating sins, vices and virtues. The Church provided checklists for penitents, examining their conscience before making a 'good' confession. Already one such formula existed in the Seven Deadly Sins, regularly found in illustrations in the thirteenth and fourteenth century. Included was Judas' sin of greed, sometimes called avarice. And despair featured prominently in an alternative list of the Seven Vices. Again Judas' was the example regularly quoted, but he was not alone. In Giotto's fresco cycles in the Scrovegni Chapel in Padua, despair takes female form. In 'Desperatio' (1306), a nameless woman hangs herself by her scarf from a bending crossbeam. Yet the echo of Judas is there, not least because, in the moment of the woman's death, a demon hovers to carry away her soul to eternal torment, as it does in countless illustrations from the period of his last moments.

What is notably absent from all these images of Judas that began appearing in greater numbers from the fourteenth century is any reference to that moment in Matthew's gospel when he tries to return the thirty pieces of silver and ends up throwing them on the floor of the Temple sanctuary. While there was a seemingly inexhaustible taste for depictions of Judas clutching the coins, the appetite for seeing him giving them back was slight. It would have shown his remorse and thereby blunted the message that he died in utter despair. The one notable exception is the Basilewsky Situla, a late tenth-century holy water bucket, elaborately carved in ivory to mark the visit of the Holy Roman Emperor, Otto II, to Milan, which is now in London's Victoria and Albert Museum.

North of the Alps

The modern temptation when picturing medieval Europe is immediately to associate its bankers, financiers and moneylenders with the persecuted Jewish community. Shakespeare's Shylock in

The Merchant of Venice casts a long shadow. And, indeed, it is true that Europe's Jews were vastly over-represented in the growing medieval money trade, though not necessarily out of choice. Christianity's moral and doctrinal reservations about usury made it an area of commerce that those in the pews tended to avoid. Yet, as a money economy grew, someone had to do it, and since laws excluded Jews from many other options for earning a living, including owning land, they had few other possibilities (despite the Talmud's own hard line on usury and the charging of interest).

Logically it should therefore follow that, in characterising the new merchant-banker class as Judases, Italian artists would include recognisable Jewish stereotypes. Judas the greedy money-grabber would be conflated with Judas the Jew, already a familiar figure in Christian rhetoric. Yet largely they didn't. Why? Because the majority of these Italian nouveau riches were Catholics rather than Jews.

There were, overall, only a tiny number of Jews in medieval Italy, and most were down in the south of the country, rather than in the commercial hub further north. And for those who did migrate to Tuscany, life was generally different from that experienced by their co-believers north of the Alps. 'The Italian Jews,' writes historian Janet Robson, 'at least before the fifteenth century, were largely spared the outbreaks of anti-Semitic violence that regularly afflicted the Jewish communities of England, France and Germany.'[17]

In these other lands, however, as Robson suggests, Jewish lives were blighted by expulsions and pogroms. Even when allowed to reside there, they lived in the presence of threat and hostility. There had been recorded Jewish settlements in German lands since the fourth century. Under Charlemagne in the eighth and ninth centuries, they had enjoyed civil liberties and relatively few religious restrictions, but their position was never secure. With every negative turn of events – plagues, invasions, wars – a hard-pressed population and their opportunistic rulers would seek out a scapegoat on whom to blame all current ills. Often that scapegoat was the Jews.

When the First Crusade was gathering, rallying to the papal cry at the end of the eleventh century and determined to teach a lesson to Jew and Muslim alike by reconquering the Holy Land, European Jews found themselves the target of troops as they made their way southwards across the continent to the Near East. Thousands of Jews died along the route as a result.

In the middle years of the fourteenth century, the Black Death, one of the most devastating pandemics in human history, killing between 75 and 200 million people across Europe, prompted yet more outbreaks of anti-Semitic violence and killing. The cause of the disease bemused doctors, so Jews once again provided a ready scapegoat in the public mind. They were blamed for poisoning the wells and cast – like Judas – as the traitors in the heart of their communities. In 1349, established Jewish communities were slaughtered in revenge attacks in Mainz and Cologne – both major trading cities that thrived on financial services provided by Jews.

In such a climate, the association of Judas, Jews and untrustworthy moneylenders was regularly, almost unthinkingly made – in literature, in heads and hearts, and in churches. In the porch of the fourteenth-century Gothic Minster of Freiburg, in the borderlands between modern France and Germany, a Last Judgement scene features a typically devilish Judas, carrying his swag bag. He's the moneyman. Alongside is his death scene, at Hakeldama. Here, he is surrounded by a group of men, all identifiable as Jews by their clothing. The greed that brought about Judas' suicide is equated to the greed of Jewish bankers and moneylenders. And so the money-grabbing, satanic Judas becomes a readily identifiable Semitic character.

This process had already been in train for many centuries in northern Europe. The Stuttgart Psalter, a ninth-century illuminated parchment manuscript, takes as its inspiration the Psalms. Such works were both devotional – something to study in order to know better God's word – and widely regarded by their wealthy owners as an amulet, capable of warding off evil. The Stuttgart Psalter contains a striking image of Judas at the Last Supper.

Judas seen in profile at the 'Last Supper', from the ninth-century Stuttgart Psalter.

As he leans forward towards Jesus, a demon is down by his feet, as if pulling his strings, while a blackbird – a usual symbol of the devil – hovers by his mouth. That much is standard, but while Jesus is seen three-quarter face, under his halo, the unadorned Judas is in profile. He is rarely in medieval times seen otherwise. To depict only half the face, it was understood, was to suggest that the individual was two-faced. And who could be more so than Judas? Showing him in profile, moreover, also played on a popular superstition that those who could do you harm had an 'evil eye' that could bewitch or possess. To escape its trap, you must avoid the gaze of the 'evil eye' or somehow cover it up to stop it being effective. Picturing Judas in profile in the Stuttgart Psalter therefore ensured that the traitorous apostle's 'evil eye' was hidden. Yet, even when out of sight, its menace remained.[18]

And a profile also handily allows the nose to be emphasised. Perhaps the oldest of all caricatures of the Jews is that they have large, hooked noses. Jesus, of course, was Jewish, yet the Stuttgart Psalter gives him a neat, modest ski-slope in the centre of his face. Judas, by contrast, is so well blessed that his conk could provide a perch for the devilish blackbird should it need to land.

As well as sharing what were taken to be typical physical features of Jews, Judas was increasingly shown in the same distinctive clothes they wore. In the early sixteenth-century Wüllersleben Triptych, originally an altarpiece by Valentin Lenderstreich for a parish church in eastern Germany,[19] Jesus' agony in Gethsemane is chronicled. As Judas approaches the garden, he stands apart from the other apostles because his robes are a bright, jarring yellow. In medieval symbolism, that was the colour of treachery, and also by design the colour prescribed for Jews (and Muslims) by various anti-Semitic edicts issued by the church authorities, first in northern Europe and later too in Italy. It was to be the outward and unmistakeable sign, decreed by the Fourth Lateran Council of 1215, that those wearing it were outsiders, foreigners; people to be held at arms' length and not trusted.

Judas looks away in the triptych and so is seen in profile, his nose large and hooked, in contrast to Jesus, whose flawless face, transfixed in prayer, is fully visible. He also sports long red hair. In medieval colour coding, this became both another of his instantly identifiable characteristics, and shorthand for the human incarnation of evil. Red was one of the devil's shades. It was also a ready indication of sinfulness. Mary Magdalen, the redeemed prostitute

Judas betrays Jesus in Gethsemane from the early sixteenth-century
Wüllersleben Triptych.

of the gospels, usually wears red. It was the colour of blood –
Jesus' blood that Judas caused to be shed, or Judas' own, spilt on
the soils of Hakeldama. In a vivid description in the Middle
English 'Ballad of Judas', red is the colour of his whole head, after
'he tore his hair until it was bathed in blood', once he had lost the
thirty pieces of silver to his treacherous sister.[20] And finally red was
the colour of ostentatious wealth, the preserve of the newly rich.

There is more anti-capitalism in the Wüllersleben Triptych.
Judas is clutching an outsized bag for the thirty coins, as if his
very life depended upon it, even though it is smeared with blood.
The evil of money is made plain.

These messages are, to modern eyes, subtly conveyed. You have
to know the code to understand what is meant, and they could
easily be missed, but they would have been much more instinc-
tively understood in their own time. Catholicism was, in this age

of illiteracy, a religion of signs and symbols, with a whole, well-known language of its own.

In the high art of altarpieces, pulpit carvings and psalters, this coding was done in such a way as to form part of the whole, but in popular forms of piety, widely circulating at the time, crude depictions of 'Judas the Jew' as nothing more and nothing less than a greedy moneylender abounded. The *Biblia Pauperum* ('Paupers' Bible') was intended for an audience of local priests and monks, who had only limited literacy, but sufficient to use these texts to preach and teach to congregations who could neither read nor write. Popular in the later medieval period, they covered the key passages of the Old and New Testaments with many more pictures than words. And the words that were included were in the vernacular. (In France, the equivalent was the *Bible moralisée*.) Sometimes they would integrate scriptural texts into the whole in cartoon-like bubbles coming out of the mouths of the main characters.

These 'picture bibles' were originally hand-copied. From the 1430s, though, they were roughly printed on blocks, often in black and white, and so were able to reach a larger audience still. Many copies have survived in various libraries, where Judas can be seen with his ever-present bag of money, his hidden evil eye, and the same unmistakeable glint of greed about him as a villain in a comic book. As he receives the thirty pieces of silver from the Jewish chief priests, he is indistinguishable from them, his beard as long as theirs, full and luxuriant with elaborate curls. Jesus, by contrast, is either clean-shaven, or sports a very modest amount of facial hair. And sometimes Judas will even wear the pointed, conical hat, or *pileus*, of the Jewish high priests.

On public display

Freer and more vivid licence was employed in bringing Judas direct to the masses in miracle, mystery and passion plays, the great public spectacles of the medieval age all across Europe. The first would explore Jesus' miracles through dramatic re-enactments; the second the story of his life; and the third focused just on his arrest, trial, death and resurrection. All had their origins as performances inside churches, where clerics staged them in an effort to bring the texts of the New Testament more fully alive for congregations by adding touches of theatre and music. As they grew in popularity, though, the drama and song element expanded and moved the plays away from a scrupulously faithful rendition of the gospels. Local communities would join forces, under the guidance of their priest, and take to stages in the public square with the aim not only of educating but also of entertaining. The mystery plays, in particular, were to become the preserve of bands of travelling players, who would criss-cross the countryside, drawing vast audiences with scripts that had enjoyed little ecclesiastical scrutiny.

It was the passion plays that gave the most prominence to Judas, since many of those twenty-two gospel references fall in the build-up to Jesus' death on the cross. Hyam Maccoby accuses them of the worst crimes against the Jews. 'It was undoubtedly the passion plays', he writes, 'that contributed most to the development of the Judas-image and its potency as an instrument of anti-Semitic indoctrination.'[21]

The earliest passion plays came in the tenth century, when they would take place in churches alongside Holy Week and Easter services. A celebrated example was put on by the Benedictines of Saint Gall in Switzerland. The gospel would be read, augmented by music and short re-enactments. As it evolved, though, it became a spectacle in its own right. By the late thirteenth century, the Saint Gall Passion had Judas dying at the end of a rope and then flamboyantly using it to cascade down into hell.

It was standard, as Maccoby suggests, for the passion plays to indulge in ever more extreme and incendiary depictions of Jews. The early sixteenth-century text of the Alsfeld Passion Play from central Germany, for example, adds the nasty twist that the thirty pieces of silver were not even silver. The Jewish chief priests are so untrustworthy that they trick Judas out of his already paltry reward with counterfeits.[22] Later, in the same text, Jews are seen holding a council of war with Satan, ready to do his bidding. They are creatures of the devil, just like his earthly representative, Judas.

The mystery plays, too, routinely took all sorts of liberties with the authorised version of Judas. The travelling players who performed them had spotted in Judas a potential crowd-puller. Every inch the Jewish caricature with his long beard and yellow robes, he carried his money-bag as if it was an extra limb. Annette Weber describes in her essay, *The Hanged Judas of Freiburg Cathedral*, how the actor playing the traitorous apostle would don absurdly elaborate padding under his yellow robes, so as to include sheep's intestines and even, on occasion, a live blackbird. At the moment of Judas' death, the actor would release a strap in the padding and his insides would split open on stage, in a cascade of bloody goo, as the devil's bird would fly out to gasps of astonishment from the audience.[23]

This absurd portrait of a bloated, poisoned Judas owed an obvious debt to Papias' description of him. It might have been penned at the end of the second century, but his *Expositions of the Sayings of the Lord* – with its graphic, repulsive image of a pus- and worm-infested Judas 'bursting asunder' – remained in circulation throughout the late medieval period. From Papias, too, arose another popular medieval staple about Judas, namely that he had his own distinctive and unpleasant smell. It is seen, most graphically, in a fifteenth-century engraving of the Last Supper, by the Dutch master known only by his initials as IAM of Zwolle. In a chaotic scene round the table, Judas is clearly identified – as ever – by his money-bag, while the apostle sitting next to him is holding his nose to shut out the smell. He might as well be putting a peg on it.

On stage, and in life, that same 'Judas odour' was also attributed to the Jews. The *foetor iudaicus* was said only to disappear when a Jew converted to Christianity, thereby purging him or her of the stench of infestation by the devil (who was himself reputed to reek of sulphur). Because he could never escape hell, or receive God's forgiveness, Judas' pong was the most pungent of all.

The medieval obsession with Judas' bodily functions knew no limits, and no reason, as can be seen in the Church of Saint-Sébastien de Plampinet in Névache in the Hautes-Alpes area of southeast France. In a work dated to around 1530, a hanging Judas gives birth to an infant at precisely the moment he is dying, with a demon acting as midwife. The newborn is to be carried off, it is implied, to continue Judas' treachery into the next generation. No matter that men don't give birth to children. Or that dying by strangulation is incompatible with labour. The church's disdain for science served it well when demonising the traitor.

The Saint-Sébastien de Plampinet Judas is, however, a model of restraint compared with another depiction to be found 100 miles away in La Brigue in the Alpes-Maritimes area, close to the Italian border. At the ancient French Catholic shrine of Notre-Dame des Fontaines, site of a spring where the allegedly miraculous powers of the water have been drawing in pilgrims since the twelfth century, a fresco cycle of the Passion was painted in primitive style in the 1490s by Giovanni Canavesio. His hanging Judas looks plain deranged, eyes flashing madly, half in fear, half in threat, his hair a spiky mop. As he breathes his last, a miniature adult – with a shadow of a beard – spills out of his open stomach, along with a stream of sweet-potato-like entrails. A golden-winged monkey/demon is on hand to catch the child. The total effect is startling, utterly revolting and utterly fascinating at the same time, when seen through twenty-first-century eyes. For an earlier generation of pilgrims who came here to honour their God and protector, it would not be easily forgotten.

The 'deranged' Judas by Giovanni Canavesio from the shrine of
Notre-Dame des Fontaines at La Brigue.

Bodily corruption

It was Papias, too, the original creator of the grotesque Judas,
who first suggested Judas' sexual depravity, highlighting his genitals as 'more massive and repulsive than anyone else's'. This
description found its way into medieval church paintings as they
sought to pin as many unpleasant characteristics onto the Jews
as possible. Jerg Ratgeb's *Last Supper* (1519), part of the celebrated Herrenberg Altarpiece, once in Stuttgart's Stiftskirche

Jerg Ratgeb's sixteenth-century *Last Supper*, with its wanton Judas.

but now in the city's museum, has a predictably yellow-clad, red-haired, stereotypically Jewish Judas, but with an unusual addition – an all-too-visible erection poking through his robes. This indictment of blasphemous wantonness, when participating in the first Eucharist, is completed by the cards and dice that are falling from his grasp to the ground under the Last Supper table. He gambles while Jesus is offering the bread of life to future generations.

And this personification of Judas as a sexual predator – among the gravest of all sins according to traditional church teaching – was taken up with gusto in the mystery plays, where the actor playing the traitor would go for laughs as he displayed his elaborate codpiece. To his long list of negative accomplishments, Judas was now being made the scapegoat for sexual excess and sin.

Another physical detail much emphasised was Judas' mouth. Here the original source might have been the sixth-century *Arabic Infancy Gospel of the Saviour*, also still in circulation. In it the child Judas bites his playmate Jesus, and so, in his medieval stage persona, Judas would often bare his terrible teeth, emit a blast of foul-smelling breath to complement his bodily odours, and noisily chomp rather than chew at the bread offered at the Last Supper, all the time smacking his lips. He was carnal and animalistic rather than spiritual.

The overlap between the stage Judas and the Jewish stereotypes of the medieval age was matched by the extent to which the traitor among the twelve apostles also took on attributes ascribed to the devil himself, so powerful an ogre in the medieval imagination. It was a small step, for example, from the scaly skin often given to the devil to the rough, spotty skin routinely allocated to Judas. In his study of fourteenth- and fifteenth-century French passion plays, the American academic Jeffrey Kahn describes how some would feature demons on stage actively egging on Judas' despair. Once he had succumbed at Hakeldama and killed himself, they would pounce and boil up his body in a cauldron for a satanic feast.[24]

If this sounds more like a scene from a contemporary horror film than a play about Jesus' death and resurrection, then the medieval audience would have taken more seriously such talk of demons. The notion of a satanic feast, with Judas' body as the main course, played on a widespread popular fear that such secret gatherings were common. It was a view promoted vigorously by the heresy-seeking monks who ran the Holy Inquisition at the pope's behest from the twelfth century onwards. Their intended target was anyone who challenged the church's authority – be they pagans, Jews, or internal dissidents such as the Cathar ascetics of southern France. But all were damned by the self-same charge that, like Judas, their treachery in defying Rome could only be explained by the fact they were in league with the devil, attending on him when night fell with satanic rituals. And there was, of course, that image of Judas scurrying out into the dark night to do his evil deeds in John's gospel. 'As soon as Judas had taken the piece of bread, he went out. Night had fallen.'[25]

In torturing dissidents into confessing to an association with the devil, one device said to be popular with the Holy Inquisition was the 'Judas chair' or 'Judas cradle'. It allowed the naked victim first to be hoisted up, in a sitting position, by belts and ropes, and then lowered onto what was in effect a sharpened pyramid, fixed on top of a stool. When the weight of the body was pressing down onto the spike through anus, vagina or scrotum, the 'heretic' was then rocked. It must have been agonising – at best causing terrible pain and tearing, at worst a haemorrhage and death.

It's a gruesome picture, much repeated in later literature, and still promoted in the various 'Torture Museums' that have sprung up of late in Tuscan hill towns, including Volterra. But there is considerable doubt that such a device ever really existed. Robert Held, in his history of the Inquisition, produces an illustration of the Judas chair in operation, from circa 1680,[26] but others point to the absence of any earlier medieval records of it being employed, and suggest that it might instead have been talked up as a piece of anti-church propaganda, used in post-Reformation carnivals to show the depravity of the Church of Rome.

And it is to Judas' role in the Reformation that we must turn. But before leaving the medieval church behind, there is one country still to explore – England.

Q

Quail

Among the animals used by hunters to lure others to their deaths is the Judas quail. When blinded and caged, its distinctive distress call draws other birds towards the guns. The association of Judas with a quail may also be a glancing anti-Semitic reference back to the bevy of quails that were twice sent by God (in Exodus and Numbers[1]) to feed the starving Jews as Moses led them through the desert to freedom.

R

Relics

In the medieval heyday of pilgrimages, when believers would walk across whole continents to deepen their faith, every self-respecting abbey or monastery en route would draw in visitors with the promise of a saint's relic. And so grew up the story – purely fictional – that the 'black bones' of Judas Iscariot had somehow been preserved, and found their way into a secret collection at the Duomo in Milan. A brief revival of the tale in the 1890s caused the cathedral authorities to issue an official denial. 'There is not, nor ever was, a relic of Judas Iscariot. Neither could such a relic be kept here, for it is contrary to the principles of our holy religion.'[2]

CHAPTER NINE

An East Anglian Journey in the Company of the Arch-Traitor

'I loathe all my life, so live I too long;
My treacherous turn torments me with pain.'

'Remorse of Judas' in the York Mystery Cycle[3]

Thanks to Noel Coward, Norfolk has acquired a reputation for being very flat.[4] It's not true, or at least not universally so across the whole county. East Harling in the southwest floats sleepily on what is unmistakeably a hill, amid vast, rolling arable fields. Back in the Middle Ages, when the wool trade and the huge flocks it required made Norfolk the most densely populated and economically prosperous part of the country, East Harling was the bustling host to a busy sheep market. One remnant of its glory days is still visible from miles away as I approach on a sunny June morning. The fairy-tale lead-and-timber spire that tops off its vast fifteenth-century church, all ornate buttresses and battlements, stands out on the horizon, guiding me in like a runway beacon.

With prosperity came civic pride, and Norfolk boasts the largest concentration of medieval churches anywhere in the world. Of the 921 originally recorded, almost all in the sturdy local flint, many with distinctive rounded towers, 659 remain, even though the wool trade is now a distant memory. Among their number is Saint Peter and Saint Paul, East Harling.

It's little short of a mini-cathedral. By my Boy Scout's reckoning, it could now comfortably seat the entire population of East Harling several times over. As well as its overpowering size, it has everything to be expected in such a historic place of worship: a hammer-beam ceiling in the nave; the eye-catching remains of a rood screen, no doubt ripped out in the plain-and-simple puritan zeal of the post-Reformation; a long-gone local benefactress sleeping soundly at its centre in an elaborate tomb; a picture-postcard countryside graveyard; and (on the downside) rather too much evidence of over-enthusiastic Victorian renovation. But what is truly remarkable about Saint Peter and Saint Paul is the fifteenth-century stained-glass window in its chancel, one of the largest in both county and country to remain mostly in its original form. And at the heart of the window stands Judas Iscariot.

It was commissioned in the 1470s, as part of a bigger renovation of the original church on this site that had been recorded in the Domesday Book. Footing the bill was Anne Harling, the wealthy, pious lady of the manor who today lies in a stately tomb on the altar with Sir William Chamberlayne, a Knight of the Garter and the first of her three husbands. There is some suggestion that this extraordinary window may originally have been in the Lady Chapel, before being removed to the safety of the attic of the local manor house to sit out the post-Reformation stripping of the altars, subsequently to be returned to the church and sited this time in the chancel.

As its theme, it takes the life of the Virgin, a familiar enough subject of the time. Not too many miles to the north lies the Marian Shrine of Walsingham, until the Reformation one of the greatest in Europe, visited by every English king from Edward I to Henry VIII. In line with their love of calibrating everything for the faithful, medieval churchmen had dreamt up around Jesus' mother various formulations, including lists of five 'joyful', five 'sorrowful' and five 'glorious' mysteries, or episodes, that she was said to have

The 'Judas Kiss' stained glass panel in the Church of Saint Peter and Saint Paul, East Harling, Norfolk.

experienced in her life. These were to be meditated upon in a cycle of prayers, all the time recording your progress by working your fingers round a chain of rosary beads. Mary's willing acceptance of God's will in the many traumas she endured was intended as a model for the faithful of how they should act. The Mary panels in the East Harling window were then a guide to living a Christian life and the pitfalls that might be encountered on the way.

As my eyes work from left to right, top to bottom, everything is in its familiar place as it is in the gospels: the Annunciation, the Visitation, the Nativity, the Adoration of the shepherds, then of the Magi. Today, they make for a colourful selection of traditional Christmas cards, on sale at a table at the back of the church. But 600 years ago, they gave dramatic form to Mary's exemplary story for a largely illiterate congregation.

This window has had more than one coming and going. As

well as being spirited away in the post-Reformation period, it was removed once again in 1939, to spare it from stray German bombs intended for nearby RAF airfields, and only returned when the Second World War had ended. The current vicar, the Reverend Sarah Oakland, interrupts her Sunday lunch to let me into the locked church, and furnishes me with a pair of binoculars to examine the details of the window. As she does so, she confesses to marvelling at how, in its various transits, such an ancient and delicate glass jigsaw didn't crumble and shatter. There are a few panels that did become jumbled when it was put back together again, and a small number that have gone missing, including the one featuring a portrait of Anne Harling, but the main thrust of the narrative is exactly as it ever was.

The second and third rows of panels follow the first in the same orderly gospel fashion – the presentation of the infant Jesus at the Temple by his parents, their losing then finding him there as a twelve-year-old, and the wedding feast of Cana. All are part of Mary's biography in Mark, Matthew, Luke or John, and here all feature her prominently. But then, sticking out like a sore thumb in the middle of it all, comes the Judas kiss. It is the only main panel where Mary is absent. What's it doing here?

Jesus' agony in the Garden of Gethsemane was a prescribed part of Mary's sorrowful mysteries, but in medieval sequences the focus would have been on Jesus praying to his heavenly father to be spared his forthcoming trial and death. That was logically the source of Mary's sorrow – that she couldn't comfort her son when he felt so distraught, so fearful of what lay ahead, his sweat 'falling to the ground like great drops of blood', according to Luke.[5] In the background there might also have been a glimpse of the line of guards approaching, led by a distant Judas, but here in East Harling Jesus' agony is exchanged for Judas' kiss of betrayal as the source of Mary's pain. The gospels may not associate her at any point with the false apostle, but this window does.

The prescribed lists of mysteries for saying the rosary were certainly still flexible in the 1470s, open to artistic and benefactor interpretation (in the window's nativity scene, I've just noticed, two hitherto unmentioned midwives have been thoughtfully and practically added to the cast in the Bethlehem stable). The watchful eye of the local bishop, guardian of orthodoxy, was hours away by horse. So including the kiss is not *so* very strange, merely a bit of poetic licence. Still its Mary-less presence does feel curious when, by contrast, she has been crudely inserted into the stories told in subsequent panels (for example, Pentecost), even when none of the gospels records her as being there. Why not pop her in the background as the Judas kiss is landed on her son's cheek? Yet, out of all the panels, this one was judged sufficient in itself not to require her, a mark surely of the power that Judas exerted over the popular imagination, and of the central role his betrayal played in everyday Christian belief in the medieval period. His crime was judged terrible enough on its own, to have sufficient moral force as a bad example, without having to happen under Mary's perfect gaze.

Once the vicar has returned to her Sunday lunch and left me all alone, I kneel at the altar rail in the chancel and alternate between picking out details with the binoculars in the panels of the window above me, and reading through the various accounts of Anne Harling's life that Sarah Oakland has given me. What I'm hoping to find is something in the latter to explain why Harling, or her three husbands, might have particularly wanted the Judas kiss included among the panels: a buried reference to a personal political or economic misfortune that might have made them acutely aware of the cost of betrayal?

I search in vain. On her shared tomb with Sir William, Anne Harling is described as blessed in her first marriage. 'Heretofore they lay,' reads the jaunty epitaph, 'better was he, or better she, 'tis very hard to say'. The various booklets, too, tell of how she bore being widowed three times with fortitude and perseverance, of how her inability to have children inspired her to endow a local school, and of how her second spouse, Sir Robert Wingfield, managed to navigate the turbulent waters of Edward IV's court, where he was a senior courtier, without losing his head. Later, when elsewhere I consult surviving manuscripts that reveal Anne Harling's own interest in literature,[6] the impression is confirmed that there is no biographical prompt for the inclusion of the Judas kiss in this sequence of Marian windows.

The answer, instead, seems to lie in her taste for devotional, and particularly penitential works. Anne Harling was much concerned by the fate of souls in purgatory, seen in the medieval mindset as not so much a waiting room for heaven as a slightly milder version of hell, still filled by longing and the torment of separation from God. In Judas' despair, did she find a reminder of that pain?

The panel, though, is perhaps better seen not through the prism of Anne Harling's own life, but more generally as an everyday fifteenth-century view of Judas and how easy it is to go astray. Indeed, as I move back to take in the whole window in its setting, as it would have been seen by the congregation in the pews, the traitor stands out prominently from the mass of figures who grace the other scenes, on account of his luridly golden yellow robes.

It is once again the standard depiction of Judas the Jew, in the colours prescribed by Christianity for his race, and on this evidence as prominent here as in other parts of Europe. There are other splashes of the same colour in one of the figures at the foot of the cross for the crucifixion, singled out presumably as Jewish too, in line with the prevailing view of the Jews' guilt in Jesus' death.

Back at the altar rails, I examine one by one every detail of the Judas panel. I am working my way down a by-now familiar list. By the light of the torches that the soldiers carry in the background, along with their halberds and spears, Judas is seen in profile, embracing and being embraced by a three-quarter-faced Jesus, illuminated by his halo. In side view, Judas' face is partially obscured by a linking finger of lead tracery that runs up between what is his prominent nose (though not hooked) and his long flowing locks of red hair. The two men's greeting, in line with Luke, is an attempted kiss rather than a completed one, but flesh does meet flesh where their arms entwine in an act of great familiarity. I can't help wondering if it is an offer of comfort to Judas on the part of the calm-faced Jesus, in the midst of the chaos of figures around them.

There is a gap between their two heads, a curiously dark-coloured opaque segment of glass that separates their two faces. It is impossible to decipher. It may be the breastplate of one of the soldiers gathered behind them, or a piece inserted to fill a gap caused by the several dismantlings and reinstallations of the window down the ages. Or it may hint at a darker, now-lost presence. The devil and his demons are otherwise wholly absent.

Judas' face is a dusky, fleshy colour, in contrast with the lily white of everyone else's, except for Malchus, the Jewish servant of the high priest, whose ear has been severed by Peter. Malchus has an almost demon-like quality to his gargoyle-ish features. This repeats another medieval tradition – seen, notably, in the Chichester Psalter in its portrait of the betrayal of Jesus. Malchus, in this earlier (c. 1250) manuscript, is shown as blackened and animal-like, far more of a devilish creature than Judas himself. And in the Chichester Psalter, it is the soldiers accompanying Judas who share Malchus' menacing skin tone, the mark presumably in the artist's eyes of the Jews, rather than a pale and youthful Judas, who is therefore left somewhere in the no man's land between the assailants and their victim in Jesus.

East Harling's Malchus, though, shares his skin tone only with Judas, and he also wears a very prominent purse or money-holder on his belt, making him the connection between Jews and finance. Judas, for once, is without his bag of thirty coins.

Is this therefore a more nuanced anti-Semitic message? It may be, but the climate at the time in England could hardly be counted as significantly more welcoming to Jews than in the rest of northern Europe. The Magna Carta of 1215 – usually hailed as a step forward in establishing the rule of law and guaranteeing freedoms – also included a clause limiting the amount of interest that Jewish moneylenders could charge.

Blood libel

A train from the all-but-abandoned Harling Road railway station, a fair step away from the church, heads back to the county town of Norwich. In the medieval period it is said to have had over sixty churches. There, in 1144, the murder of a twelve-year-old apprentice tanner, known to history as William of Norwich, set off a wave of anti-Jewish feeling. William had disappeared shortly after delivering goods to a merchant who was part of the city's small and recently arrived French-speaking Jewish community, which enjoyed the protection of the sheriff and local notables. The accusation – not unique to Norwich, but heard loudly elsewhere in Europe at the time – arose that William had been seized as he went about his work and then murdered by Jews who wanted to use his blood to make *matzo*, traditional unleavened bread eaten during the Passover.[7]

To modern ears, the 'blood libel', as it is known to history, is a monstrous accusation, especially since there appears to have been not a shred of evidence for the charge of ritual murder laid against Norwich's Jewish community. Equally, it sounds a bizarre idea to make up, but it reveals a long history of prejudice and hysteria. Once, the early Christians had been accused by their persecutors of much the same practice, of spilling blood as they ritually ate bread, a result of a crass misunderstanding of their belief that the bread and wine of the Eucharist didn't just represent the body and blood of Christ, but were in some complex theological sense almost literally that.

The slings and arrows that had been thrown at the early church in a failed effort to discredit and destroy it, therefore, had subsequently been transformed by it, once it had gained power, into weapons to use against its opponents. So similarly blood-soaked charges were directed against Jews, fed by Christian preachers who also returned time and again to the image of Judas the Jew; how his grubby, blood-splattered betrayal had led to Jesus' agonising death in return for thirty pieces of silver, and more broadly to the Jews' crime of deicide.

In Norwich, when such images were invoked by preachers, the crowds were whipped up into such a frenzy that they were soon declaring William a saint and a martyr. Such was the level of suspicion and hostility that surrounded Jewish communities, whatever official tolerance they had been granted. Even that was not to be relied upon, and could be rescinded to pander to popular opinion, with the Jews expelled from England in 1290 and only allowed to return in 1655.

Norwich, too, was the home of the thirteenth-century poet, the Franciscan Walter of Wimborne, originally from Dorset. His lengthy part-satirical, part-religious popular verse survives to paint a lurid picture of the prevailing attitudes towards Jews and Judas at this time. In 'Of Simony and Avarice', Friar Walter begins by naming and shaming Judas as the source of what he sees as the plague of greed and avarice – for which read bankers, merchants and moneylenders – that is sweeping and corrupting Europe. Judas' betrayal of Jesus, he claims, produced the seed that grew into a bitter crop that was now being harvested. With the spilling out of his entrails like raw sewage on the soil of Hakeldama, Judas infected first its soil, then the soil of Judea (and by association all Jews), before the stinking pestilence was carried by travelling Jews all over Europe, afflicting both church and state.

> *Of old, when Judas died by hanging,*
> *The flow of his guts polluted Judah.*
> *Today, an effusion of shit more fetid stinks*
> *Than the smell of a sufferer of the king's disease.*[8]

Here, once more, Judas and the Jews are being routinely scapegoated for all the problems of society, right up to the financial crimes of kings with their incessant demands for more taxation. And present, too, in Friar Walter's words, is that same scatological association between Judas, excrement and bowels, captured in the image of the Judas chair.

From Norwich, it is one more short East Anglian hop to the university city of Cambridge to see and touch more evidence of Judas' place in medieval England. Many of today's university colleges have their origins in religious foundations or bequests, and their libraries contain priceless medieval books. Saint John's College is no exception. Founded in 1511 out of the estate of the devout Lady Margaret Beaufort, mother of Henry VII, four-times married, but from 1499 living as a nun under a vow of chastity, its original aims were as much religious as educational.

One of its librarians, Mandy Marvin – a navy chaplain's daughter, she points out, and thus well versed in the scriptures – ushers me through into the rare books' collection to examine a priceless early fourteenth-century text, containing both hymns and gospel readings, believed originally to be have been part of a psalter from Canterbury, and given to the library by Edward Benlowes, a fellow of the college, in 1631. 'Its colour palette,' she warns, as she opens the ancient leather-bound volume on a foam support to protect its spine, 'is a bit limited. There are red, orange, green and blue pigments, and that's about it.'

If she is managing my expectations, it's to no avail. They soar as I handle the book. There are few things that can so instantly compress centuries as the feel of an old book. To touch *Canticles: Hymns and Passion of the Christ* is to travel through 700 years as two different English illustrators chronicle Jesus' passion in square, spare, sparsely decorated miniature panels that sit within a French text 'in very fine hand', reports M.R. James, the twentieth-century medieval scholar, best recalled now for his ghost stories, who catalogued this and other treasures of Saint John's library. The handover from one illustrator to the next comes at folio 50. The first artist's work is slightly rougher, though curiously more modern, the facial expressions so cartoon-like that they bring to mind the incongruous image of The Gambols strip cartoon in the *Daily Express*, which my father used to buy religiously. The second artists work is better, more refined and intense, and begins with the last and undoubtedly the most intriguing of the manuscript's three depictions of Judas (as with most medieval accounts, Judas' remorse, in his attempt to return the money, is omitted as potentially too problematic for what is undoubtedly intended as a clear-cut damnation of the wretch).

Judas' first appearance, by name, is a sinister illustration of him receiving his booty from the chief priests, immediately identifiable with their stereotypical long beards, prominent noses and pointy hats. The sickly, sinister grey shade of Judas' face is arresting – which is code, M.R. James notes in his catalogue, for the fact that he is to be seen as a 'wicked Jew'. And just in case anyone should be in doubt about what that means, Judas wraps his grasping hands greedily around the coins as they are passed to him.

So far, so typical for the times and their deployment of Judas. Likewise the next folio, as I turn the pages gingerly, of the Last Supper. It is another them-and-us arrangement, without any real precedent in the gospels, but shaped by contemporary prejudices that sought to fence off Jews and outsiders as 'other'. Jesus and the other eleven apostles are gathered, exuding holiness, behind the table. Judas kneels, conspicuously separate and alone, on the other side, in the foreground. Jesus has to lean right over to give him the sop of bread. As he does so, the devil, a winged beast, enters into Judas.

And then to the final portrait of Judas, the debut of the second artist, who immediately sets a more stark tone. To the right of the panel, Judas hangs from a fig tree on Hakeldama. As was often the habit, the two versions of his death are united, because as the rope tightens around his neck, Judas is simultaneously slashing open his own stomach with an outsized knife, allowing his entrails to spill forth like the snake in the Garden of Eden. His facial expression is both tortured and resigned.

What is more unusual, though,[9] is that Judas' last moments, usually described as lonely, are here witnessed by three onlookers, calm and unmoved by the horror unfolding before them, making no attempt to intervene and rescue Judas, save for one pointing a finger, as if signposting an example that is not to be copied at any cost.

Their unexpected presence first makes me think of the tradition that the other apostles went into hiding in the caves at Hakeldama, following Jesus' arrest. Is this them emerging to be confronted by the body of their former colleague? Yet, there's no look of surprise on their faces, which certainly would have been within this second artist's range, and there's nothing to identify them as apostles. Neither do they have anything exaggeratedly Jewish about them – according to the stereotypes of the age. Their role, it seems, is to focus the viewer's attention on the lessons of Judas' despairing demise.

Because of that 'limited palette' there are no very firm deductions that can be made about the colours of robes. In the first

From the early fourteenth-century *Canticles: Hymns and Passion of the Christ* in the library of St John's College, Cambridge: Judas receives the thirty pieces of silver; Judas at the 'Last Supper'; and Judas dies at Hakeldama, in the presence of three nameless witnesses.

depiction of Judas, he has red hair, in accordance with medieval prejudices, but later it goes brown, while Jesus is given red locks. The purpose of this manuscript seems to have been not so much crudely to stigmatise Judas, though it does reflect the spirit of the times in this regard, but rather to cast him as a warning to all comers. 'My impression', confides M.R. James in his catalogue notes, 'is that it was meant for the owner of the book (an Abbot perhaps) to study during the long services of Good Friday and Easter eve.' And, presumably, to remind himself not to take any steps down the same path as Judas.

Part Three:

Judas – God's agent

S

Simnel Cake

The simnel, a two-layered fruit cake eaten around Easter, dates back to the thirteenth century, and is thought to be named after the variety of flour originally used in making it. It is traditionally made for Easter Sunday. In Victorian times, the habit took hold of decorating it with eleven marzipan balls, for the eleven apostles who stayed loyal to Jesus, with a space left vacant to symbolise Judas' betrayal.

T

Thirteen

Fear of the number 13 – triskaidekaphobia, to give it its scientific name – is one of those continuing superstitions whose origins are disputed. One theory is that it came down to us from Norse mythology, where a benevolent gathering of 12 gods turned sour when the mischievous deity, Loki, pitched up and made 13. Another looks to the Last Supper, where Jesus plus his 12 apostles made 13, an ill-fated number to have round the table because one was the betrayer Judas.

CHAPTER TEN:

How Judas Became an Enlightenment Hero

'A kissing traitor. How art thou proved Judas?'

William Shakespeare: *Love's Labour's Lost* (5:2)

The economic prosperity spreading out in waves from late medieval Italy carried with it many other changes, including – originating above all, from Florence – what is now referred to as the Renaissance, an artistic, philosophical and cultural movement that gathered pace from the late fourteenth century onwards. In the broadest of terms, the Renaissance brought with it new optimism about humanity's potential, and people's capacity, alone and collectively, to be and do good, in contrast to the doom-laden, fearful obsession with sin and damnation that had so gripped the imagination of the medieval church and medieval Europe.

The hallmarks of the Renaissance were a new spirit of curiosity and independence of thought. It is tempting to see it as a revolution against Catholicism's control over every aspect of life, but it is more accurately regarded as more a loosening of the straitjacket, the start of embracing a freedom to think and look afresh that, at this stage at least, often took place with the blessing and patronage of clerics and church institutions. Old ideas and stereotypes were revisited, including those that damned Judas Iscariot to hell and used his example to scapegoat all who stood outside the church and its control. As the world evolved, so too did interpretations of Judas' personality, motivations and crimes.

Some even dared to wonder if he should really be regarded as a criminal at all.

It began slowly, with just the occasional voice raised to challenge the consensus in the later medieval period. The Spanish Dominican, Vincent Ferrer, roving missionary, renowned orator, counsellor to popes and miracle worker, preached in the late fourteenth century on what he presented as Judas' tragedy. Rather than consign him to the fires of hell ever after, Ferrer suggested, why not allow Judas to be redeemed? He fixed his gaze on that neglected gospel episode when a remorseful Judas had tried to return the thirty pieces of silver. Ferrer wondered how that might have played out differently. In his imagined version, after being turned away by the chief priests, Judas sets off to seek forgiveness from Jesus, but is blocked by the crowds gathered on Calvary to witness the crucifixion.

'[He] said in his heart, "since I cannot get near Christ with my corporeal feet, at least I shall meet him on Calvary by journeying in my mind, and once there I shall humbly beg pardon from him"; and that he did this by hanging himself with a noose, and his soul flew thence to Christ on Calvary aforesaid, and therefore he begged for pardon, which Christ granted at once; and that from thence Judas rose with Christ into heaven, where his soul is blessed with those of the other elect.'[10]

The idea of Judas' suicide being a fast track to seek and receive forgiveness from Jesus was not a new one. As we have already seen, others had already suggested, albeit rather less magnanimously than Ferrer, that by hanging himself before the crucifixion (to follow the chronology of Matthew's account), Judas was therefore in hell when Jesus descended from the cross to the underworld to save all the tortured souls before his own resurrection. But here, in Ferrer's account, the noose of Hakeldama becomes an instrument of redemption, not an exit of despair. Judas' place in heaven is the unmistakeable sign of Jesus' unflinching forgiveness, and the welcome that awaits even the most notorious of sinners. Neither ghoul nor monster, this Judas is simply one more flawed human being, capable of being saved.

This willingness to look again – characteristic of Renaissance thought – was, unsurprisingly, not always welcomed by the church authorities. Vincent Ferrer might later have been declared a saint, but his remarks about Judas got him into trouble with the Inquisition, guardians of orthodoxy. The Inquisitor from Aragon, in Ferrer's native Spain, initiated a heresy trial against him on account of what he had said. He was only saved by an intervention from Pope Benedict XIII, to whom he acted as confessor, and who ordered his acquittal and the burning of all papers that indicted him.[2] Others, without such a prominent champion in the church's hierarchy, and engaged in another prominent aspect of Renaissance endeavour, the study of science and astronomy, discovered to their cost there were limits to official tolerance of new thinking. The Dominican, Giordano Bruno, for example, embraced philosophy, mathematics and astronomy in his personal quest for greater understanding of the world, but ended up burnt at the stake by the Inquisition in 1600.

There was, then, a tension between the fresh spirit of enquiry and tradition. A line had to be walked, as seen already in the writings of Dante, product of Italy's new capitalism, who died in 1321. His use of Italian rather than Latin in his *Divine Comedy*, its constant harking back to the Classical world of antiquity for wisdom, its quasi-scientific curiosity around the structure of the universe that caused the heavens above and hell below to be divided into different layers – all these marked Dante out as among the first Renaissance men. Yet his bleak picture of Judas as the worst of traitors was a thoroughly medieval one. Indeed, it could be argued it was Dante's inclusion of Brutus and Cassius alongside him in Lucifer's jaws that struck the truly radical note.

How much progress was made, under Renaissance influence, in

the succeeding centuries can be glimpsed, though, by comparing Dante's Judas with the picture of him presented 200 years later by Desiderius Erasmus, the most celebrated of the new breed of Christian humanists. This Dutch Catholic priest eschewed the usual labels for Judas as Satan's tool, or traitorous pariah, and instead saw him simply as a man who made the wrong choices. Judas was, Erasmus said in his *Colloquies* of 1518, a 'ruffian'; not a word that necessarily suggests approval, and certainly not saintliness, but one whose sins should be judged as on a par with Pontius Pilate and Caiaphas the high priest. Judas had, Erasmus said of his last hours, 'run mad with Horror of the Fact [he] had committed'.[3]

This is all of a piece with Erasmus' wider dismissal of the medieval notion of the devil – traditionally Judas' manipulator and boss – as a real, living, breathing creature who skulked around in dark corners, all sulphur breath and cloven hoof, ready to seduce those who did not place all their trust in the church. 'Consider as the devil,' Erasmus wrote in *Enchiridion Militis Christiani* (1501), 'anything that deters us from Christ and his teaching'.[4] If there was malice within Judas, then, it was of his own making.

So how did the Renaissance reshape Judas' biography? One of its most intriguing contributions came in relation to the Judas kiss.

A kiss is more than a kiss

The Dominican Friary of San Marco in Florence was, for ten years from 1436, both home and workplace to Fra Angelico. Endowed by Cosimo de'Medici, a member of the city's wealthiest merchant-banking dynasty, this religious complex contains some of the artist's – and the early Renaissance's – most significant works. In his fresco cycles of Jesus' passion, death and resurrection are two particularly striking images of Judas. The first comes in *Last Supper*, a simple, almost naïve representation, only just into three dimensions, with muted colours. It has Jesus distributing the bread to a group of seated apostles. Four more of their number kneel to one side (and a female figure, usually taken to be the Virgin Mary or Mary Magdalen, hovers to the left). The only sign that one of this quartet is Judas is his dark halo, rather than the golden rings given to everyone else present. Gone is the heavy symbolism of medieval art that felt obliged to trumpet Judas' difference. So his robes are dull (rather than yellow), his hair is the same shade as those around him (rather than red); while he continues to be seen in profile, so are his companions, and his nose is not exaggerated, his mouth nothing more than the

Fra Angelico's *Capture of Christ*, from the Friary of San Marco in Florence.

usual thin slash, and he carries with him no identifying money-bag or demon companion.

Fra Angelico takes the same approach later in *Capture of Christ*. Once again, all the old Judas baggage is jettisoned. His cloak is this time the same neutral colour as that of Peter, seen wrestling with Malchus. There is drama in the scene, but not the flat, medieval helter-skelter chaos of faces and tussles. In its place Fra Angelico brings an almost meditative focus on the reality of the moment between the two men when – following Luke's account – Judas reaches forward to try to kiss and thereby betray his master, while Jesus looks back at him. This is no symbolic brush on the cheek, to show the guards whom to arrest, and congregations whom to hate. Instead, the artist invests it with a special intensity, using light and perspective to add depth and personality.

While Luke does not permit an actual kiss, Mark and Matthew both do. They use the Greek word *kataphileo*, which usually translates as a warm or vigorous kiss, a 'smacker' in modern-day parlance, rather than the more usual *phileo*, used for the straightforward social kiss of greeting, today's 'air-kiss'. So what is it that they had in mind?

We're back once again to the mystery of that Judas kiss, never properly explained in the gospels, where it is largely superfluous, since the soldiers would have known all too well who Jesus was – the natural leader figure in a group of hapless fishermen, and the one who had already drawn so much attention to himself in the preceding week on the streets of Jerusalem and in the Temple.

Theologians had long struggled to find a justification for the kiss. In an eighth-century, Gnostic-influenced text written in Coptic, *Homily on the Life and Passion of Christ*, formally attributed to the fourth-century Christian leader Cyril of Jerusalem, and claiming to draw on documents found in the Virgin Mary's house, it was suggested that Jesus, as Son of God, had the power to change his features at will. Therefore Judas had to kiss him that night in Gethsemane to prevent him transforming himself and escaping.[5] (By which logic, of course, he might also have tricked Judas before he landed the kiss.) And in a fourteenth-century tome, *Meditations on the Life of Christ*, erroneously attributed to the Franciscan Saint Bonaventura, it was written that Jesus made it a rule, every time one of the apostles who had been apart from him returned to the fold, that he must be greeted with a kiss. This was, of course, a fabrication, with no authority in the canonical or apocryphal gospels, based on assumptions about the social customs of the time, but it shows how keenly a watertight explanation was sought for the kiss.[6]

Neither elaborate justification quite convinces, so in the absence of anything compelling, medieval (and some later more traditional) artists continued therefore to infuse the kiss with every sort of menace, with demons, with anti-Semitic symbols, with odours and perversion, even with Judas' alleged predilection for biting, with his insanitary mouth, fleshy lips, and with the glint of a greedy, possessed traitor finally publicly revealing his dastardly betrayal. Fra Angelico, though, is having none of it. He brings a plain human tenderness to the encounter: Judas tentative as he stretches forward; Jesus making no attempt to dodge the embrace (as is the detail of Luke's account). It is as if both men know what must happen, but in the same instant both regret it.

That is an astute and plausible reading of the gospels. A Renaissance sensibility transforms the infamous but puzzling act into something intimate and believable. Instead of a charade of a kiss, Fra Angelico returns the gesture back to its obvious meaning, a sign of closeness. Without the jostling crowd of bodies and swords and lanterns around the two of them, there is a sense of being admitted to something private in this encounter between Jesus, who after all had chosen Judas as an apostle, and the traitor who had spent three years of his life in the thrall of the one with whom he is about to break forever – and almost immediately regret it.

Quite how far Fra Angelico's depiction represents a step change in attitudes to Judas can be measured by comparing his work with *Judas' Kiss* by Giotto, often labelled the first Renaissance artist. The work is found as part of his celebrated fresco cycle in the Arena Chapel in Padua, and was completed around 130 years earlier, before Fra Angelico got to work in San Marco. Giotto's plump Judas is dressed in a vast enveloping yellow cloak, with red hair, altogether the stereotypical Jew as understood by viewers. And he is pressing his face in on Jesus in an aggressive, almost snout-like way.

Subsequent Renaissance artists followed Fra Angelico's lead on the kiss (if not on Judas' dark halo – in pursuit of naturalism, they pensioned it off, along with the golden ones for the 'good' apostles). In continuing to heighten the realism and the human frailty of this moment, they allowed themselves sufficient leeway to provoke and challenge the usual line on Judas. Two landmarks stand out. Caravaggio comes at the very end of the Renaissance period, almost at the dawn of the Baroque. His *The Taking of Christ* (1602), painted for a wealthy noble patron (rather than the church), was subsequently lost for 200 years, and then rediscovered in a Jesuit refectory in Dublin. It is best known for including a rare self-portrait of the artist. On the right of this depiction of the Judas kiss stands a young man (Caravaggio was thirty-one when he painted it), holding a lantern that illuminates events in the scrum in front of him. Perhaps it was just vanity that prompted him to include himself in the scene, or a playful reference to his own noted technique as a painter in using strong patches of illumination against a black backdrop. Others, though, have suggested that he might have wanted to imply he was casting new light on his subject matter.

The canvas has the realism that came with Renaissance art,

and its exploration of human interaction, but it possesses a startling dynamism that goes well beyond the plain naturalism of Fra Angelico. Caravaggio's Judas is no monster, but a flesh-and-blood, rough-looking, working man; balding, with a heavy, wrinkled brow and full beard. His attempted kiss is being gently resisted by a paler, ethereal Jesus, who looks ready to faint in the tumult that surrounds them in the Garden of Gethsemane.

Behind Jesus, Saint John, the 'Beloved' apostle, is making ready to run away (as told of a nameless follower in Mark's gospel). As 'the Beloved' departs, Judas closes in. Who is loyal, who is disloyal, the artist seems to ask? John, so revered by the church, is about to abandon Jesus just as Judas betrays him.

Caravaggio was bisexual, a theme taken up in Derek Jarman's acclaimed 1986 film about him, and that has subsequently led to a suggestion that the Jesus-Judas-John triangle in this painting carries a homoerotic charge. Above Judas' and Jesus' heads is an arc of material, like the huppah under which a couple marry at a Jewish wedding. Is John the Beloved fleeing because he has been replaced in Jesus' affections with another – namely Judas?

It is certainly a stretch, as theories go, and even if any of it is true, then Caravaggio neither condemns nor demonises, though the church would certainly have done so then as now (even if wider society in 1602 was perhaps more tolerant than might be imagined). The highly polished, black-armour-clad arm of a soldier that reaches round the advancing Judas towards Jesus' throat may, in this particular reading, represent the intolerance and crushing power of the law, be it church or civil. And Caravaggio's own presence may therefore signal not his attitude to sexuality, but his own (and humanity's) guilt in the damning of Judas, whose crime becomes less about greed and more about spurned love. It all remains speculative and ambiguous, open to the projections of a twenty-first-century viewer.

Caravaggio's *The Taking of Christ* (1602).

Ludovico Carracci's *The Kiss of Judas* (1589).

And the same verdict applies to another apparently erotic depiction of the same period, Ludovico Carracci's *The Kiss of Judas* (1589), painted for a wealthy patron in his native Bologna. In it, a wan, pale-skinned Jesus, bare-shouldered but buff, with his full red lips pursed in expectation, is kissed by a yellow-clad Judas, his eyes closed, his skin much darker and his hand, which rests on Jesus' exposed flesh, gnarled as if by hard labour. The focus of the painting is almost exclusively on the two of them. A confrontation is going on around them, illuminated by a lamp, but they are in their own world.

Over Jesus' head, a length of rope is shaped into a halo by a pair of hands attached to a body that is out of sight. Does Carracci's tableau condemn or celebrate a same-sex attraction? The halo/rope could be a symbol that Jesus is above the fray, or a reminder that Judas will soon die for his sins, which may include being gay. If it is the hangman's rope, then an addition can be made to the list of the 'crimes' for which Judas has been made the scapegoat – same-sex attraction. Already Judas had been scapegoated for what was seen as transgressive love and sexual desire, with his bulging codpiece and visible erection. What Carracci undeniably and memorably conveys with his Judas, though, is the powerful connection between love and betrayal.

Back to the future

The schism in Western Christianity that came with the Reformation, initiated by Martin Luther in the second decade of the sixteenth century, is often presented as a reaction to the excesses of the medieval church. Which, of course, it was, but such a simplistic explanation can lead to the assumption that this was the historical moment when what to contemporary eyes look like outdated superstitions in Catholicism were finally jettisoned.

In such a reading of events, the Reformation should mark the start of another chapter in Judas' biography, the moment when he put behind him his long-standing pariah status. Yet, in the short term at least, the opposite was true. The example of the evil Judas was embraced by Reformers and Counter-Reformers with equal fervour.

Long before Martin Luther came into the world in 1483, witches, dissidents and other outsiders were being tortured and burnt as devil-worshippers by the Holy Inquisition on behalf of the Catholic Church. Luther's dispute with Rome, his bitter break with the Pope, and the strife that coursed across the continent in the first half of the sixteenth century, did not discredit the Inquisition; rather they gave it new energy. It led the Catholic fightback, or Counter-Reformation, vigorously promoting the idea that the devil and his demons were everywhere on the prowl, notably in the ranks of Judas-like Protestant traitors, working to corrupt those who showed the same weakness as the false apostle. And from the lips of the Reformers, too, the accusation of 'being a Judas' was regularly heard, directed at the Catholic authorities.

Luther, an Augustinian monk when he nailed his 95 Articles on the door of the church at Wittenberg in October 1517, led what was as much a practical and political revolt against the corruption and abuses of the Church of Rome as it was a theological rebellion. His views on the devil were, if anything, more hard line than standard Catholic paranoia. He recounted his personal struggles with Satan in the most graphic and realistic terms, including describing how he once left a stain on the wall of the room in Wartburg Castle where he had been staying, still visible to visitors today, when he had been forced to throw an inkpot at Satan to drive him off. No longer quite so visible, but just as memorable, was Luther's belief that his own constipation (a frequent theme in his writings) was caused by the devil, with demons possessing his bowels. It is an image that could be lifted straight from centuries of depictions of Judas' death, as told in the Acts of the Apostles.[7]

For Luther, then, as for Catholic theologians, Judas should only be seen as an instrument of the devil. 'Because he thus gave place to sin,' he says in his *Sermons on the Passion of Christ*, '[Judas'] carnal security finally brought him so far that the devil completely possessed him and urged him on to the attainment of his outrageous purpose of betraying his dear Lord.'[8] Luther also emphasised as forcefully as any bishop in Rome the malign connection between Judas and the Jews – 'Judas' people' as he labels them in his *Psalms*.[9] Indeed, Luther's anti-Semitism arguably surpasses all that had gone before. In his 1543 treatise, *On Jews and Their Lies*, he calls them 'base, whoring people' and 'venomous serpents'. He proposes burning all synagogues and expelling Jews from all Christian lands.[10]

His description of 'Judas Scarioth' is by no means original – full of the usual stereotypes of foul odours and intrinsic malice – but Luther's language is extreme, even by Papias' standards, and scatology was his stock-in-trade. In another violently anti-Semitic pamphlet, *Schem Hamphoras*, he writes: 'Cursed goy [non-Jew] that I am, I cannot understand how they [Jews] manage to be so skilful, unless I think that, when Judas Iscariot hanged himself, his guts burst and emptied. Perhaps the Jews sent their servants with plates of silver and pots of gold to gather up Judas' piss with other treasures, and then they ate and drank his offal, and thereby acquired eyes so piercing.'[11]

Back to the 'evil eye', and why Judas could only be seen in profile. These old prejudices remained unchallenged, even as the Reformation was transforming the religious landscape of northern Europe. And it is not just the Jews that Luther attacks by reference to Judas' treachery. Since the papacy is his principal enemy, it too can be brought down by likening it to Jesus' betrayer. 'See the pope, for instance,' he remarks in his *Sermons on the Passion of Christ*, 'he has the very bag of Judas hanging from his neck, and is so fond of money and possessions that he takes them in exchange for the gospel, which he betrays and sells.'[12] Here, then, the scapegoat of Judas, so long an instrument used by the Catholic Church, is being deployed against it.

Luther's unflinchingly medieval attitude to Judas was shared by others among the Reformers who broke away from Catholicism. In post-Reformation England, for example, the Elizabethan communion service continued to warn sinners to stay away from the altar 'lest after taking that holy sacrament, the devil enters into you, as he entered unto Judas, and fill you full of all iniquities and bring you to destruction of both body and soul'. The French Protestant reformer, John Calvin, meanwhile, saw Judas as damned from the very beginning, in line with his own belief in predestination – that every individual's chance of eventual redemption is predetermined by God. Such a view left no place for the free will taught by the Catholic Church. So Judas did not choose, for whatever reason, to betray Jesus. Instead, this 'base and wicked man' was, Calvin insisted, doing nothing more and nothing less than as God intended – not that it mitigated his sin in any way whatsoever, or spared him damnation.

'Why did our Lord deliberately choose Judas, who, he perfectly knew, was unworthy of the honour, and would be his betrayer?' questions Calvin in his *Harmony of the Gospels* of 1555. '[This] is met by the following reply. Our Lord expressly intended to prevent future offences, that we may not feel excessive uneasiness, when unprincipled men occupy the situation of teachers in the Church, or when professors of the gospel become apostates. He gave, at the same time, in the person of one man, an instance of fearful defection, that those who occupy a higher rank may not indulge in self-complacency.'[13]

Calvin also tackled in the same commentary the question of why Jesus included Judas among the apostles in the first place, in preference 'to honest and faithful ministers'. It was more a case, he writes, that 'Christ . . . raised him to an eminence from which he was afterwards to fall, and thus intended to make him an example and instruction to men of every condition and of every age, that no one may abuse the honour which God has conferred upon him, and likewise that, when even the pillars fall, those who appear to be the weakest of believers may remain steady.'[14]

Enlightened times

If the Reformation and the Counter-Reformation saw a return to the time-honoured presentation of Judas as rotten to the core, those first signs of a re-evaluation of his role, witnessed earlier in the Renaissance period, were not lost forever. In the age of Enlightenment, starting at the end of the seventeenth century, the old stereotypes of Judas were ultimately not so much questioned and probed, as they had been in the Renaissance, but treated with derision. This all-encompassing movement – philosophical, cultural, political, economic and social – grew ever bolder in challenging the church's long-standing teachings, practices and prejudices. It insisted on testing notions of Jesus, the devil and even God against the sum total of human knowledge and experience; against science, and against logic. It preferred reason to faith, and science and scepticism to superstition and scapegoating. Many Enlightenment figures publicly turned their back on the churches altogether.

Because of the advances the Enlightenment spirit produced in science in particular, the shackles on the late medieval mind were thrown off, making real and unfrightening what had previously been imaginary and terrifying. The causes of disease, for example, were explored, rather than blamed on possession by the devil. The skies were surveyed not for angels with harps on clouds in heaven, but for the sun, the stars and the planets. The unknown was no longer per se a threat, but a challenge. And if the devil was downgraded, then Judas too had to be rethought.

His by-now standard role as Satan's tool, or 'Judas the Jew', the foul-smelling moneylender clutching his bag of coins, was obsolete for many in an Enlightenment age that loudly trumpeted its rejection of crude anti-Semitism. This was, indeed, a major shift, as Hyam Maccoby acknowledges. 'Jews were allowed into the professions, instead of being channelled into moneylending and then vilified as moneylenders. They were finally even given citizenship, allowed to vote and to attain positions of leadership. Many Jews accepted these developments with the highest enthusiasm.'[15]

It was not, though, Maccoby adds, the hoped-for new dawn of tolerance and respect. Anti-Semitism, he argues, had deep, deep roots in the human subconscious, planted by Christianity and fed by the scapegoating of Jews through their connection with Judas. And so it continued to fester, but was no longer so naked. 'Beneath the veneer of enlightenment, the old, deeply instilled myth continued to assert that the Jews were not like other human beings.'[16]

What the new thinking did mean, as the 1600s turned into the 1700s, was that the familiar unthinking caricatures of Judas no longer went unchallenged. *The Jew of Malta*, by English playwright Christopher Marlowe, first performed in 1592, nods at both old and new ways of seeing Judas. The eponymous anti-hero, Barabas, richer than everyone else put together on the island of Malta, is betrayed by his Turkish slave, Ithamore, with the words: 'The hat he wears, Judas left under the elder when he hanged himself.' Does the line send up the caricature of 'Judas the Jew', or reinforce it? You can read it either way. Ithamore could be cast as just as much of a Judas himself, proving an arch-betrayer in the course of the play, while Barabas (rather like Shylock in Shakespeare's *Merchant of Venice*, said to be influenced by *The Jew of Malta*) is not intrinsically evil, but one driven to act badly when his fortune is unjustly seized.

As the Enlightenment progressed, argues the French historian Leon Poliakov in his 2003 *History of Anti-Semitism from Voltaire to Wagner*, the significance of Judas in such debates faded. In some cases he is replaced by another figure, the 'Wandering Jew', a more nuanced, usually more straightforwardly tragic creature. The original medieval legend of the Wandering Jew – sometimes called Ahasver – was that he had taunted Jesus as he carried his cross to the place of execution on Calvary, and was therefore damned to immortality, walking the earth until Jesus' return in the Second Coming at the end of time. In some versions, he was said to be the doorman at Pontius Pilate's residence. But in the Enlightenment, this story was adapted to reflect instead the Jews' experience of exile from their ancient homeland, of persecution and of expulsion. 'Judas, in the Christian imagination, was a traitor, an unspeakable being, who in the collective person of the Jews, suffered well-deserved punishment in the shape of the ghetto, the badge, all the forms of social and legal ostracism', writes Poliakov. But the Wandering Jew was different. 'If he had acted like a Jew, had no fault other than his unbelief, a fault which he deeply regretted, even yearning to become a Christian.'[17]

Yet any distinction between Judas and the Wandering Jews was lost on some, such as the nineteenth-century Scottish poet, Robert Buchanan. His best-known works include both 'The Wandering Jew' and 'The Ballad of Judas Iscariot', where the unquiet soul of the betrayer wanders the earth looking for a place to bury its corpse.

For days and nights he wandered on
Upon an open plain,
And the days went by like blinding mist,
And the nights like rushing rain.
For days and nights he wandered on,
All thro' the Wood *of* Woe;
And the nights went by like moaning wind,
And the days like drifting snow.

'Twas the soul of Judas Iscariot
Came with a weary face—
Alone, alone, and all alone,
Alone in a lonely place!

He wandered east, he wandered west,
And heard no human sound;
For months and years, in grief and tears,
He wandered round and round.

For months and years, in grief and tears,
He walked the silent night;
Then the soul of Judas Iscariot
Perceived a far-off light.

Judas is finally welcomed into a bright wedding by a forgiving bridegroom (Jesus) carrying a lamp.[18]

The Enlightenment's leading figures grew ever more confident in ridiculing the churches. They increasingly drew on the techniques once used by clerics and thereby damned the whole edifice of institutional religion – and these included the scapegoat Judas. Along with the Judas name, his defining traits – greed and treachery – were attributed by the new thinkers to senior churchmen.

In this battle, Jonathan Swift might have been expected to side with the churches. He was an ordained priest of the (Anglican) Church of Ireland, but he was practised at turning his satirical eye on its shortcomings, prompted in some measure by his personal disappointment at his lack of advancement through its ranks. Yet neither was he a natural ally of the age of the Enlightenment. His best-known work, *Gulliver's Travels*, includes a damning judgement on some of its prized beliefs.

In his poem 'Bishop Judas', first published in 1735, the clerical title character is presented as surpassing Jesus' despised betrayer with his own hypocrisy and lies.

> *By the just vengeance of incensed skies,*
> *Poor Bishop Judas late repenting dies.*
> *The Jews engaged him with a paltry bribe,*
> *Amounting hardly to a crown a-tribe;*
> *Which though his conscience forced him to restore,*
> *(And parsons tell us, no man can do more,)*
> *Yet, through despair, of God and man accurst,*
> *He lost his bishopric, and hang'd or burst.*
> *Those former ages differ'd much from this;*
> *Judas betray'd his master with a kiss:*
> *But some have kiss'd the gospel fifty times,*
> *Whose perjury's the least of all their crimes;*
> *Some who can perjure through a two-inch board,*
> *Yet keep their bishoprics, and 'scape the cord:*
> *Like hemp, which, by a skilful spinster drawn*
> *To slender threads, may sometimes pass for lawn.*[19]

Judas' 'crime' paled, in Swift's eyes, in comparison to those of a clerical class he labelled 'a new set of Iscariots'. This poem was not an attack on one bishop who had done him wrong, but on the conduct of the entire hierarchy. As such it shares the same suspicion for all forms of organised Christianity exhibited more bluntly in the writings of Thomas Paine. But Paine took the argument further forward, notably in his celebrated tract *The Rights of Man* (1791), but also in his 1793 pamphlet, *The Age of Reason*. The latter proposed that all revealed religion was bogus, and should be replaced by a loose form of deism.

Since he did not believe that Jesus was God, Paine had little interest in Judas as his betrayer. He was amused, though, in reporting on the outbreak of the French Revolution in July 1789, by accounts of crowds in Paris after the storming of the Bastille discussing the close etymological link between the word 'Iscariot' and the French for 'aristocrat'. The two were as bad as each other in their eyes. In the tumult of revolution, the stain of Judas damned not only the institution of the church, but also the whole privileged class that depended on it.[20]

Paine could see a wider purpose for Judas in revealing quite how hollow were the claims of the churches. His 'Remarks on R Hall's Sermon' sets out a polemical and deliberately inflammatory case in favour of Judas as a positive role model that seems designed to goad clerics by turning their own words and beliefs on them. 'The Christian system of religion is an outrage on common sense. Why do not Christians, to be consistent, make saints of Judas and Pontius Pilate, for they were the persons who accomplished the act of salvation? The merit of a sacrifice, if there can be any merit in it, was never in the thing sacrificed, but in the persons offering up the sacrifice – and, therefore, Judas and Pontius Pilate ought to stand first on the calendar of saints.'[21]

Paine was not content with exonerating Judas by lauding *his* sacrifice, and the part it played in Jesus' death and resurrection (where, in conventional Christian tellings since the time of Saint Paul, the focus has always been on Jesus' sacrifice). He also sought to make the Judas of the gospels into an alternative role model to replace Jesus his master. From an example of how not to be, Judas was becoming someone to emulate for positive reasons. It was a short step, as Paine had, to move from absolving and even applauding Judas to turning him into a hero.

The Romantic movement, starting at the end of the eighteenth century, was a reaction against many things – the Industrial Revolution, aristocracy, even the ideas of the Enlightenment that inspired the French Revolution. It had, though, its own radical, iconoclastic edge, and took a particular delight in overturning social and religious conventions. The English essayist, Thomas De Quincey, knew both the Romantic poets Coleridge and Wordsworth. His 1821 autobiographical *Confessions of an English Opium-Eater* had made his name and reputation in post-Revolutionary times as an independent-minded controversialist. Among the many much-remarked-upon essays he published subsequently was his 1852 treatise on Judas.

The case he lays out for the apostle begins straightforwardly enough, picturing Judas as sharing the conviction of all twelve apostles – when they were called to join Jesus – that his mission was to lead an earthly kingdom. They were all mistaken, but 'if he erred, so did the other apostles'. De Quincey goes on: 'But in one point Judas went further than his brethren, viz., in speculating upon the reasons of Christ for delaying the inauguration of this kingdom.' He proposed – something that might once have cost him his life at the hand of the Inquisition as a blasphemer – that Jesus was a flawed character and that Judas saw through him. Jesus might have been 'sublimely over-gifted for the purposes of speculation, but, like Shakespeare's great creation of Prince Hamlet, not commensurately endowed for the business of action and the sudden emergencies of life'. Jesus was, De Quincey argued on the basis of his own particular reading of the gospels, 'indecisive' and 'morbid' by temperament.

So what he needed was Judas to 'precipitate his master into action'. Or at least, that is what Judas deduced from his first-hand observations of Jesus and the rising tide of Jewish expectation that saw Jesus as the promised messiah, able to shake off their Roman overlords. If Judas had a defect, De Quincey noted, it was an all-too-human one. He had not realised the 'true grandeur of the Christian scheme'.[22]

De Quincey's Judas was first and foremost a political revolutionary, the radical among the apostles, the one (as a Judean) with his eyes more firmly on Jewish political hopes than the Galilean fishermen, closer in fact to the Sicarii, those knife-wielding Jewish zealots sometimes quoted to explain the word Iscariot. By contrast Jesus was distant, distracted and, De Quincey implies, irrelevant, a nod perhaps to his own view that the church in mid-nineteenth-century England no longer had a role.

Judas' motivation in betrayal was, De Quincey argues, that he wanted to precipitate a Jewish uprising and believed that the otherworldly Jesus required shoehorning into playing the leading role. Instead of seeing Judas as treacherous, he is labelled 'audacious in a high degree'. He contrived Jesus' arrest as a way of forcing his charismatic leader to put himself at the head of a latent Jewish revolt against Roman rule. Either his arrest would cause Jews to take to the streets or, face to face with the high priests, he would make common cause with them. 'The crime, though great, of Iscariot has probably been too exaggerated. It was the crime of signal and earthly presumption, seeking not to thwart the purposes of Christ, or to betray them, but to promote them by means utterly at war with their central spirit.'[23]

De Quincey even had a new and positive take on Judas' ever-visible money-bag. Again, it owed more to his own political outlook in booming, commercial, mid-nineteenth-century England than to any insight into first-century Jerusalem. 'As the purse bearer, [Judas'] official duty must have brought him every day into minute and circumstantial communication with an important order of men, viz., petty shop-keepers. In all countries alike, these men fulfil a great political function. Beyond all others, they are brought into the most extensive connection with the largest stratum by far in the composition of society.'

So here is the template for Judas the political radical, the fixer with his ear better tuned to popular concerns than his religious leader's. He is an anti-Establishment figure who stood outside the churches and the status quo. It was to signal the start of a whole new chapter in Judas' biography.

U

Ullulaq

As a first name, Judas is today almost extinct outside Judaism, but Judas Ullulaq (pronounced Ooloolah) was one notable exception, a celebrated Inuit artist in his native Canada and beyond. One of three brothers, who all made their name as sculptors, his works in stone, with inlaid animal bone (and occasionally his own extracted teeth), include Arctic animals and shaman figures taken from the legends he grew up with in the Thom Bay area of the Nunavut Territories. They are now in national collections. Judas Ullulaq died in 1999.

V

Valentine

In German folklorish traditions, dating back to the fourteenth century, Judas is given a birthday – Judastag. This is variously placed on 1 April (one of a set of three ill-fated days in the calendar, along with 1 August, when Satan is kicked out of heaven, and December, when Sodom is destroyed) or 14 February, Valentine's Day. The explanation for the latter is lost, but may have something to do with his original love for Jesus, which then turned bad.

CHAPTER ELEVEN:

The Judas Myth and Modern Anti-Semitism

A learned hate is hard to unlearn.

Brendan Kennelly: *The Book of Judas* (1991)[1]

Life stories rarely have a single, straight trajectory. We all have various, often contradictory aspects to our characters, and in that respect Judas is no exception. Thanks to the Enlightenment, to revolutions and to Romanticism, he had started, as the nineteenth century turned into the twentieth, finally to live down his centuries of being Satan's tool and a propaganda device in Christian anti-Semitism. He was even becoming fashionable in some secular quarters for the first time – a radical hero.

But the past has a habit of coming back to haunt us. In the parallel universe of mainstream Christianity, a very different image of Judas continued to hold sway, and to be used much as it always had been – as a reproach, as a weapon against enemies, and as a scapegoat. Yet in this era, organised religion was under threat as never before. The ideals of the French Revolution had set in train a movement among European nations that resulted in a trend towards the separation of church and state. Catholicism sided with those who opposed this trend, joining forces with embattled conservatives across the continent in opposing aspirations to democracy and greater economic and social freedoms. In the clashes that resulted, the traditional Judas returned to play his part, demonstrating the malign hold on the collective imagination that he still exercised.

In France, following the national trauma of humiliating collapse in the 1870 Franco-Prussian War, followed by the annexation of Alsace and part of Lorraine into a united Germany, the church was part of a coalition of pro-royalist, pro-military and generally pro-tradition forces as they squared up to the progressive, tolerant, secular forces shaping a Third Republic out of the ignominy of defeat. France was a deeply dispirited nation, torn between its recent past as the bringer of liberty, equality and fraternity to the world, and an older image of itself as the land of Saint Louis, the canonised thirteenth-century monarch whose memory invoked the seamless co-operation of church and throne.

Division and tension led in turn to the search for a scapegoat to explain why the country found itself at such a low ebb. *In extremis*, it proved easier to search out some individual or group on whom to pin the blame with charges of betrayal, rather than to look in the mirror and accept a collective failure. And so, as often before, when times got hard, a finger of accusation was pointed at the Jews, and the cry went up yet again that they were the descendants of Judas.

In particular, suggests Hyam Maccoby, it was the rise of nationalism in the nineteenth century that fuelled anti-Semitism and renewed interest in Judas. '[It] has been a great spur to this identification, since almost every national group of Christian background whose aspirations have been disappointed is ready to blame it on those "traitors" the Jews, and for evidence cite the arch-traitor, Judas.'[2]

What made it more potent in defeated France was the presence of a small number of high-profile Jews at the top of the political and economic ladders in the Third Republic – a result of the radical reforms of the French Revolution that almost 100 years earlier had broken new ground in conferring full civic rights on Jews.

Many were secular, not practising their religion, but that counted for nothing in the eyes of their accusers. If Judas' very name and his possible origins in Judea had been sufficient in the eyes of the church for so many centuries to define him as the agent of the Jewish establishment, now race, origin and religion once again became muddled in a fog of accusation and prejudice. In the years after 1870, there was a marked upsurge in anti-Semitic literature in France – pamphlets, newspapers and books. Edouard Drumont's 1888 *La France Juive*, pandering to every stereotype of the Jews as the enemy within, sold one million copies and was still being reprinted twenty-five years later.

On the back of that success, Drumont started his own popular daily newspaper, *La Libre Parole*. It gave prominence to Judas in name and medieval image as the symbol of what it argued vehemently was the Jews' contemporary betrayal of France, a treachery that had contributed to national defeat. The age-old prejudices of a society that had been shaped for centuries by Christianity were rearing up at this time of crisis to reveal themselves as not rejected, but simply buried not far below the surface. Among them was a version of Judas as Satan's tool.

This whole fearful, ugly backlash boiled over in 1894 in a national scandal known to history as the Dreyfus Affair. Captain Alfred Dreyfus, a Jewish officer on the Army's General Staff, was charged with selling secrets to the hated Germans. The evidence against Dreyfus was thin – a handwritten note that bore only a passing resemblance to his own script (the real perpetrator was later identified) – but the fact that he came from disputed Alsace counted against him. He was suspected of being a fifth columnist who wanted to aid the German takeover of his homeland.

Far more potent, though, in the eyes of his accusers was that he was Jewish. When asked to explain why this privately wealthy, secular individual would endanger the good life he enjoyed with his wife and children amid the haute bourgeoisie of Paris by selling secrets to an enemy power for money he didn't need, they returned time and time again to the religion of his birth and how it naturally predisposed him to greed and treachery, just as once it had caused Judas to betray Jesus for the measly sum of thirty pieces of silver. No matter to them, as Piers Paul Read has pointed out in his study of the Dreyfus Affair, that the accused saw himself as a hero of secular French republicanism and values of the Enlightenment, rather than of Jews and Judaism.[3]

Despite the shortcomings of the evidence against him, and a farcical military-run legal process, Dreyfus was found guilty of the charges against him and sent off to the hellhole of a prison known as 'Devil's Island' off the coast of French Guiana. Before he was dispatched on a convict ship to serve out a life sentence (there had been loud demands that he be executed), he was subjected on 5 January 1895 to a public dressing-down, where he was ceremonially stripped of his military rank and decorations at the École Militaire in Paris. Maurice Barrès, the novelist, anti-Semite and right-wing politician, prominent among the anti-Dreyfusards, relived the spectacle in an essay entitled 'La Parade de Judas'. Crowds that gathered outside the military school had, he reported, chanted 'Coward', 'Dirty Jew' and 'Judas'.[4]

Drumont, too, was busy stoking the fire of hatred with repeated reference to Jesus' betrayer. *La Libre Parole*'s headline for 10 November 1894 read, '*À propos de Judas Dreyfus*'. Underneath was an illustration of Drumont picking up a broken, puppet-like figure of Dreyfus, with the hooked nose of medieval caricatures of Jews, and a German helmet, with the caption: 'Frenchmen, this is what I have been warning you about for eight years.' Drumont was in his element. In another edition of his paper, soon after Dreyfus' arrest, he wrote: 'Judas sold the God of mercy and love . . . Captain Dreyfus has sold to Germany our mobilisation plans and the name of our intelligence agents. This is all just a fatal running to type, the curse of the race.'[5]

Every well-known detail of Judas' story was deployed against Dreyfus. In an 1898 pamphlet on the affair, François-Réné de La Tour du Pin concluded with a reference to the Jews' guilt in the death of Jesus: '[We] must never lose sight of the fact that France is the kingdom of Christ, and that if the deicide nation comes near it, it can only be to give it the kiss of Judas.'[6] Meanwhile, the Catholic daily, *La Croix*, run by the Augustinian religious order and enjoying a rising circulation throughout the affair, made much the same connection when it rejected Dreyfus' insistence that he was a French patriot. 'His cry of Long Live France,' it said, 'was the kiss of Judas Iscariot.'[7]

Bernard Lazare, one of the earliest in the ranks of prominent pro-Dreyfusards, had a theory as to why Judas' name was heard so much throughout the affair. 'They [the anti-Semites]', he wrote, 'needed their own Jewish traitor to replace the classic Judas.'[8] Because the church caricature of a monstrous Judas had been steadily dying out since the eighteenth century, his ghastly image seen less often, even the wounding power of his name diminished, he was now being given new life by putting a fresh and living face to the name, that of Captain Dreyfus – or 'Judas Dreyfus', as Drumont would have it.

The creation of new Judases had, of course, been happening from Italian merchant-bankers to French aristocrats during the Revolution, but now in fin-de-siècle France it was given a particular and sustained virulence by the rise of a powerful popular press, keen to exploit old enmities and suspicions. That said, it was also in the press that the pro-Dreyfusards ran their rival campaign in his defence, demanding that he be released and pardoned – and, by association, that the Third Republic should resist the forces of reaction and hatred.

It took over a decade for them to achieve a victory, with Dreyfus finally cleared in 1906. One key moment in the fightback was the publication in January 1898, in the newspaper *L'Aurore*, of Emile

Zola's *J'accuse*, a passionate denunciation by the novelist of the injustice that had been visited on Dreyfus, and of anti-Semitism in the highest echelons of state and society. This, in its turn, prompted anti-Jewish riots all over France, with the unrest lasting not for days but for weeks and even months. Zola had to flee the country to avoid prosecution, such was the depth of the hatred that *J'accuse* had unleashed. In the town of Saint-Jean-de-Maurienne in the southeastern Savoy department, the annual Mardi Gras procession that year featured two mannequins, one of Judas and the second of Zola. The stain of the apostle's treachery was being spread to others.[9]

Even when Dreyfus had been returned to his family, feted in liberal society, and eventually pardoned, the wounds caused in France by the affair were slow to heal. The question of whether he was a victim or a traitor continued to hover over Dreyfus, just as elsewhere it was being asked about Judas Iscariot himself.

The makings of a hero?

Away from France, as the nineteenth century gave way to the twentieth, Judas was increasingly being looked at in new and more favourable ways. These picked up on the insights of De Quincey in casting Judas as a much-misunderstood and much-maligned figure. Those who were rallying to his defence tended to have few formal ties with organised religion. Indeed, far from seeing Judas written off as irrelevant, as might have been expected, the loosening of the church's influence in society seemed only to increase interest in him.

There was, of course, an obvious polemical spur for this. Judas' adaptability as a weapon to be turned against the churches had been established as long ago as Jonathan Swift and the treacherous 'Bishop Judas'. Those intent on diminishing further the powers, prestige and privileges of religion therefore saw in championing Judas a means of advancing their cause by presenting him as another victim of ecclesiastical intolerance.

But there was something more than mere point-scoring that kept Judas current. His story still possessed an ability – for good, for ill, and in illuminating the vast grey areas in between – to rise from the pages of the gospels written almost 2,000 years ago and say something relevant to everyday life. He intrigued as the other eleven apostles couldn't. Not even Saint Peter – in the past often juxtaposed with Judas as the good apostle against the bad, understandable doubt against unforgivable treachery – continued to exert such a pull on imaginations. In Judas' story there was psychological complexity, grit over the issue of motivation, and that still-unanswered question mark over his exact purpose in Jesus' life. Did his betrayal of his master reveal him as evil, or was he part of a preordained, divine plan?

The English composer, Sir Edward Elgar, was the son of a Catholic mother and agnostic father. In a 2007 broadcast essay, the pianist and composer Stephen Hough argued that Elgar's own struggles with the Church of Rome were 'central to understanding his music'.[10] Since childhood Elgar had been drawn to the tale of the disciples, and to Judas in particular. He finally got round to tackling the subject in *The Apostles*, his austere 1903 oratorio.

This choral work has six soloists, each recounting their experience of being alongside Jesus on his journey from Galilee to death on a cross in Jerusalem. Judas' account stands out, not least because the crucifixion is framed by his suicide, rather than vice versa. 'The finest music . . . is given to Judas,' writes Elgar's biographer Michael Kennedy, 'almost amounting to a self-portrait of the depressive Elgar.'[11]

Here, then, is a first glimpse of how the twentieth century treated the story of Judas – Elgar's suggestion that his actions, as reported so tersely in the gospels, could be seen through the prism of depression. Part of the composer's own depressive streak centred on his faith and his struggle to integrate Catholicism into his broader outlook on the world around him. In the first decade of the twentieth century, the Catholic Church was at its most reactionary. The 'Modernist Controversy', a Vatican-inspired witch-hunt aimed at those Catholic theologians who were attempting to find common ground between science, philosophy and religion, was making it appear medieval to most onlookers, as it decried just about everything to do with the modern world.

At a simple level, Elgar's portrait of Judas is conventional, chillingly so when a glockenspiel sounds out the cold shimmering of the thirty pieces of silver being weighed out. In line with Luke and John's gospels, he is presented as possessed by Satan, but Mark and Matthew are acknowledged too with the accusation of greed. 'What are ye willing to give me and I will deliver him unto you?' he propositions the chief priests. Yet, alongside such a familiar take, Elgar also endeavours to get under the skin of Judas, to reveal his psychological state, his remorse and his eternal fate. He seeks neither to excuse nor to exonerate. That Judas did what he did, as reported in the gospels, goes unchallenged. Elgar's concern is why he did it, by reference to the apostle's turbulent emotions and agonised mental state.

The two-part oratorio begins at dawn with Jesus summoning his apostles to him. Peter (baritone) and John (tenor) offer sugary responses about embracing light and life and love, but Judas (bass) strikes an awkward pose. 'We shall eat the riches of the Gentiles, and in their glory shall we boast ourselves.' From the start Elgar has Judas aspiring almost greedily to earthly power by working with Jesus. And this continues as Jesus delivers the beatitudes. To 'Blessed are the poor', Judas responds with a political statement about the rulers of the day, 'he poureth contempt upon princes'. To 'Blessed are the merciful', Judas replies as the social reformer. 'The poor is hated even of his own neighbour: the rich hath many friends.' His concerns are of this world.

When part two turns to the betrayal itself, Judas' outwardly conventional acceptance of the money is contrasted with what is going on inside him. As he accompanies a troop of soldiers to arrest Jesus in Gethsemane, his doubts and contradictions are expressed as thoughts taking wing and flying to Jesus. 'Let Him make speed, and hasten His work, that we may see it; He shall bear the glory and shall sit upon His throne, the great King, the Lord of the whole earth.' Still he is hoping that Jesus will seize political power (on the De Quincey model). He therefore wills the betrayal to result in Jesus making common cause with the chief priests, thus satisfying Jewish aspirations for a rebellion against the Romans.

Elgar's is a tortured Judas. 'My punishment is greater than I can bear,' he laments, 'mine iniquity is greater than can be forgiven.' As, in the background, Jesus' trial builds up in stages to his crucifixion, it is Judas who dominates proceedings, utterly lost in a wilderness of his own making. 'Whither shall I go from Thy Spirit?' he cries out. 'Or whither shall I flee from Thy presence?' Elgar bases these musings on lines taken from the Psalms. Rather than heading for hell, Judas spirals downwards, emotionally and psychologically, into the depression that the composer himself knew all too well. 'Mine end is come – the measure of my covetousness; over me is spread a heavy night, an image of that darkness which shall afterwards receive me: yet am I unto myself more grievous than the darkness.' With those words he goes to his lonely death, not so much the vile traitor of history, but a victim of his own inner conflicts.

It was a theme that came ever more to dominate portraits of Judas in the early decades of the twentieth century. Some writers took it much further than Elgar. They sought not only to give Judas the benefit of immortal doubt, but to bolster his case by showing him in the context of a bad but charismatic Jesus. A striking and controversial example came with the long title piece of the 1929 collection *Dear Judas and Other Poems* by the American Robinson Jeffers.

Published when Jeffers was at the height of his fame, having the year before produced his celebrated narrative poem, 'Cawdor', 'Dear Judas' puzzled and disappointed his erstwhile admirers among the critics (and was later omitted from collections of his poetry), and brought him directly into conflict with the churches. In the late 1940s, a theatrical adaptation of 'Dear Judas', planned to be staged in Oakland, California, was abandoned when the local Catholic bishop threatened the two leading actors with excommunication. Another production suffered the same fate in Boston, on the East Coast, before finally it managed to open in New York in 1947 (only to close two weeks later).

What sparked all the controversy was Jeffers' bold reversal of the roles of Jesus and Judas in what is, in effect, a forty-page modern passion play in verse. Jesus is the brilliant but flawed leader. This time he is the one who is in mental turmoil – caused by confusion over the identity of his father. And it is Jesus not Judas who is set on a political victory over the Romans. Judas, by contrast, is a depressive loner with a tender conscience.

Neither figure is heroic, nor divine (one reason why Christians took such exception to the poem), but the two are bound inextricably together. 'I know you are neither God nor God's son/But you are my God', Judas tells Jesus at the start, as he gives him the kiss of betrayal in Gethsemane.[12]

Jeffers, the son of a strict Presbyterian minister, had a lifelong respect for belief, even if he had rejected it for himself, and later was to express surprise at the offence 'Dear Judas' had caused. He had, he said, deliberately set it within the dream-like structures of the Japanese Noh theatre tradition in an attempt to distance himself from any charge of attacking religion. And, in turning the Judas story on its head and then reassembling it in a wholly new order, he still followed the gospels. Judas is shown growing disillusioned with Jesus, notably in regard to the episode of the expensive ointment in Bethany. It acts as the trigger for his betrayal of Jesus to the high priests. That is what John's gospel says, too, but in Jeffers' poem Judas' motivation is not greed or anger or even satanic possession. Instead he has seen through Jesus in that moment, and recognises him as vain, dangerous, egotistical and set on his own glory. Judas recognises Jesus as a politician not a prophet.

And it is this unattractive Jesus who suggests that Judas betray him – because he believes it will hasten his own rise to power. Judas could, of course, refuse, but he agrees because he sincerely believes it will prevent a Jewish rebellion, not provoke one. 'Too many have made rebellions before: they are drowned in blood', he warns Jesus. He calculates that the chief priests will hold Jesus for 'three or four days for the city peace and dismiss him'.

But he misjudges what will happen. Jesus dies and Judas is blamed for a death he never intended, and for a betrayal that was not his idea, but a ruse dreamt up by the man he turned in. That is, Jeffers explains, how Judas has earned himself eternal enmity, and why his conviction as a traitor by Christianity is fundamentally unsound.

Jeffers puts the standard interpretation of Judas' actions on the lips of Mary, Jesus' mother.

That I will curse you? Because you betrayed my son, because you are infamous, because no viper is made
Venomous, nor reptile of the slime loathsome, to your measure?

Then he goes on to explore behind these words what betrayal actually means. Again, he reverses the familiar narrative, leaving Mary to confess to betraying her son, and absolving Judas of any blame. If Jesus was flawed, she argues, then she caused him to be so by the way she brought him up.

225

*I will not curse you, Judas, I will curse myself. I am the first who
    betrayed him. The mothers, we do it
Wolf-driven by love, or out of compliance, of fat convenience.*

Judas might, therefore, be allowed a happy ending, but Jeffers
sticks to the suicide of Matthew's gospel, though he reshapes it in
the light of history's enmity.

*I am going a little distance into the wood
And buy myself an eternal peace for three minutes of breathless-
    ness, never to see any more
The tortured nailed-up body in my mind, nor hear the useless
    and endless moaning of beasts and men.*

For Jeffers, there can be no liberation for Judas because the
death of Jesus haunts him to his grave. That much is there in
Matthew's gospel. But 'the useless and endless moaning of beasts
and men'? Is that the manipulation of Jesus' memory by the
churches? Jeffers had little time for them. Or might it also be their
use of Judas' image and story as a weapon to attack others? The
poet offered no definitive answer. 'It seems to me to present', he
said later of 'Dear Judas', 'in a somewhat new dramatic form, new
and probable explanations of the mythical characters and acts of
its protagonists.' Later, in programme notes for the short-lived
New York stage production, he described his Judas as 'sceptical,
humanitarian, pessimistic and sick with pity'.[13] Not the stuff of
heroes, then, but no traitor, and above all recognisably human.

The Nazi Field of Blood

Elgar, Jeffers, and many others in the first four decades of the
twentieth century led the way in examining Judas' story afresh,
with psychological insight rather than recourse to crude

stereotypes. But the old Judas was not so easily discredited and banished. As the Dreyfus Affair had demonstrated, he carried with him too much ballast not to resurface periodically in stormy waters. Just as Robinson Jeffers in the United States was making the case for Judas' rehabilitation, the Nazis in 1930s Germany were promoting the medieval template of 'Judas the Jew', the traitor within, as part of their determination to obliterate the country's Jewish minority.

Judas is there in *Mein Kampf*, Hitler's poisonous manifesto, published in two volumes in 1925 and 1926 as the National Socialist Party was on the rise. Proposing a 'Storm Detachment' of party loyalists to 'educate' the German people in line with his own prejudices, Hitler writes that such a task must be carried out openly, not by stealth.

> Secret organisations are established only for purposes that are against the law. Therewith the purpose of such an organisation is limited by its very nature. Considering the loquacious propensities of the German people, it is not possible to build up any vast organisation, keeping it secret at the same time and cloaking its purpose. Every attempt of that kind is destined to turn out absolutely futile. It is not merely that our police officials today have at their disposal a staff of eavesdroppers and other such rabble who are ready to play traitor, like Judas, for thirty pieces of silver and will betray whatever secrets they can discover and will invent what they would like to reveal.

It is fleeting, and makes no direct link between Judas and the Jews. Taken in isolation the reference to the traitor is simply being employed as a kind of cultural currency, an existing and immediately recognisable archetype of betrayal. Elsewhere, however, the Nazi propaganda machine laboured to load that association with anti-Semitism, in line with the party's ideology of blaming Germany's post-First World War humiliation, and the economic and social turmoil that followed, on a Jewish conspiracy. It is well illustrated by a radio broadcast made in January 1939 by Walter Frank, a leading Nazi ideologue and director of the Reich Institute for History of the New Germany, which was busy refashioning the past with anti-Semitic slurs.

'Jewry is one of the great negative principles of world history,' Frank explained, 'and thus can only be understood as a parasite within the opposing positive principle. As little as Judas Iscariot with his thirty pieces of silver coins . . . can be understood without the Lord whose community he sneeringly betrayed, . . . that night side of history called Jewry cannot be understood without being positioned in the totality of the historical process where God and Satan, Creation and Destruction confront each other in an eternal struggle.'[14]

Images of 'Judas the Jew', complete with the full panoply of racist, medieval caricatures, were used in public information advertising campaigns (examples can be seen in the displays at Yad Vashem, Israel's Holocaust memorial). There is an unmistakeable connection between what such propaganda said about the Jews and what writers from Papias onwards had claimed of Judas – that he was dirty and disease-ridden. The Nazis promoted the notion that the Jews constituted a threat to public hygiene.

Once Hitler had taken power in 1933, German classrooms resounded with slogans such as, 'Judas the Jew betrayed Jesus the German to the Jews'.[15] And adults were given the same message in the most notorious of Nazi propaganda films, 1940's *Jud Süss* ('Süss the Jew'), directed by Veit Harlan. The principal character, a Jewish moneylender and villain, has so many of the marks of Judas that the parallels would have been unavoidable to the estimated 20 million Germans who went to the cinema to see it. A costume drama, set in the eighteenth century, partly based on a historical character, but also using a 1925 novel by Leon Feuchtwanger (ironically a Jew), and with substantial input from Joseph Goebbels' propaganda ministry, *Jud Süss* follows Joseph Süss Oppenheimer as he wins the trust of Karl Alexander, the Duke of Württemberg, and becomes his treasurer. Oppenheimer, like the greedy medieval Judas, is inseparable from his money-bag. So great is his greed and treachery, indeed, that he uses the trust placed in him to betray the duke (and by implication the whole German nation), when he manipulates Württemberg's finances in a way that bankrupts the economy but fills his own pockets and those of a menacing group of associates, all of them caricatures of Jewish moneylenders, with long beards, hooked noses and the 'evil eye'. And just in case anyone missed the association with Judas, Oppenheimer's end is met dangling from a rope.[16]

So powerful and influential was *Jud Süss* judged that, in 1945, Veit Harlan stood trial for war crimes. He successfully defended himself, and was found guilty only on other minor charges. He went on to make further films, but remained a controversial figure until his death, with *Jud Süss* banned from ever being shown. 'Judas stars in Nazi propaganda films', writes the cultural historian Susan Gubar, 'not because he betrayed Christ but because, having done so, he was depicted for centuries in European art with traits that became the stock in trade of anti-Semitism.'[17]

Judas was, in this reading, just one of the tools that the Nazis employed towards their own particular ends. But others allocate him a bigger role. Hyam Maccoby regards the effect of 2,000 years of Christian efforts to conflate Jews and Judas the betrayer as being to prepare the ground for the horror of the Holocaust and its six million victims. 'The image of Judas made Hitler's crimes possible,' he writes; it 'fertilised the field of blood Hitler harvested'. There was, he argues, 'a direct connection' from Judas to Hitler, from the 'hate-filled portrait of the treacherous betrayer of the Lord' to 'the culmination of that indoctrination of Jew-hatred'.[18]

The philosopher and novelist, George Steiner, endorses this view in his collection of essays, *No Passion Spent*. Before Steiner's birth in 1929, his Viennese Jewish parents had moved the family first to Paris and then to New York to escape the rising threat to their safety posed by Nazism. Steiner sees Christianity's innate hostility to Judaism as distilled into hatred of Judas. He even dates it back to a precise moment – when, in John's gospel, the false apostle departs into the night after being given the sop of bread at the first Eucharist[19] – 'a totality of ostracism and malediction from which the Jewish people were never to escape', Steiner writes. 'The "final solution" . . . is the perfectly logical, axiomatic conclusion to the Judas-identification of the Jew . . . That utter darkness, that night within night, into which Judas is dispatched and commanded to perform "quickly" is already that of the death-ovens.'[20]

Historically the Nazis were, indeed, the latest in a long line to exploit the deep-rooted Christian prejudice against the Jews by recourse to Judas. But there are other considerations to bear in mind when assessing Steiner and Maccoby's charges. Unlike those who had previously used Judas as a weapon of anti-Semitism, Hitler and his inner circle were neither Christian zealots, nor, for the most part, could they count on the support of the churches. Indeed, they had a profound distrust of Christianity – personally and politically. While they appreciated the contribution that its roots in Germany, going back over many centuries, and with its elaborate rituals and trappings, offered to their favoured image of an Aryan master race, their relationship with, for example, Catholicism was a complex one. There were shared concerns (in particular the Church's fear of 'godless' Soviet communism that led it to agree a concordat with Hitler's Germany in 1933), but increasingly in the late 1930s that turned to hostility, with Pope

Pius XI at the start of 1939 putting the finishing touches to an outspoken attack on anti-Semitism that was also intended as a denunciation of the Nazis. But Pius XI was on his deathbed as he set out his thoughts and died before he could make them public. His successor, Pius XII, notoriously buried the text.[21]

Some senior Nazis even had their own chequered history with Judas. Joseph Goebbels, Reich Minister of Propaganda in Nazi Germany from 1933 to 1945, had had ambitions as a playwright as a young man. His first effort was a 1918 verse drama entitled 'Judas Iscariot: A Biblical Tragedy'. Far from embracing a hate-filled medieval image of the Jewish traitor, it took a thoroughly modern line that can be traced back to De Quincey. Goebbels' Judas was really a revolutionary mover and shaker who became disillusioned with Jesus' failure to lead his people against the tyranny of Roman rule. His driving force was political idealism, rather than avarice, and he saw Jesus' promise of eternal salvation as simply tricking the masses.[22]

The nuances of the history of Judas in the Nazi period are well illustrated by the example of the Oberammergau Passion Play. A hangover from those medieval passion plays that had once been so popular with an illiterate population, it continued to be performed in the Bavarian village of the same name once every ten years. Legend had it that it started in 1634 when the village wanted to find a way of thanking God for sparing them from the plague, but modern historians have cast doubts over quite how accurate that account really is.[23] In 1860, in an effort to attract more visitors (it proved successful – Thomas Cook organised package tours there when a railway station opened in 1900), the text was rewritten, updated for changing times by first an ex-monk, Othmar Weis, and then by the village's long-serving Catholic priest, Father Joseph Alois Daisenberger.

The overall effect was to return to a simpler and more naturalistic interpretation of the gospel texts, which downplayed the crude, low humour of the older version, some of it enjoyed at Judas' expense. The treacherous apostle was to remain unambiguously a thief and deceiver, but his supporting cohort of devils and demons was much reduced, if not entirely disbanded. The real betrayers of Jesus, in the new script as in the old, remained the Jewish authorities, the Jewish population of Jerusalem and the compliant Roman authorities. This was in tune with the gospel accounts, and was nothing so unusual or extreme that it deterred European politicians and royalty from taking their seats at Oberammergau once a decade.

The updated script was not entirely devoid of Judas-baiting. One early twentieth-century visitor lampooned the sight on stage of 'Judas hanging himself under a red umbrella'. Another recorded that the death scene on Hakeldama was followed by a cascade of fake rocks that revealed a band of devils, vomiting fire and exulting over the dead body of their collaborator.[24] And a 1910 cartoon in the *Simplicissimus* series showed a British visitor confusing fact with fiction and punching the actor who played Judas on the streets of Oberammergau.[25]

The rise of Nazism, however, changed the whole backdrop to the 1934 performance, the 300th anniversary season. Goebbels' propaganda ministry was keen to promote it as an example of 'pure' German culture and organised a campaign under the banner, 'Germany is calling you'. There were even visits to the play by the Führer himself. What he watched was Judas face his final despair with the lines, 'O, earth, open and swallow me up! I can no longer exist.' Some historians, with hindsight, have noted potential parallels with Nazi plans for the Holocaust.[26]

Yet the local organising committee in Oberammergau had strongly resisted demands from the government for changes to the text they had been using since 1860, to match the official ideology of hatred of Jews. And while several of the cast were prominent National Socialists, the actor who played Judas when Hitler attended was a known opponent of the regime. His soliloquy (after Jesus has been anointed with expensive ointment at Bethany) showed Judas not as a greedy Jew but, in the modern way, as a political radical. 'The master's conduct to me is very inexplicable,' says Judas. 'His great deeds allowed us to hope that he would restore again the kingdom of Israel. But he does not seize the opportunities that offer themselves, and now he constantly talks of parting and dying, and puts us off with mysterious words about a future which lies too far off in the dim distance for me.'[27]

Even as the Nazis were trying to use the story of Judas to further their own murderous ends in relation to the Jews, there were, then, dissenting voices among Christians. And these were heard too among German Christian theologians in those troubled decades of the first half of the twentieth century. There were remarks they routinely made, in scholarly pronouncements based on the gospels, about Judas, his betrayal and his Jewish connections. Not all were flattering, and to contemporary ears some have a definite ring of anti-Semitism about them, but to assume that they were a contribution to Nazi propaganda is too easy.

In 1942, for example, Karl Barth, a well-known Protestant theologian, Swiss-born, but teaching at a German university, published his second volume of *Church Dogmatics*, in which, *inter alia*, he repeated the traditional case against Judas that dated all the way back to Saint Jerome in the fourth century. Judas stood for the Jewish rejection of Jesus. 'The basic flaw', Barth argued, 'was revealed in Judas.'[28]

So can Barth be judged as contributing to the demonisation of the 'flawed' Jews by the Nazis by such a remark about Judas? Well, he would have been horrified by such a suggestion. At the time of publication, Barth was living back in Switzerland because his vocal opposition to Nazism had seen him removed from his academic position at the University of Bonn. Moreover, if that single remark is taken in context, Barth can be seen to be making a very different argument about Judas. 'The basic flaw was revealed in Judas, but it was that of the apostolate as a whole.' In other words, all twelve apostles were Jews, and all had their moments of doubt about Jesus' conduct, notably over the episode of the expensive ointment at Bethany which Barth is considering. 'Peter and Judas,' Barth emphasises, 'stood side-by-side on the same footing.'

Judas by name

A final and moving perspective on Judas' place in Holocaust history opens up as I search through the archives of Yad Veshem in Jerusalem for references to the traitor in Nazi propaganda. In the catalogue, I notice that under Judas there are many others with the same name. While to call your child Judas had long been regarded as anathema in every Christian community because of the association with the betrayer, among Jews it has continued to be used, just as it had been for centuries before Judas Iscariot (or Judas, son of James) was even mentioned in the gospels as being among the apostles.

So, among those recalled at Yad Veshem for their wartime courage in sheltering Jews from the Nazis are a Belgian couple, miner Cyriel Dewachter and his wife Zulima. At their home in Houthalen in Limburg province, they hid three Jews from 1942 until the end of the war: Mirla Neumann and her son Erich, and one Abraham Judas who, the archive reports, used to sew leather bags in his secret room on the upper floor of the Dewachter house to help defray the cost to their hosts of having three extra mouths to feed.

Judas as a first name is there too in the index, among those who did not survive the Nazis and who are commemorated forever in the 'Pages of Testimony' in the archives. Two are Algerian Jews:

Judas Ben Lamou, born in north Africa, later moving to Versailles in France, where he married Rachel, and was, subsequently murdered at Auschwitz at the age of fifty-two; and Judas Ben Racassa, born in Oran, named after his father, later working as a greengrocer in Paris, and married to Elisa. He was put to death aged fifty-seven in Auschwitz. The details provided are sparser about Judas Meyokas, from Champigny-sur-Veude, who died aged forty-eight in Auschwitz in 1944.

None of these three entries includes a photograph, but among a file of surviving passport-sized pictures taken from the Jewish community in Brest-Litovsk in Poland by the Nazis is one of Judas Karszenbaum. He was given his name by his parents Lejzor and Chana and died with it aged twenty. The face of this Judas is that of a gentle, smiling teenager with the sidecurls (or *payot*) worn by Orthodox males, who looks out at me with hooded eyes.

W

Wine

The Sottano winery in Mendoza in Argentina produces a well-regarded red wine – from the Malbec grape – named after Judas. Dark and dense, according to experts, its colour is said to recall the blood-red imagery that accompanies Judas' name.

X

X-rated

Like the devil, Judas continues to be a name and image to conjure with in the world of horror films, mostly recently the 2013 British independent movie, *Judas Ghost*, where a group of ghost-hunters are trapped in a village hall and – as the blood starts flowing – face slaughter.

CHAPTER TWELVE

Giving Judas a Second Glance

'Tis but a game of mutual homicide,
Who have cast lots for the first death, and they
Have won with false dice – Who has been our Judas?

Lord Byron: *Marino Faliero, Doge of Venice* (1821)

Judas' guilt-by-association in the Holocaust might – indeed, some would argue, should – have seen him pensioned off once and for all in the post-1945 era. What it certainly did cause was the out-lawing of the 'Judas the Jew' stereotype from all but those most extreme fundamentalist Christian fringes where anti-Semitism continues unabated and unashamed. With such a large chapter in his poisonous past jettisoned, however, other readings of Judas' story have been able to flourish. Now that he is no longer the resident scapegoat of institutional Christianity, or shorthand for anti-Semitism, Judas is enjoying a vivid old age. His name remains readily recognised, far beyond the confines of churchgoers, while, freed from the constraints of official doctrine or dogma, the known elements in his story are in a constant state of revision and reinvention.

Jorge Luis Borges, the Argentinian essayist and short story writer, published extensively before, during and after the Second World War. He highlighted in particular Germany's 'chaotic descent into darkness', attacking the Nazis' racist ideology, and their corruption of culture to inflame anti-Semitism. It is within this context that his enigmatic short story, 'Three Versions of Judas', appeared in 1944.[1] Its structure is typical of Borges' output, written as if it is a scholarly factual account of a writer and his *oeuvre*, but that writer is fictitious. The 'deeply religious' theologian, Nils Runeberg, lives in the Swedish city of Lund at the start of the twentieth century and tackles the gospel story of Judas 'with a singular intellectual passion',[2] determined to make his academic reputation. In all, Runeberg pens not one but three attempts to explain Judas' motivations, each reworking what he had previously proposed in an effort to win universal approval. It is, in Borges' telling, a doomed task.

There has been, ever since the short story appeared, much debate about quite what Borges was saying. 'Three Versions of Judas' could just as easily be taken as an exposé of the pointlessness of biblical scholarship, seeking absolute truth from texts that, because of their nature, can never yield it, as it could an attack on the machinations and inventions of institutional religion itself, endlessly reshaping its holy books in an ultimately futile effort to make an impact, or to improve the human condition. Or it may be a reflection on how hard it is, given the available material, to arrive at a final, definitive version of Judas.

Runeberg's first Judas is, pretty much of his time, not the devil-fuelled traitor of the medieval church, but the figure who had become increasingly popular since the Enlightenment. De Quincey is even name-checked. In handing over Jesus, Runeberg writes, the political revolutionary Judas might even be seen as a noble hero, keen to 'set in motion a vast uprising against Rome's yoke'. Of the betrayal, Runeberg describes it as 'a predestined deed . . . which has its mysterious place in the economy of the redemption'.

This first version, too, represents the more contemporary theological view of Judas. This holds that since Jesus is the Son of God – as John puts it 'the word was made flesh, he lived among us, and we saw his glory, the glory that is his as the only Son of the Father'[3] – everything that happens to him on earth must be part of God's plan. And so Judas' betrayal is Runeberg's 'predestined deed' – an integral part of that divine plan that will see Jesus rise from the dead and save humankind. That is why Jesus tells Judas after identifying him as the betrayer, 'What you are going to do, do quickly.'[4] Judas is playing his part, working from an already agreed script, doing God's work, rather than the devil's.

Borges then offers a second version of Judas. When Runeberg's first theory is published in 1904, the short story tells, it is widely refuted, not just by the local 'sharp-edged bishop', but also by others who remain unconvinced. So Runeberg tries again, evolving his thinking now to see Judas as motivated by 'an extravagant and even limitless asceticism'.

It is a portrait that has a touch of Gnosticism to it. This Judas 'renounces honour, good, peace, the Kingdom of Heaven, as others, less heroically, renounced pleasure. With a terrible lucidity, he premeditated his offence . . . [he] sought hell [because he thought] happiness, like good, is a divine attribute and not to be usurped by men.' So the choice to betray Jesus is his and his alone. He is not following God's plan, but is using his own free will, albeit, as he would see it, to a divine purpose. He is not malicious or greedy, or any of the other negative qualities that had been attributed to him down the centuries. Instead he is sacrificing himself, knowing the consequences, realising that the promise of heaven is hollow, and that 'happiness [is] not to be usurped by men'. This second Judas is a realist, or even a pessimist.

When this version again falls flat on publication, Runeberg puts forward his third and most radical alternative, arguing that if God really did choose to take human form, then he would have picked the vehicle of Judas, rather than Jesus, since Judas more completely reflected all that man was capable of – for good and for ill. There are hints here of the theory Robinson Jeffers had advanced in 'Dear Judas', of a Judas–Jesus role reversal. And as Jeffers had discovered, this third take on Jesus by Runeberg is regarded by his audience as blasphemous. He has failed to explain Judas convincingly and, as a consequence, is degraded. He becomes a lost soul, 'intoxicated by insomnia'. He wanders the streets of Malmö, where he dies of an aneurysm. 'To the concept of the son,' Borges writes, 'he added the complexities of evil and misfortune.' As indeed Judas does by his role in the gospels. Borges is far too subtle a writer to provide a straightforward 'answer' to the questions he raises, in this enigmatic short story, but what it does demonstrate is both the allure of Judas, in terms of the challenge of trying to make sense of him, and, as Borges would have it, the inevitability of failure.

That warning, though, did not deter others. Greek writer Nikos Kazantzakis presents another memorable Judas in his 1953 novel, *The Last Temptation of Christ*. It was condemned by the church in his homeland – something that once would have crushed a book and its writer, but which in the latter half of the twentieth century had the opposite effect, endearing the novel to a large, admiring international audience.

Kazantzakis has Judas and Jesus working together in doing God's will, the former a red-bearded blacksmith once more cast as a Jewish zealot, who regards the Roman forces occupying his homeland as 'criminals'. It is that political, nationalistic conviction that leads him to break with Jesus over his message of turning the other cheek. 'Are we supposed', Judas asks him, 'to hold out our necks like you do your cheek, and say, "Dear brother, slaughter me, please"?'[5] This is an earthy, real-world Judas.

Kazantzakis echoes the gospels' portrait of an evil betrayer to the extent that Judas is literally two-faced, one aspect 'sullen and full of malice', the other 'uneasy and sad'. Yet for all his very human mixed-up feelings about Jesus, Judas remains in this

telling unmistakeably God's agent, what Kazantzakis character-
ises as the 'sheep dog', who guides the sometimes vacillating Jesus
to his planned sacrifice of himself for the sins of humankind.
Sheep dogs are, of course, far removed from treachery. 'We two
must save the world', Jesus tells Judas.

In what was to prove the most controversial section of
Kazantzakis' novel when it was adapted for the cinema in 1988 by
Martin Scorsese, Jesus has a dream before his ordeal on the cross.
Christianity teaches that Jesus is both fully human and fully
divine. In the dream, Kazantzakis explores the tensions that this
sets up within him. In his reverie, Jesus imagines what would
happen if he rejected his divine destiny. He could marry Mary
Magdalen. It was the scene of them consummating their bond
that caused religious fundamentalists to boycott cinemas where
the Scorsese film was shown. But the storm about their on-screen
lovemaking obscured what was potentially an even bigger volte-
face. In Kazantzakis' reworking of the gospels, it is Judas (played
in the film by Harvey Keitel) who is now no longer the traitor but
the guardian of Christian orthodoxy. He brings Jesus sharply
back to reality from his dream. And, as Jesus fondly imagines a
reunion with his elderly apostles at the end of a long life, it is
again Judas, standing by 'a withered, lightning-charred tree', who
rebukes his master and accuses *him* of being a traitor. 'Your place
was on the cross. That's where the God of Israel put you to fight.'

Judas' role may change radically, but the essential story of
Jesus' sacrifice remains the same in Kazantzakis' telling. Judas is
not required to be an evil betrayer for Jesus to die and rise from
the dead, but there is an alternative role he can play in casting
light on the Christian story. *The Last Temptation* is, arguably, a
novel about human frailty, Jesus' as much as Judas', and how our
weaknesses potentially distance and distract us from God. In a
century that had already witnessed two world wars, the Holocaust,
and the dropping of atomic bombs on Japan, it had a particular

resonance. As the most worldly of the twelve, and the most reviled, Judas provided Kazantzakis with powerful raw material to refashion.

And there is another intriguing reworking of Judas' story in Shūsaku Endō's deeply reverent 1966 novel, *Silence*. Like Kazantzakis and Graham Greene, with whom he has been regularly compared, Endō took religion as a central theme in his fiction and his life. Internationally admired, and said to have narrowly missed out on the Nobel Prize for Literature in 1994, he was one of Japan's tiny Catholic community (fewer than 1 per cent of the population).

Silence has a historical setting and tells of a Portuguese Jesuit missionary priest, Sebastião Rodrigues, who comes in the seventeenth century to nurture the crop of Catholic converts struggling to grow in the hostile soil of Japan. The authorities do not welcome such missionaries, and so he is smuggled into the country by Kichijiro, a devout convert. His 'face with its fearful eyes like a spider',[6] Kichijiro turns out to be Rodrigues' Judas when he betrays him to the magistrate for a handful of coins.

So far, so straightforward, as a representation of Judas, but Endō then reimagines the Calvary narrative. The captured Rodrigues is forced by the Japanese authorities to watch as fellow Catholics are tortured and killed. He can save himself, they tell him, by the simple act of stamping on an image of Christ – called a *fumie*. In his distress, Rodrigues cries out to God to end the suffering he is witnessing, and to give him the courage to resist his tormentors, to be truly Christ-like.

'Men are born into two categories,' he records in his prison diary, 'the strong and the weak, the saints and the commonplace, the heroes and those who respect them. In time of persecution the strong are burnt in the flames and drowned in the sea; but the weak, like Kichijiro, lead a vagabond life in the mountains. As for you (I now spoke to myself) which category do you belong to?

Were it not for consciousness of your priesthood and your pride, perhaps you like Kichijiro would trample on the *fumie*.'

Kichijiro, Endō's Judas, is then simply 'weak' in his faith. But what about Rodrigues, the Jesus-like figure? Real life, the novelist suggests, is much more complicated than goodies and baddies, the pure and corrupt. However straightforward such clear categories sound when reading the gospels, or living them out in ordinary times, they become unattainable when under duress. Rodrigues hears no voice of God to keep him on the path of the righteous. It is he, not Judas, who succumbs to despair. And it is he who betrays his Lord. Sensing the futility of martyrdom without knowing that God is on his side, he allows himself to be persuaded to recant.

As soon as he has done it, though (in another parallel with the Judas of the gospels), he regrets his actions. He is now no better than Kichijiro, he tells himself. He is Judas. That is how easy, he realises, it is to cross the line between good and evil.

In the final scene of the novel, Kichijiro comes to Rodrigues and asks him if he can hear him confessing his sins. As one who has renounced his priesthood by his denial of God, he is no longer allowed to do so, but Rodrigues reasons that to say no would be a failure to show Christ-like forgiveness to his betrayer. He shares his dilemma with the still-silent God. 'But you told Judas to go away: "What thou dost, do quickly". What happened to Judas?'

And, finally, Rodrigues gets his longed-for reply from God, but it is not the message he is expecting. God denies rejecting Judas. 'I did not say that,' the voice tells Rodrigues. 'Just as I told you to step on the plaque [the *fumie*], so I told Judas to do what he was going to do.' What Rodrigues has taken to be his own, and Judas' betrayal, is nothing of the sort. It is God's work, and it comes at a cost. 'For Judas was in anguish,' the voice says, 'as you are now.'

Released from hell

If those outside clerical ranks, some devout, some not, were revisiting Judas' betrayal in such powerful ways, what of the mainstream churches themselves in the post-war years? Was there any response to this growing chorus that suggested Judas had been done an injustice by all the blame heaped on him over the centuries?

Mostly, there has been silence on the subject of Judas. It is, in one sense, an improvement on noisily condemning him, and using his example to scapegoat others. And that silence may have been intended as a form of atonement for their sins over the centuries in promoting the image of 'Judas the Jew' with such appalling consequences. Even on those occasions when the twenty-two gospel passages in which he features come up in the rota of readings for mass, Judas is today generally overlooked as a topic for homilies, theological tracts, bishops' letters or papal pronouncements. It is as if he is an embarrassing skeleton left over in the cupboard from an earlier age of intolerance. If no one mentions him . . .

On a more positive note, a transformation has taken place in relationships between Christianity and Judaism, reversing almost two millennia of hostility. There have been practical gestures – the removal in 1960 by Pope John XXIII of the reference to 'perfidious Jews' from Catholicism's Good Friday liturgy. In medieval times, it had been followed by violent attacks on Jews and Jewish homes and businesses.

Five years later, as part of the landmark Second Vatican Council's commitment to modernise the Catholic Church, the declaration *Nostra Aetate* was published by Pope Paul VI, formally acknowledging the close ties that bind Judaism and Christianity. It had been the early church's anxiety to deny these, and so to separate itself from its own roots, that had fuelled the promotion of Judas as a scapegoat to damn all Jews. So, in that same spirit of atonement, almost 2,000 years after the event, Catholicism declared that the Jewish people bore no collective guilt for Jesus' death.

Perhaps it should come as no surprise, given his toxic role in Christian anti-Semitism, that *Nostra Aetate* made no reference at all to Judas. Elsewhere, too, significant mentions by Christian leaders of Judas have been few and far between. When they do let his name slip, the connotation is still usually negative. In April 1971, for instance, when Pope Paul VI was giving a Maundy Thursday reflection lamenting the number of priests and nuns who had left the active ministry to get married as a result of the changes instigated by the Second Vatican Council, he chose to describe them as 'Judases'. Re-reading the story of the treacherous apostle, he said, he had not been able to prevent himself thinking of 'the escape of so many brothers in the priesthood'.[7] It was a new entry to the list of wrongdoers – in the eyes of the church authorities, at least – whose 'crimes' could be bemoaned by scapegoating Judas.

With the dawn of the new millennium, however, there has been a small shift in attitudes within Catholicism towards Judas. Oberammergau, still going strong, commissioned a new script for a special staging of its passion play in the year 2000. Previously tough on Judas, albeit with some mitigation, the new version, in Act VII, features the 'Despair of Judas'. The title may be impeccably medieval, but the words are not. The choir sings out: 'See Judas fall into the darkness below. Why does no brother hold him tight? Gracious Lord grants mercy to the ostracised.'[8] Judas is now presented as a reminder of God's mercy towards the marginalised. That is another new role for him.

The impending publication – in *National Geographic* in 2006 – of the rediscovered *Gospel of Judas* gave added impetus to whatever slight revisionist tendencies existed in the upper echelons in Rome. Monsignor Walter Brandmüller, the German head of the Vatican's Committee for Historical Science, was reported as having told fellow Bible scholars at the start of that year that he believed Judas was ripe for a re-reading. While the *Gospel of Judas* would contain 'no new historical evidence', he confidently (and accurately) predicted, it may yet 'serve to reconstruct the events and the context of Christ's teachings as they were seen by the early Christians'.[9]

Monsignor (later Cardinal) Brandmüller subsequently rejected as exaggerated reports that he was part of an official 'campaign' to rehabilitate Judas. He even dismissed the *Gospel of Judas* as 'a sort of religious novel', but that earlier intervention did at least prompt another Vatican insider, the Italian writer and senior layman Vittorio Messori (who had co-written a book with Pope John Paul II) to raise his voice too. Referring to Jesus' observation in Matthew's gospel that it would have been better if Judas hadn't even been born, he said: 'Jesus' words about Judas are tough [but] Judas wasn't guilty. He was necessary. Somebody had to betray Jesus. Judas was the victim of a design bigger than himself.'[10]

So Judas is no longer taboo in the Vatican, nor is he utterly reviled by all, but any talk of the authorities revisiting his case as a potential miscarriage of justice is premature. Pope Benedict XVI, John Paul's successor, published in 2007 the first of the three-part exploration of the life of Christ that became the defining act of his papacy. The theologian-pope did offer a few more crumbs of comfort than his medieval predecessors might have done over the arguments traditionally deployed against Judas. 'The light shed by Jesus into Judas' soul was not completely extinguished. He does take a step toward conversion: "I have sinned", he says to those who commissioned him. He tries to save Jesus, and he gives the money back. Everything pure and great that he had received from Jesus remained inscribed on his soul – he could not forget it.'[11]

That is as far as Benedict was prepared to go. He gave no

ground to those who argued that Judas was God's agent, doing what had already been decided for him. Instead, he returned to the favourite medieval image of 'Judas desperatus'. 'Now he [Judas] sees only himself and his darkness; he no longer sees the light of Jesus, which can illumine and overcome the darkness. He shows us the wrong type of remorse: the type that is unable to hope, that sees only its own darkness, the type that is destructive and in no way authentic.'[12]

If Benedict refused to be moved by the pleas to reconsider Judas' role, the 'Preacher of the Papal Household' was. By tradition, the Good Friday sermon in Saint Peter's is delivered by the Preacher of the Papal Household, always a Capuchin Franciscan Friar, and for the last thirty years Father Raniero Cantalamessa (his surname means 'sings the mass'). His 2014 oration took as its theme, 'Why did Judas become a traitor?'

The short, uncontroversial answer given by Father Cantalamessa was 'love of money'. Then, however, he ventured into more contentious areas. 'Judas began with taking money out of the common purse,' he said, quoting John's gospel. 'Does this say anything to certain administrators of public funds?'[13] This pointed question took the congregation back to the dawn of capitalism in medieval Italy, when Judas with his money-bag was used to scapegoat the emerging class of merchant-bankers. The church's suspicion of the money economy has never wholly gone away.

Father Cantalamessa next went on to mention drugs barons, the Mafia, arms manufacturers and those who organise the sale of human organs as being potential beneficiaries of a careful reflection on the lessons of Judas' example. And he had one more sensitive target. The false apostle, he argued, was recalled whenever 'a minister of God is unfaithful to his state in life'.

This preacher had in previous years caused headlines by referring from the same pulpit to the scandal of child sex abuse by priests as, for too long, something swept under the carpet else-where in the Vatican. On this occasion, it was thought that his remark was likening Judas' betrayal to that of paedophile priests.

Finally, he chose to pose a question that had been debated for 2,000 years – whether Judas was in hell. The gospels offer no definitive statement (on Judas, or anyone else who might be there), but it has long been taken as read by Christianity. Father Cantalamessa, though, stressed there was always the chance of repentance, right up to the very last minute, and said that he, for one, hoped therefore that Judas had taken up that offer in his final moments in Hakeldama.

That, of course, was the opposite of the impression Pope Benedict had given in his published remarks on Judas a few years earlier. While the disparity between the two can hardly be described as a major schism, it did at least give the topic an airing. Hell is another of those taboos in mainstream Christianity, gener-ally considered too medieval and condemnatory to name check at a time when the emphasis is on a God of love. Even the devil is rarely mentioned. No Pope since Paul VI in the early 1970s has managed more than the odd fleeting reference to Satan.

Some Catholic traditionalists, however, refuse to collaborate in the silence, and line up instead with those Evangelical and Pentecostal churches which trumpet a literal reading of the gos-pels on the subject of the devil, and of hell. It exists, they assert, and contains the worst of sinners such as Judas. The conservative American Cardinal Avery Dulles, a distinguished Jesuit theolo-gian, argued in an essay published just before his death in 2008 that the language of scripture about Judas 'could hardly be true' if he had been saved from damnation. He rejected any notion of an empty hell – i.e. one without Judas – as the 'thoughtless opti-mism' characteristic of the modern age.[14] Some clerics still require Judas to be held up only as a cautionary example to believers.

The question of where Judas is spending eternity is not only of interest to cardinals and traditionalists. It also intrigued the American playwright, Stephen Adly Guirgis, though he came up with a very different answer. Raised Catholic, like Kazantzakis, Greene and Endō, he takes faith as one of his central themes, and is almost alone in Broadway, London's theatre land and elsewhere in successfully mining the once ubiquitous, now almost forgotten, seam of religious drama, the modern-day inheritor of the mystery and passion play tradition. Adly Guirgis' *The Last Days of Judas* opened in New York in 2005, following in the footsteps of his *Our Lady of 121st Street* and *Jesus Hopped the 'A' Train*, a parable set on Death Row. His urban argot may be expletive-ridden, but his purpose is serious.

In *The Last Days of Judas*, his chosen vehicle is an unusual courtroom drama, with an appeal being heard in purgatory from Judas, who is petitioning to be allowed out of hell. Among the various disreputable witnesses called are Judas' traditional fellow inmates, Satan, Pontius Pilate and Caiaphas. Mary Magdalen pops up to share that Judas was 'Jesus' favourite, too . . . almost an alter ego to Jesus . . . the shadow to Jesus' light'. But the court's decision is not the real point. That is posed most directly by Judas' widowed mother, here called Henrietta, as she recalls burying her son in the soil of Hakeldama after his suicide, with no one else willing to help her. 'If my son is in hell,' she wails, 'there is no God.'

Adly Guirgis suggests that since there is no limit to God's forgiveness (the gospels make the point repeatedly), then Judas too must be forgiven. The logic is hard to deny, but it is a conclusion some in the churches still resist. Judas, they say, remains a special case.

Burning bright

With formal religious attachment in steep decline in the West, and the teaching of the gospels now patchy in many schools, polls suggest many now are ignorant of the most basic details of the gospels. In the United Kingdom, a 2012 newspaper survey found that 21 per cent of those questioned were not able to say what happened on either Good Friday or Easter Sunday. 'Something to do with rabbits' was one response. And 23 per cent were not able to identify Jerusalem as the location for the events of the Easter story. Judas, though, continues to poll rather better. In the same survey, 55 per cent identified him as the betrayer of Christ.[15] His name recognition – that most prized of twenty-first-century commodities – remains high.

And that is despite the fact that – within living memory – some age-old associations with his name have died out. In my hometown of Liverpool, a port city and therefore more international than most in the customs that have washed in with the ships, there was a ritual that survived well into the twentieth century in the streets of Dingle, in the south end of the city, close to the docks, of marking Good Friday morning by carrying round a Judas scarecrow door to door, collecting pennies. Then the cry would go up, 'Burn Judas', and a bonfire would be lit.[16]

It was something my mother's generation could recall happening well into the 1930s, and there are police reports from 1954 of officers intervening to stop 'Judas fires' being started. 'It is comic', the records note, 'to see a policeman with two or more Judases under his arm, striding off the Bridewell and 30 or 40 children crowding after him crying Judas!' Another source claims a sighting as late as 1970.[17]

It shares most of the characteristics of the wider British habit on 5 November of first parading then burning a 'guy', representing Guy Fawkes, the Catholic conspirator whose Gunpowder Plot of 1605 was an attempt to blow up the Protestant monarch, James I, and the Houses of Parliament. And it is a short journey from Judas' treachery to Guy Fawkes'. But the origins of this tradition in Liverpool seem to have been visiting sailors from

Portugal, Spain, Greece, or even Latin America, landing in Liverpool over Easter and sharing their own customs. They had long been doing something very similar in other ports. An 1874 illustration from *The Graphic* and an 1884 report from *The Times* both describe Portuguese sailors flogging a Judas effigy on the deck of their ships in London docks on Good Friday,[18] but by the early twentieth century such spectacles had ceased. Why it persisted longer in Liverpool is hard to know. The city's heightened religious divide – with Catholic and Protestant populations at loggerheads well into the 1970s – may well provide some context.

'Burn Judas' was street theatre. Moving indoors to popular theatre, Judas gained another new lease of life in 1970 with Andrew Lloyd Webber and Tim Rice's *Jesus Christ Superstar*, a musical so popular that star-laden revivals continue to this day. Its Judas is a composite of nineteenth- and twentieth-century interpretations that follow the structure of the gospel narrative but turn him once more into a misunderstood anti-hero. He is the rebel who feels let down when Jesus embarks on a divine rather than a political mission, but he is also in love with Jesus – he reprises 'I Don't Know How To Love Him', Mary Magdalen's ballad from earlier in the show. His insistence on following his own conscience, however mistaken he may be, casts him as victim, not villain, and leads to his lonely death by hanging from a tree, but it is mitigated when he rises to join in the final chorus.

Judas' credits in recent decades could fill pages: from New Zealand literary novelist, C.K. Stead, and his 2006 *My Name Was Judas*, where the betrayer has survived into old age to reflect sceptically on Jesus' claims to divinity,[19] to the more populist Jeffrey Archer and his attempt the following year (co-authored with a senior Vatican advisor) to recreate Judas' tale through the eyes of his son, Benjamin;[20] from a transsexual Judas, now known as Judith, in Monty Python's 1979 send-up of Jesus, *Life of Brian*, to

The Graphic reports on Portuguese sailors flogging a Judas effigy in London Docks on Good Friday (1884).

Terrence McNally's 1998 play, *Corpus Christi*, which shifts a gay Jesus and his all-gay apostles to Texas to face their persecutors. Though all base their characterisations to some degree on the gospels, and all reach very different conclusions, the proliferation of Judases, many of them controversial, some high profile, reveal an enduring quality about him – that his story is both compelling and capable of infinite adaptation. He dances to the music of time.

Y

Yellow

There are many theories as to why yellow became so synonymous with Judas that there are now pots of fashionable paint on sale called Judas Yellow. Was it because yellow stars were given to Jews to wear from the thirteenth century onwards and Judas was cast by Christianity as the stereotypical Jew? Or because yellow was close to gold, the colour of riches but also of greed, Judas' sin? Or because in nature yellow can be the colour of treachery, the alluring yellow of Laburnum blossom that disguises its poison?

Z

The Zodiac

With the zodiac's twelve signs, and twelve houses to each chart, astrologers have inevitably been tempted to draw parallels with the twelve apostles (despite Catholicism's official disapproval of horoscopes). Judas was allotted Pisces in recognition that he was temptable, but later remorseful, and that he gave way to despair.

CHAPTER THIRTEEN

Three Contemporary Versions of Judas

There were things the man said that filled Iehuda with fire, as if his blood had turned to flame.

Naomi Alderman: *The Liars Gospel (2012)*

Hyman Maccoby concludes his 1991 study of Judas Iscariot's role in fuelling anti-Semitism with a plea that the apostle's name be banned because its history means it will always serve as a term of racial abuse, on a par with derogatory phrases once used for black people. 'Every time the word "Judas" is used to mean traitor,' he argues, 'the anti-Semitic conviction latent in the expression is made manifest. To call someone a Judas is to say, "you are as bad as the Jews when they betrayed Judas". Jewish evil is thus established as a universal benchmark for the ages.'[1]

His argument goes too far for most, though, including that minority of Jews who still call their children Judas. And what of all the stage, screen and fictional Judases who would have been lost in the decades since his book was published if his plea had been answered. Some of what he wanted to achieve, though, has come about. Those once routine references to 'Judas the Jew' are no longer heard. Whether some still harbour them in their hearts is harder to know. The Dreyfus Affair and Nazi Germany demonstrate that, just when the 'old' Judas appears finally dead and buried, he can rear up again to inflame prejudice with disastrous consequences. 'The devil's deepest wile', the French poet Baudelaire once wrote, 'is to convince us that he doesn't exist.'[2]

A casual trawl of the internet, especially among fundamentalist Christian groups in the United States, confirms that 'Judas the Jew' rhetoric still occasionally surfaces, drawing on that interpretation of the gospels – once strongly endorsed and encouraged by the church authorities but now disowned – that makes all sorts of assumptions about his background to cast him alone as an archetypal Jew, and ignores the fact that Jesus and the rest of the apostles were Jewish too.

There are other details about him in the gospels – plainer, more straightforward, and unique to him – that require no such leaps, and it is these aspects found in the accounts of Mark, Matthew, Luke and John that still resonate regularly in contemporary uses of Judas' name and example. In the British House of Commons, for example, in 1975, the maverick Conservative Member of Parliament, Elaine Kellett-Bowman, a near contemporary of Margaret Thatcher, surprised onlookers and fellow members listening politely to her florid denunciation of the Labour government for betraying local tax-payers involved in a dispute in Derbyshire by flamboyantly flinging thirty pieces of silver onto the clerks' table that separated opposition and government benches.[3] One coin hit a junior minister in the eye. Kellett-Bowman was roundly condemned and ridiculed – her card was probably marked as a result, since she never rose to high office – but no one needed to ask her to explain the origin of her protest. It was readily understood.

In Hyam Maccoby's terms, could her gesture be taken as anti-Semitic? She would certainly have denied it. Was inferring that the front bench ministers she faced were Judases tantamount to libel? The laws of libel and defamation do not apply, of course, in the precincts of the Houses of Parliament, but might there have been a case if the incident had happened elsewhere?

In 1907, John Murray, the grand old man of British publishing, brought out in three volumes *The Letters of Queen Victoria*. The book had the blessing of the royal family, six years after the death of the long-serving monarch, and became the great literary event of the season. Its price – three guineas, or thirty-three shillings – was, however, regarded as extortionate, as the reviewer in *The Times* noted. (The backdrop to the remark was an ongoing battle between authors and publishers over the allegedly excessive mark-up on books.) Had the newspaper left it at that, Murray would have had to suffer in silence. However, it later published on its letters' page a complaint, signed with the nom de plume 'Artifex', accusing Murray of exploiting the late queen in an act of 'simple extortion' to gain 'thirty-two pieces of silver'. That was, it implied, his profit on the sale of each copy – its true cost to him being just one shilling.[4]

Murray sued for libel, claiming he had been tarred by implication with the name Judas Iscariot. The four-day trial, in May 1908, made headlines. It turned out that 'Artifex' was in fact a *Times* leader writer, who had been put up to penning the letter by a Mr Hooper, the manager of the paper's readers' Book Club, who was in the forefront of the campaign against publishers' mark-ups. When Hooper was called as a witness, he refuted any suggestion that the mention of thirty-two pieces of silver was intended to call to mind Judas. 'I should say he [Murray] was not compared to him,' he protested. It was simply 'a bright way of putting it'. The judge, Mr Justice Darling, was having none of it. Though the name Judas had not been stated, he ruled that the implication was clear and Murray had been libelled. The publisher was awarded £7,500 in damages, a verdict that caused a standing ovation in the court.

English legal precedent, then, suggests that to imply someone is like Judas Iscariot, even if you don't actually say the name aloud, is defamatory, if you cannot prove a close resemblance.

Causing the death of the Son of God, as Judas' role is still popularly understood, is quite a benchmark to meet. Yet the accusation is still heard, sometimes making headlines, rarely contested, and always hurting. Here are three contemporary versions of Judas.

(1) Bob Dylan

Bob Dylan makes several appearances in Judas' story in the twentieth century. The suggestion, in one of the verses of his protest song, 'With God On Our Side', that Judas was doing God's work (mentioned in the Prologue) may not have been strikingly original, but his fame gave it more prominence than any who had uttered it before, reaching a different audience from readers of political pamphlets or literary novels. Dylan was the major figure in the world of contemporary music when he released 'With God On Our Side' in 1963.

That much-remarked-upon reference to Judas was to rebound on him spectacularly three years later when, on 17 May 1966, at Manchester's Free Trade Hall, a discontented concert-goer wrote himself a place in musical history when he cried out, into the lull between numbers, to accuse Dylan of being a 'Judas' himself. In 1963, the fresh-faced Dylan had accompanied himself on 'With God On Our Side' on harmonica and acoustic guitar. Three years later, he had swopped his acoustic guitar for an electric one. It was regarded by diehard fans as an out-and-out betrayal. They wanted him to remain unchanged. That he didn't came to symbolise a wider loss of innocence as Dylan (in their eyes) crossed from anti-establishment icon to embrace the corporate mainstream.

The singer's own response on the night in 1966 was defiant. He shouted at his band to play the next track ('Like A Rolling Stone') 'fucking loud' on their electric guitars. Fittingly its lyrics are about someone having to alter course because they had grown disillusioned at how they have turned out. The description could have applied either to Dylan himself, as he sought to move on with his music, or also just as easily to Judas, in that modern reading of him as the revolutionary who grew tired of Jesus' talk of establishing a heavenly kingdom when there were Roman overlords to expel from Israel.

'By doing something new, by doing something unexpected,' writes the psychoanalyst and academic Adam Phillips in his essay 'Judas for Now', 'Dylan was Judas . . . In retrospect we can see that what sounded like a betrayal was innovation. Something was betrayed – the folk-music tradition – to make something else possible. This Judas was bringing a new vision, a new sound.'[5]

What is striking about Dylan's own reaction is not so much his fury on the night itself. That is understandable in the heightened atmosphere of a music gig. Rather it is that his anger about being called Judas was still close to boiling point almost fifty years later, in an interview with the American magazine *Rolling Stone* in 2012. Despite all the accolades, the sales and the plaudits of the intervening five decades, justification if it were needed of his wisdom in changing to electric, he launched into a tirade against 'wussies and pussies' who questioned his muse. 'These are the same people that tried to pin the name Judas on me. Judas, the most hated name in human history. If you think you've been called a bad name, try and work your way out from under that. Yeah and for what? For playing an electric guitar. As if that is in some way equitable to betraying our Lord and delivering him up to be crucified. All those evil motherfuckers can rot in hell.'[6] Judas clearly still has quite some power to wound.

(2) David Oldfield

In 1998, Tony Abbott was still climbing the ladder of preferment in Australia's Liberal Party that would later elevate him to the prime ministership in 2013. Among his closest aides until recently had been David Oldfield, but two years earlier Oldfield had been exposed as secretly working with one of Abbott's opponents, Independent MP, Pauline Hanson, to help her set up her rival, populist One Nation Party. It briefly captured the public's mood (and the Liberals' votes) on the issue of immigration levels. Oldfield later joined One Nation and sat as its representative in Parliament.

Abbott shrugged off the betrayal at the time it happened in 1996, but this devout Catholic, who trained for three years to be a priest, is well known for his plain and sometimes incautious remarks. He was famously challenged by the Labor prime minister, Julia Gillard, in October 2012, in her spirited, off-the-cuff attack on his casual and repeated misogyny that went viral around the world (but didn't stop Abbott later winning the general election).

Uncharacteristically, Abbott waited two years to take his revenge on Oldfield, and when he did, he reached for the name of Judas. In 1998, he was taking part in a run-of-the-mill debate in the House of Representatives when he revealed quite how much the betrayal had hurt. 'Politics makes for odd bedfellows,' he said, 'and even the best of us get saddled with our personal Judas.'

In some legislatures such a reference might have been deemed 'unparliamentary', but in the macho world of Australian politics, it only added to Abbott's appeal. For his part, Oldfield – who moved on from politics to become an outspoken popular broadcaster – kept his thoughts private.

(3) Luis Figo

In 2002, the Portuguese star, Luis Figo, was being hailed as the best footballer in the world. He had moved in 2000 for £37 million from his club Barcelona to their bitter rivals, Real Madrid. Fans at

Barcelona took a very dim view. For them, it was not so much a commercial transfer as the most colossal betrayal ever. And, in popular culture, that made Figo a Judas.

There is a long history of fans reacting in this outraged way to losing their favourite sportsmen and -women, but Figo's experience stands out. In November 2002, he returned to the Barcelona ground, Nou Camp, with his new club for '*El Clásico*', as every game between Spain's two biggest teams is known. Fans inevitably greeted him with chants and banners assailing him as 'Judas'. The barrage of sound from the 120,000 in the stadium was so strong at one point that Figo put his hands over his ears.

It was, though, just the start. Another of the banners read, 'Figo because of you, I had to kill my dog.' The accusation was bizarre, and unexplained, but it was as if, wrote the football pundit, Sid Lowe, who witnessed the events, Figo had done 'a deal with the devil'.[7] Every misfortune could be blamed on him, and he was adjudged to taint everything. There was, Lowe reports, a joke going round the city of Barcelona before the match. Figo was given his wage packet at Real and remarked to the cashier that it was very heavy. 'Yeah, well,' he replied, 'thirty pieces of silver weighs a bit.'

When Figo moved closer to the crowd at one stage in the match so as to take a corner, he was pelted with a barrage of bottles, mobile phones, coins and cigarette lighters. Strangest of all the missiles, though, was a *cochinillo* – the severed head of a suckling pig. It landed face up on the pitch near to Figo, and made a perfect picture for the newspapers around the world the next day. Who, it was asked, would have gone to all the trouble of smuggling a pig's head in through security? It would require quite some planning and premeditation. And to what point?

In medieval Europe, the pig's head was deployed on occasion as an anti-Jewish symbol – a reference to Jewish dietary laws that prohibit the eating of pork. Though Figo wasn't Jewish, one possibility was that at least one member of the crowd had decided he was not just a Judas, but 'Judas the Jew'. That may be attributing too much premeditation and prejudice to overheated football fans, but the echoes are curious. Figo later professed himself bemused and wounded. 'It never even enters your head that someone could go into the stadium with a *cochinillo* . . . that's not sport; I understand rivalry and that goes beyond it . . .'

Saint Judas?

In *The Big Bang Theory*, the hit US comedy about four socially awkward science geeks at California Institute of Technology, one of the episodes, endlessly repeated on TV, always makes me think of Judas Iscariot. The oddest character of all in this quartet of oddballs, Sheldon Cooper, introduces his girlfriend, the almost-as-geeky-but-not-quite Amy Farrah Fowler, to one of his favourite films, Steven Spielberg's *Raiders of the Lost Ark*, the first outing for adventurer Indiana Jones (Harrison Ford). Amy tries hard to like it so as to further her pursuit of the emotionally detached Sheldon, but her scientist's objectivity wins out over her instinct to indulge him when, at the end, she points out the 'glaring story problem'. 'Indy' plays no role in the outcome of the story, she says. The Nazis' attempts to steal the Ark of the Covenant would have failed with or without his intervention. 'If he weren't in the film,' Amy notes, 'it would turn out exactly the same.'

She might deliver exactly the same verdict on Judas' role in the gospels. Yes, he has more than his share of dramatic and memorable moments (in comparison to the other apostles), notably that kiss and then his grisly death. And yes, the portrait that the gospels paint of him has attracted so much attention down the centuries that his name is still instantly recognisable today, remains synonymous with betrayal, and carries a rare power to wound those labelled modern Judases. But would Jesus' fate have been any different if Judas hadn't been there at all? Or if he'd remained in the ranks of the faceless apostles about whom next to nothing is known?

The Jewish authorities would certainly have found a way of arresting Jesus, the man his followers hailed as the new messiah, without Judas. His subsequent conviction – as reported in the gospels – involved no appearance by Judas as a star witness for the prosecution, the insider revealing secret plans and discussions within the Jesus movement. Therefore, without Judas, Jesus' trial, death and resurrection would have followed as before. And Christianity in their wake. So Judas' betrayal was, in practical terms, unnecessary.

There are two ways of facing up to this. The first is to accept that events are not always necessary in order to be significant, or to be real. There is a school of thought – espoused most eloquently by the novelist Graham Greene – that says that the unnecessary details in the gospels are the true ones, because they serve no other agenda. In telling of Judas' betrayal, the gospel writers might simply have been repeating what had happened, as passed down in the oral tradition of the early Christians over forty years. They then struggled to make sense of it – hence the variations in the accounts from Mark, through Matthew to Luke and John.

The second is to ask, if there is no practical need for a betrayer, then what of the betrayal itself? Or the handing-over, as some translators of the Greek in Saint Paul's letters would have it, though the gap between the two seems narrow enough when dealing with passing to a hostile authority someone who trusts you. Paul's letters, which predate the gospels and are the closest in time to actual events in Jesus' life, speak only of him being betrayed. They do not attribute it to any one individual. Indeed, the closest they come to naming a culprit is when Paul subsequently writes of God 'giving up' his son for the benefit of humanity. That's the big picture, and Paul is very much a big picture man.

Can God betray? Christianity would say no. So Jesus' betrayal must be part of his plan. The individual who does the betraying is God's agent and should not carry any blame. That is the message of Paul's letters, but it is a challenging one that sits uneasily with many listeners. Human nature likes to blame, likes to identify and punish wrongdoers, likes to separate out the good and the bad. That is why Christians have long been so drawn to the figure of the devil.

The teaching of the church (and of Judaism and Islam, all monotheist faiths) is that God is omnipotent, responsible for everything, blessings as well as betrayals, and that the devil is absolutely not his opposite and equal, but rather doomed to defeat. It is there in the Book of Revelation that ends the New Testament. But the practice of the church has been more pragmatic. It cannot quite stomach allowing God to take responsibility for the bad things that happen, for what many call the evil in the world, so that is hived off and attributed to the devil.

There is an argument that makes Judas part of that process. Saint Paul has Jesus' betrayal as a small part of the divine plan, not something worth dwelling on, but, when the gospel writers came subsequently to follow that narrative in their accounts, they baulked at reporting God as having sullied his hands by handing over his son. And so they put a human face to the betrayer.

In Paul's account, the nameless betrayer is doing God's will, and therefore is his agent. In the gospels, and for 2,000 years in the theology of the church, Judas the betrayer is Satan's tool. His actions result not from God's prompting, but from a variety of motivations, all embraced with free will, that ultimately lead back to the devil pulling his strings. These are the two Judases of this biography. They both still exist, and feed off each other.

The gospel Judas, though, opened up a whole range of other

possibilities as the early Christians shaped their church. Satan's tool, the human face of evil, of despair, the unforgiveable one who rejected Jesus, even after being called to be an apostle and to share in the first Eucharist, became the scapegoat. He was the one on whom was projected the things the church, in every age, considered wicked or threatening, most often the whole Jewish race, an attribution made solely on a disputed interpretation of Iscariot.

Yet the gospel Judas remains an intriguingly contradictory character. The four writers build him up by degrees. Mark, the most reliable historically, since he wrote first, is also the briefest in dealing with Judas. He names him straightaway as the betrayer, but then gives him no plausible motive for going to the chief priests. They are, moreover, the ones who suggest paying him for his act of betrayal. Matthew reverses this and has Judas demand money, introducing the charge of greed that has stuck like mud ever after. And he adds the unforgettable detail of the thirty pieces of silver. However small a sum that might have represented, its symbolic power has been immense.

Matthew's portrait is nuanced. He also allows Judas remorse, when he has him try and fail to return the 'blood money', a detail often overlooked by medieval artists, and he alone accords him a tragic ending, his lonely death by suicide, later amended in the Acts of the Apostles to become a more public humiliation of bursting asunder with poisonous innards spilt on the ground. It is only with Luke and John, third and fourth chronologically in the gospel accounts, that Judas is painted into a corner as unremittingly bad. Luke makes him unambiguously the tool of Satan, and John develops the connection, casting Judas on the basis of no named evidence as a cartoon baddie, the duplicitous, self-serving, heartless, crooked treasurer of the Jesus movement.

As the gospel Judas evolves, he gathers maleficence and becomes ever more a role model for Christians of how not to be and how not to act. And so outside circumstances started to shape the figure of Judas. John's elaborate embroidering on the other three gospels was influenced by the concerns and conflicts in the emerging Christian Church at the start of the second century, just as Mark had reflected the world of 70 CE when he put pen to papyrus. The great driving force behind developing further the gospel Judas was the tensions between those who saw Jesus' legacy as part of Judaism, and those who saw it as something separate and ultimately a rival to the faith system that had produced it. 'Judas the Jew', a curious construction since every one of the twelve original apostles was a Jew, became the scapegoat onto whom the early Christians could project negative images of Judaism itself.

That is one of his lives, the one that gained most traction down the ages, to terrible effect right into the twentieth century, but the twenty-two references to him in the gospels have given rise to many other incarnations because, despite their brevity, they contain sufficient question marks and gaps to invite every generation thereafter to come up with their own answers for their own times. These are the many Judases who have moved through 2,000 years of history: Judas the merchant-banker with his money-bag; Judas the closet gay giving Jesus a passionate kiss; Judas the hen-pecked husband; Judas the sex maniac; Judas the corrupt cleric; Judas the comic idiot of the passion plays; Judas the reactionary, standing out against change; and Judas the revolutionary hero, chasing an earthly paradise. The list is long and is still getting longer.

What is it about the Judas of the gospels that has made all this possible? It is that recognisable humanity at the heart of his story, separate from the purpose of the gospels and from the core Christian story, that rests in the description of a friendship between Judas and Jesus. There is something very intimate about sitting around a table with someone and breaking bread together. It is an experience everyone has had. And going on an adventure with someone, leaving your home town, crossing the country and arriving in a big city. Then that friendship turns sour and becomes destructive. We have all been there as well. Whether we choose to admit it or not, there is a sliver of Judas in all of us. It is what makes him so compelling.

And all of us, too, at some stages in our lives, have been betrayed, or experience what has happened to us as a betrayal, whether it be at work, in our families, or a broken relationship. And betrayal leaves us raw. That is why we respond so readily to other stories about betrayal – of King Arthur by his illegitimate son, Mordred, or of Shakespeare's Othello by his intimate advisor, Iago. And it is why the Judas of the gospels has had such a resonance inside and outside Christianity, and continues to do so in more secular times.

Judas produces mixed reactions. Since we all know the pain of betrayal, we want to see him punished. Yet, since we have all, at some time, been cast by others as betrayers, even if we regarded ourselves as acting for the best, we are open to versions of Judas' life that rehabilitate him. That is why the reappearance of *The Gospel of Judas* in 2006, accompanied by headlines about reversing a historical miscarriage of justice in his case, had such immediate and universal appeal.

Yet even that positive re-reading of the lost gospel was a betrayal of what is actually said. 'I felt that the team's interpretation may have been so well received by our society', cautions Professor April DeConick, who noted the errors in translation that allowed this to happen, 'because a heroic Judas may allow for collective healing in the aftermath of the atrocities of World War Two.'[8] It is back to context.

And the very word betrayal can mean many things to many people. 'In psychoanalysis', writes Adam Phillips, 'betrayal is called, variously, weaning, the birth of a sibling, the Oedipus complex and puberty. At each of these developmental stages, in the psychoanalytic story, the child suffers what feels like a breach of trust, a loss of entitlement, a diminished specialness.'9 So the flexibility of the gospel Judas even matches the flexibility of the very concept of betrayal itself.

Perhaps one day, if the fledgling reform movement under way in the Vatican gathers steam, the many faces and roles of Judas might be acknowledged. He could even be allocated a golden halo (rather than Fra Angelico's black one) as, for example, the patron saint of those who lose a loved one to suicide, or as the symbol of Christianity's counter-cultural message of forgiveness for an unforgiving modern world.

Canonisation of Judas, though, while it would give his biography another eye-catching twist, would, I fear, diminish him. For the appeal of his life story is surely his ambiguity: that he can speak to both the betrayed and the betrayer in all of us, that he can represent treachery and progress simultaneously, that he can be scapegoated by both the churches and their opponents to their own ends, that he can be both Satan's tool and God's agent. It has made for an incident-packed life. And will continue to do so.

Sir Laurence Whistler's Judas window, Dorset

Gabriel's features adhered throughout their form so exactly to the middle line between the beauty of Saint John and the ugliness of Judas Iscariot, as represented in a window of the church he attended . . .

Thomas Hardy: *Far From The Madding Crowd* (1874)

On a crisp November afternoon, the small, strung-out Dorset village of Moreton is dozing under a blanket of autumnal leaves in red, gold and caramel. Tucked away deep in the lanes between Dorchester and the sea, it appears, at first glance, an unlikely place to have got itself into a tangle over Judas. But controversy there certainly was here, sufficient to make headlines, and it took place not 500 years ago, as is usually the way with these once notorious sites of religious disputes in the English countryside, but in the last decade of the twentieth century. Judas still has the power to divide communities.

The battleground was the local parish church. It is certainly well signposted from the village green, if absent from the skyline. Saint Nicholas' church is dedicated to a fourth-century Syrian bishop who, Christian legend holds, was the model for Father Christmas. The arrows that point to it down a narrow lane, however, quickly run out and, tramping along in my wellies, I begin to suspect that, like its namesake, Saint Nicholas' church is spoken about but never seen. Finally a dog-walker directs me to retrace my steps and turn in through the gates of the local big house, where generations of Framptons have presided for over 600 years as lords of the manor. 'You'll find it lurking behind some trees,' she says.

It's an unusual way of putting it, but accurate. Halfway up a grand drive, the thick foliage on one side parts to reveal a squat, grey, eighteenth-century church, with a small tower, standing on a slightly raised bank. It is not the sort to set hearts a-flutter, and there is, as I get closer, something decidedly odd about it. It is as if its windows are popping out of their sockets.

Saint Nicholas' fame – or infamy – rests on these twentieth-century additions. In October 1940, the building took an almost direct hit from a German bomb, dropped, it is variously speculated locally, either because the church was near to the now-closed RAF Warmwell, or because the army unit billeted up at the manor had failed to close their blackout curtains properly and the pilot had one more missile to discard before heading back over the Channel. A great hole was blown in the north wall, and all twelve stained-glass windows were shattered beyond repair.

With local enthusiasm and a grant from a post-war reconstruction fund, however, Saint Nicholas' was restored and reconsecrated ten years later. The basic shape and design remained the same but, in place of the traditional reds, blues and greens of the old nineteenth-century windows, it now featured five strikingly original, many say unique, clear sheets, engraved by the artist, Sir Laurence Whistler.

Brother of the more famous Rex, Sir Laurence was single-handedly responsible from the late 1930s onwards for reviving the intricate technique of glass engraving (using a tool to mark the glass, rather than applying caustic substances, as in the more popular glass etching), which had been popular in the seventeenth and eighteenth centuries. His enthusiasm had been born, he recalled, when he wanted, as Elizabethan gentlemen before him had, to inscribe with diamond point one of his poems on the window of a house where he was staying as a young man. Over the next sixty years, right up to his death in 2000, he developed this enthusiasm into an art form of images *and* words, using stippling to achieve on glass a delicacy that, he said, was beyond pen or pencil. 'In glass engraving, you are putting on the light not the shade. If you are drawing in ink or pencil, you are necessarily putting dark lines on a white or light surface, but glass engraving is always imagined as seen against a shadowy background, so that you are always drawing things by the light on them.'

He took on larger and larger commissions, including the windows at Saint Nicholas', which many regard as his masterpiece. After the initial five, he added to their number up until 1984, when all twelve spaces were filled, linked by the theme of light – physical and spiritual. And it is the curious, almost mystical luminosity the windows generate, seemingly too big for their frames to contain, which draws me in as I approach the church.

In the late 1980s Sir Laurence, whose studio was just along the Dorset coast at Lyme Regis, offered Saint Nicholas' the gift of a thirteenth window, of Judas Iscariot. It had originally been made for a joint exhibition he had staged with his son, Simon, who followed him into glass engraving. 'The number thirteen in itself', he said at the time, 'suggested Judas as the thirteenth disciple.'

Though the parish council originally welcomed the gift, some forty-four churchgoers, backed by their vicar, subsequently wrote in to object. Deadlock resulted and dragged on for several years until the fate of the gift was referred up to the local diocese where, again, after initially positive reactions, Sir Laurence's offer was declined. A world-renowned artist being snubbed by the church where his twelve existing windows drew in visitors from all round the globe became news. Camera crews and reporters descended.

The reasons given by the objectors were various: that the depiction of Judas hanging by the neck was too graphic ('hanging is not a very comely thing', the artist replied drily); that his dress was too modern – jeans, jumper and wellingtons – for such a historic church; that the traitor of the gospels had nothing to do with the linking theme of light found in the other windows. Some, though, seem simply to have been displaying that 2,000-year-old antipathy to Judas. They didn't want the traitor to darken the door, or lighten the windows, of their church.

A compromise was agreed with the artist, whereby the window was placed on indefinite loan by the church with the county museum in Dorchester. And there it remained for twenty years, displayed in a simple wooden frame, until 2013, when a new incumbent at Saint Nicholas', the Reverend Jacquie Birdseye, hoped that attitudes had changed sufficiently for Judas to be allowed into the church. This time there was unanimity in favour when she raised the matter, and in the summer of that year, the window was finally installed, albeit with no ceremony for fear of reigniting debate.

The sun is low in the sky as I step inside Saint Nicholas'. 'Please close this gate and door', reads a Hardy-esque notice on the porch gate, 'lest a bird should enter and die of thirst'.

It is only when confronted by something so different as the effect created by Sir Laurence's windows that I realise how conditioned I have become to expect the inside of a church of any age to be gloomy and closed off from the outside. Even the largest and most celebrated stained-glass windows change the light inside great abbeys and cathedrals, introducing a note of artifice by bathing everything in jewel-like colours. And those more ancient, or more puritan, places of worship that prefer plain glass usually frost it over to avoid the congregation becoming distracted. Sir Laurence's windows, by contrast, bring inside and outside together as one. It is as if the sacred interior is illuminated by spotlights from outside, while the engravings seamlessly join the pews with the landscape.

In the east windows, from 1955, the passage of the seasons is charted from Christmas trees to the wheat of the harvest, each with words about light from the Bible. And in the more complex Galaxy Window, the last of the twelve, at the west end, a spiral of stars travels from Alpha to Omega in a vast panel that is more impressionistic. It also seems to be imbued with pagan overtones, but these presumably didn't cause offence to the parishioners when they were installed.

The detail on each panel – often in tiny medallions, created by the engraver's tools – is extraordinary, but I'm still puzzling whether, while being awestruck by Sir Laurence's technical skill, I actually like the result, when I realise that I still haven't spotted the thirteenth window that has brought me here. There's no trace of Judas. On the piety stall is a range of guidebooks, postcards and bookmarks, all detailing Sir Laurence's achievement (and covering Saint Nicholas' other claim to fame: the grave, in its overflow cemetery elsewhere in the village, of T.E. Lawrence, Lawrence of Arabia, a cousin of the Framptons). But, as I flick through the literature, there is once again not a word about any Judas window. I am just starting to despair when I turn over one of the bookmarks. On the side that was facing up had been a motif of butterflies from the Trinity Chapel window, which I can immediately place, but overleaf, unmistakeably, is the figure of Judas, hanging from a branch, and bathed in light. It is captioned 'The Forgiveness Window'.

Feeling foolish, I now make a further, very slow, circuit of the church in search of this Judas panel, even going so far as to breach normal ecclesiastical etiquette to stand on one of the pews in case it has been lost at the bottom of the Lightning Window in the vestry, which is partially hidden by a wooden screen. But all to no avail.

At which point, with the autumn light starting to fade quickly, I retreat to the porch, where I find a telephone number for the Rev.

Birdseye. I'm looking for Judas, I explain, when she answers (which at 4 p.m. on a Sunday afternoon is excellent service). 'Ah,' she explains, 'you need to go outside to see it.'

We're back to Judas the Outsider. He may have been allowed back to Saint Nicholas after a two-decade exile, but not inside the body of the church. He has been allotted a blind window at the back, overlooking a plot of graves. It is glazed, but immediately behind it is black wooden boarding, so it can't be seen from the pews. Judas, it seems, still causes sufficient embarrassment for the worshippers at Saint Nicholas' for him to be accorded special treatment. They have put him in the most obscure place they can think of, rather like hanging an unloved decoration, handmade by a spinster aunt who is a guest every Christmas Day, on a branch at the very back of the tree.

It makes for a neat metaphor about Judas' current standing in the world – widely known, often spoken of, no longer perhaps such a pariah, but still handled with caution. But that may be to judge the parishioners of Saint Nicholas' too harshly. Having already filled all twelve available window spaces inside the church, Sir Laurence would have known that the only possible location for his depiction of Judas was here, on this lonely east wall at the rear of the building. It was the location that gave him the idea for his subject.

Later, reading his own notes on the whole dispute, I find him arguing that such a placement is not a relegation, or a half-hearted gesture of inclusion, but rather an echo of the medieval church's habit of including the 'uncouth and unholy' in corbels – brackets – and gargoyles on the external surfaces of its places of worship. The church, Sir Laurence mused, is the one place that good and evil can be thus accommodated. And the artist was keen, too, on the use of a blind window because, as he explains, he wanted his Judas to be a 'shadowy' figure, which would have been much harder to achieve if the engraving was back-lit as well as front-lit, as is the case with all his other panels.

The effect of the one-way flow of light is certainly in keeping with Judas' story. He feels more trapped in his surroundings than the other figures inside the church. Long and narrow, the panel begins with a gnarled branch from which a rope is slung, pulled tight and looped around Judas' neck as he hangs, feet swinging slightly forwards. His back is to the viewer, neatly sidestepping the dispute in New Testament accounts about the manner of his death (we don't see his stomach, so there is no call for it to burst asunder), or any charge of gratuitous violence or voyeurism. In Judas' right hand is the traditional symbol of the treasurer's money-bag, still grasped tightly even in the moment of death, though not as outsized as in some medieval depictions that strained to damn the merchant-bankers. From his left, though, open with fingers splayed, fall the thirty pieces of silver, down towards the ground where, on contact, they turn into flowers. No longer a bleak field of blood, Judas' death place is here transformed into a spring meadow, symbol in religions and beyond of regeneration, rebirth and redemption.

Judas is dressed in simple workman's clothes. This is not the monster of legend. He has become, as elsewhere in the twentieth century on stage and in fiction, a kind of everyman. We too, the engraving suggests, could have followed the same path.

The only comment that has been registered since the controversial window was installed, Rev. Birdseye tells me later, asked why the church had commissioned a new window about a gardener. Sir Laurence, I can't help thinking, would have loved the ambiguity of that response. Mary Magdalen, when she first meets the risen Christ next to the empty tomb on Easter morning, mistakes him for a gardener.[1]

The most striking feature of the window, though, is the light that streams down from the heavens and onto Judas as he dies. Contrary to those objections from parishioners, it connects this panel with the theme that unites all the others inside the church.

Judas no longer has about him something of the night. Even the worst sinner, if that is indeed what he was, can be saved by God's light. It makes for a tender scene. Sir Laurence called it 'The Forgiveness Window'. He intended his Judas, he said, to be 'timeless and relevant to any age, and to ordinary people'.

The Forgiveness Window at the Church of Saint Nicholas, Moreton,
Dorset.

Acknowledgements

I found myself recently, as part of a newspaper assignment, travelling in a car with Jeffrey Archer, the peer, best-selling novelist and former British Conservative politician. He was once a great favourite of Prime Minister Margaret Thatcher, who appointed him deputy chairman of her party, but he was subsequently jailed for perjury. We were going to visit a long-term prisoner he had befriended while behind bars. On the way home, the subject of Judas Iscariot came up. Archer had, in 2007, published his fictional *The Gospel According to Judas*. I confessed to being hard at work on a biography of Jesus' betrayer.

'Let me give you a word of advice,' he offered affably. 'You won't make any money out of it. I'd assumed that Judas' name would sell books, but my book about him was the only one of mine that failed commercially.'

So I should start by thanking him for that guidance, which, probably foolishly, I have overlooked. It's not that I don't want this book to reach a wide audience. I do. But I believe the best chance of achieving that is to write about a subject that fascinates me and then convey why to readers. And Judas and I go back a long way.

Our most sustained encounter was in the mid-1990s when I was researching *The Devil: A Biography*, later televised. They say that, for an author, one book leads naturally to the next, and in reading so much about Judas, so often seen in the medieval imagination as Satan's tool, I knew then that I wanted one day to write about him. It has just taken me twenty years to get round to it.

Another nudge in that same direction had come with an earlier encounter in 1993, oddly on a television set in Pinewood Studios, recreating the Last Supper for a British documentary fronted by the novelist, Howard Jacobson. It was called *Sorry, Judas*, and drew on Hyam Maccoby's research into Judas' role in fuelling anti-Semitism. I was sitting round a long table between the popular broadcaster Rabbi Lionel Blue and the religious historian, Karen Armstrong, munching grapes, breaking bread and sounding off. I'm not sure which of the twelve of us was meant to be Judas, but it was a hoot.

The start of the long road that has finally produced this book, however, lies in my long-ago Catholic childhood. Judas was always the apostle who attracted me most. He was like us. The other eleven seemed unapproachable, too good by half, eminently suitable when I was looking for a confirmation patron saint, but not otherwise. Judas, though, sounded real. I'm not sure what that says about the youthful me, my guilty conscience, or the state of my developing faith. Nothing too damning, I can only assume, since I still try to practise it.

There have been many others attracted by Judas, some in recent times, despite our age routinely being defined as secular, sceptical and scientific. It's another sign that something more profound, possibly spiritual (though it is a much misused word), is going on beneath the surface of declining church attendance figures and high-profile outbursts by militant atheists. The selection of writers, artists, theologians, theorists and polemicists I have explored in these pages reflects my own judgement as to who has either added to Judas' biography, or who best illustrates changing opinions about him. Others may favour different texts or paintings or tracts to the ones I have mentioned. It is a mark of Judas' continuing pull that there are so many to choose from.

And, since the building blocks of any life of Judas are the gospels, I have, again selfishly, chosen a translation of the Bible that seems to me both to bring it alive in everyday language and remain true to the original. All quotations are from the *New Jerusalem Bible*, published by Darton, Longman & Todd in 1974.

Among those who have given of their time, expertise and enthusiasm as I have been writing this book, my special thanks go to: Simon Banner; Rachel Billington; the Rev. Jacqueline Birdseye of Saint Nicholas', Moreton; Frank Cottrell-Boyce; Lucinda Coxon; Clare Dixon; Fiona Fraser; Professor Albert Gelpi and Barbara Gelpi, both of Stanford University; Robert Hanks; Guy Martin; Mandy Marvin at Saint John's College, Cambridge; Louis Michel; the Rev. Sarah Oakland of Saint Peter and Saint Paul's, East Harling; Catherine Pepinster; Sarah Newton; Toby Roberts; and Nicholas Robinson at the Fitzwilliam Museum in Cambridge.

I must also acknowledge a debt to the academics whose detailed studies around various aspects of Judas' long and evolving story have sustained my fascination for him, and informed my research: Professor April DeConick of Rice University; Professor Susan Gubar of Indiana University; Professor Karen King of Harvard; the late Hyam Maccoby, Professor Kim Paffenroth of Iona College; Professor Elaine Pagels of Princeton; and the late Géza Vermes. Above all, my profound gratitude goes to Dr Janet Robson, associate lecturer in art history at Birkbeck College, University of London, for good-humouredly sharing her expertise on the iconography of Judas in medieval Italy.

I have been wonderfully well looked after, at Hodder by my editor, Katherine Venn, and by Rachael Kichenside, Ruth Roff, Kate Craigie, Juliet Brightmore and Penelope Isaac, and elsewhere by my agent Piers Blofeld. Most of all, thank you, now as always, to my family, to Siobhan, to Kit and to Orla, who have willingly, encouragingly and often laboriously accompanied me on this journey, sometimes on the road, other times in spirit. They mean everything.

Peter Stanford
London: September 2014

Notes

Prologue

1 *Struwwelpeter* – 'Shocked Peter' – is a German children's book of cautionary, moral tales, first published in the mid-nineteenth century, but popular both in Germany and in translation worldwide for much of the twentieth century.

2 John 17:12 – rendered in some more modern versions as 'the one who chose to be lost'.

3 Pope Leo the Great, Sermo 53, *De passion Domini* 3, ch. 3 (*Patrologia Latina* 44): 'sceleratior omnibus o Juda et infelicior exstitisti' ('the wickedest and unhappiest man that ever lived').

4 Dante Alighieri, *Inferno* XXXIV: 60–63

5 For example, in my 2013 book, *How To Read a Graveyard*, I visited Greyfriars' Kirkyard in Edinburgh, scene in the seventeenth century of the massacre of 400 prisoners, which thrives on its reputation as 'the most haunted place in the whole city'.

6 Matthew 27:3–10.

7 Adrian J. Boas, *Jerusalem In The Time of the Crusades: Society, Landscape and Art in the Holy City Under Frankish Rule* (London, 2001).

8 Acts 1:15–26.

9 Joan E. Taylor, ed., *The Onomasticon by Eusebius of Caesarea* (Jerusalem, 2003).

10 Jas Elsner, 'The Itinerarum Burdigalense: Politics and Salvation in the Geography of Constantine's Empire', *The Journal of Roman Studies*, 90 (2000).

11 D. Meehan, ed., *De Locis Santis* (Dublin, 1958).

12 See Yair Bar-El et al. 'Jerusalem Syndrome', *British Journal of Psychiatry*, 176 (2000): 86–90.

13 Featured on Bob Dylan's 1964 album, *The Times They Are A-Changin'*.

14 As reported in *The Times* (12 January 2006).

15 Matthew 27:3–10.

16 Mark 14:22–25; Matthew 26:26–29; and Luke 22:19–20.

17 If not prescribed in doctrine, where the church holds that it cannot confirm or deny anyone's presence in hell, except of course the devil.

18 John 18:15–16.

19 Acts 1:20–21.

20 Matthew 4:1–11.

21 II Chronicles 28:3.

22 By the National Geographic Society on 9 April 2006.

23 Bob Dylan, in an interview with *Rolling Stone* magazine, 18 September 2012.

Chapter One

1 Luke 6:14–16.

2 John 14:22.

3 Mark 3:19.

4 Matthew 10:4.

5 See, for example, Hyam Maccoby, *Judas Iscariot and the Myth of Jewish Evil* (London, 1991).

6 John 6:71.

7 Géza Vermes, *Who's Who in the Age of Jesus* (London, 2005).

8 See Maccoby, *Judas Iscariot*.

9 Joshua 15:25.

10 See Maccoby, *Judas Iscariot*.

11 Ibid.

12 Ibid.

13 See the German vorname.com website, with a section of names that are '*verbotene*'.

14 Genesis 35:23.

15 I Maccabees 3:3.

16 Acts 5:34–39.

17 See Maccoby, *Judas Iscariot*.

18 Acts 15:22.

19 G.A. Williamson (trans.), *The Church History* (London, 1989).

20 Mark 6:3; Matthew 13:55.

21 Mark 1:29.

22 Mark 14:66–72.

23 See Maccoby, *Judas Iscariot*.

24 Frank Kermode, 'My Man', *London Review of Books*, 2 January 1997.

25 John, for example, describes Jesus making more than one visit to Jerusalem; the other three writers restrict him to one. More specific discrepancies between the four in relation to Judas will be examined in subsequent chapters.

26 Melvyn Bragg: 'Bride of Christ or Enemy of the Church?' *Daily Telegraph*, 23 March 2013.

27 Matthew 9:9.

28 John 20:2.

29 Acts 4:13.

30 More of a list of sayings attributed to Jesus than any sort of account, to judge from surviving fragments, whose actual dating is hotly contested.

Chapter Two

1 See G.F. Hill, *The Medallic Portraits of Christ, The False Shekels, The Thirty Pieces of Silver* (Oxford, 1920).

2 See R. Axton, 'Interpretations of Judas in Middle English Literature,' in P. Boitani and A. Torti (eds), *Religion in the Poetry and Drama of the Late Middle Ages in England* (Cambridge, 1990).

3 'Saint Brandan' by Matthew Arnold and 'The Last Chantey' by Rudyard Kipling.

4 David Hare, *The Judas Kiss* (London, 1998) Act II, sc. 2.

5 Mark 3:13.

6 Mark 3:13–15.

7 René Girard, *The Scapegoat* (Baltimore, 1986).

8 Mark 3:19.

9 I Corinthians 11:23–24.

10 Notably William Klassen, *Judas: Betrayer or Friend of Jesus?* (Minneapolis, 1996).

11 I Corinthians 15:5.

12 Romans 8:32.

13 Matthew 10:4–5 Luke 6:15–16.

14 John 6:71.

15 Mark 14:10–11.

16 Mark 14:2.

17 Frank Kermode, 'My Man', *London Review of Books*, 2 January 1997.

18 Mark 14:3–9.

19 Matthew 26:6–13.

20 Ibid.

21 Matthew 26:14–16.

22 Luke 22:1–6.

23 Peter Stanford, *The Devil: A Biography* (London, 1996).

24 Luke 22:6.

25 Luke 4:1–13.

26 John 1:14.

27 John 6:70.

28 John 6:66.

29 John 6:71.

30 John 12:1–8.

31 Pope Francis, since his election in March 2014, has repeated the phrase often.

32 John 12:6–7.

33 See Girard, *Scapegoat*.

34 Hyam Maccoby, *Judas Iscariot and the Myth of Jewish Evil* (London, 1991).

35 John 13:2.

36 Mark 14:20–21.

37 Ibid.

38 Susan Gubar, *Judas: A Biography* (New York, 2009).

39 Matthew 26:20–25.

40 Mark 14:22–24.

41 See Girard, *The Scapegoat*.

42 Luke 22:19–23.

43 John 6:54.

44 In 2001, as Cardinal Bergoglio, he washed and kissed the feet of twelve AIDS patients at a hospice in the Argentinian capital.

45 John 13:1–2.

46 John 13:2–3.

47 John 13:3.

48 John 13:21–26.

49 John 13:26.

50 John 13:27.

51 John 13:28.

52 John 13:28–30.

53 Mark 14:27.

54 Mark 14:43–45.

55 Mark Lawson, 'Shedding the Veil', *The Tablet*, 14 May 2014.

56 Matthew 26:50.

57 Used by James Moffatt, the Church of Scotland biblical scholar and translator (1870–1914).

58 Matthew 26:55.

59 Luke 22:48–49.

60 John 18:1.

61 John 18:3.

62 See Maccoby, *Judas Iscariot*.

63 John 18:1–11.

64 See Girard, *The Scapegoat*.

65 John 17:12.

66 Mark 14:50–52.

67 Mark 14:54.

68 John 18:15–16.
69 Mark 14:56.

Chapter Three

1 Quite how long an olive tree can live is a matter of debate among scientists. Studies carried out by the University of Crete on a tree reputedly over 2,000 years old in the village of Ano Vouves endorsed claims as to its age. There is one on Sardinia, called 'Cormac's Tree', that is said to be 3,000 years old. See E. Parker and A. Lewington, *Ancient Trees* (London, 2012).

2 Thomas Pakenham, *Meetings with Remarkable Trees* (London, 1997).

3 Published online by newadvent.org.

4 Told in Carol Drinkwater, *The Olive Tree: A Personal Journey through Mediterranean Olive Groves* (London, 2008).

5 Rowan Williams, 'Gethsemane', *The Poems of Rowan Williams* (Oxford, 2014).

6 Mark 14:35–36.

7 Mark 14:47; Matthew 26:51–52.

8 Luke 22:51.

9 John 18:10–11.

10 Mark 14:29–31; Matthew 26:33–35; Luke 22:33–34; John 13:36–38.

11 Jaś Elsner, 'The Itinerarum Burdigalense: Politics and Salvation in the Geography of Constantine's Empire', *The Journal of Roman Studies*, 90 (2000), 181–195.

12 Alfred Edersheim, *Life and Times of Jesus the Messiah* (London, 1886).

13 Leo Papadopulos (trans.), *Four Great Fathers: Saint Paisius the Great, Saint Pachomius the Great, Saint Euthymius the Great, and Saint Theodosius* (London, 2007).

14 Luke 22:28–30.

15 Luke 22:36–37.

16 Mark 14:29–31.

17 John 13:27–30.
18 John 13:31–17:26.
19 Mark 14:33.
20 Mark 14:41–42.
21 Mark 14:44.
22 Mark 14:53–54 Matthew 26:57–58.
23 Luke 22:54–55.

Chapter Four

1 Quoted in Simon Sebag Montefiore, *Jerusalem: The Biography* (London, 2011).
2 Matthew 27:3.
3 Mathew 27:1.
4 Matthew 27:2.
5 Matthew 27:3–5.
6 Acts 1:23–26.
7 Acts 1:25.
8 Acts 1:18–20.
9 When it promulgated the document Nostra Aetate.
10 Acts 15, also mentioned in Saint Paul's Letter to the Galatians 2.
11 Matthew 27:24–26.
12 Hyam Maccoby, *Judas Iscariot and the Myth of Jewish Evil* (London, 1991).
13 Ibid.
14 Frank Kermode, 'Improving the Story', *London Review of Books*, 27 May 2010.
15 Exodus 21:32.
16 Zechariah 11:13–14.
17 Matthew 27:9.
18 Zechariah 11:12–13.
19 Second Book of Samuel 20:9–10.
20 Genesis 37.
21 Psalm 41:9.
22 John 13:6–18.

23 Dennis MacDonald, *Does The New Testament Imitate Homer?* (New Haven, 2003).

24 Dan Brown, *The Da Vinci Code* (New York, 2003).

25 Géza Vermes, *The Authentic Gospel of Jesus* (London, 2003).

26 Ibid.

27 Ibid.

Chapter Five

1 All quotations, unless stated otherwise, from Marvin Meyer, *Judas: The Definitive Collection of Gospels about the Infamous Apostle of Jesus* (New York, 2007). Meyer, Griset Professor of Bible and Christian Studies at Chapman University in Orange, California, was one of the team that produced the original translation published in *National Geographic*.

2 Ed. Alexander Roberts, James Donaldson and Cleveland Coxe, *Against Heresies by Irenaeus of Lyon* (published online, 2010).

3 The words in square brackets [ ] have been added by the translators as their best effort in filling gaps in the surviving manuscript.

4 April DeConick, *The Thirteenth Apostle: What the Gospel of Judas Really Says* (New York, 2009).

5 Ibid.

6 Ibid.

7 Géza Vermes, *The Authentic Gospel of Jesus* (London, 2003).

8 Ibid.

9 Genesis 4:25.

10 Elaine Pagels and Karen King, prominent scholars of Gnosticism, in *Reading Judas: The Gospel of Judas and the Shaping of Christianity* (London, 2007), stand firm by their reading of the text that it means that Judas will indeed make it into heaven.

11 Papias, quoted in Bart D. Ehrmann, *The Apostolic Fathers, Volume Two* (Harvard, 2003).

12 Ibid.

13 Ibid.

14 Ibid.

15 Hyam Maccoby, *Judas Iscariot and the Myth of Jewish Evil* (London, 1991).

16 *The Gospel of Nicodemus*, trans. M.R. James (Oxford, 1953).

17 Ibid.

Chapter Six

1 Philip Schaff and Henry Wace (eds), *The Nicene and Post-Nicene Fathers of the Christian Church: Volume 12* (Massachusetts, 1996).

2 Pope Leo the Great, Sermo 53, *De passion Domini* 3, ch. 3 (*Patrologia Latina* 44): 'sceleratior omnibus o Juda et infelicior exstitisti' ('the wickedest and unhappiest man that ever lived').

3 Lesley Janette Smith (ed.), *The Glossa Ordinaria: The Making of a Medieval Bible Commentary* (London, 2009).

4 Edward A. Synan, *The Popes and the Jews in the Middle Ages* (New York, 1965).

5 Robert Michael, *A History of Catholic Anti-Semitism* (New York, 2008).

6 Origen, *Contra Celsum*, trans. Henry Chadwick (Cambridge, 1953).

7 Ibid.

8 St Augustine, *Tractates on the Gospel of John and the First Epistle of John*, trans. John Rettig, (Washington, 1988).

9 Ibid.

10 St Augustine, *City of God*, trans. Henry Bettenson (London, 1958).

11 Augustine may also here have been using the example of Judas to attack the Donatists, schismatic African Christians of his time, who believed that suicide was a legitimate form of martyrdom.

12 Synan, *Popes and Jews*.

13 Luke 23:34.

14 The real sources for the 'Harrowing of Hell' are, first, Peter's words in Acts 2:24 – 'You killed him, but God raised him up to life, freeing him from the pangs of Hades, for it was impossible for him to be

held in its power' – and next in the First Letter of Peter 3:19, where Jesus in death is described as going 'to preach to the spirits in prison'.

15 From Marvin Meyer, *Judas: The Definitive Collection of Gospels about the Infamous Apostle of Jesus* (New York, 2007) – a collection of translations of early texts.

16 Matthew 18:21–22.

17 Meyer, *Judas: The Definitive Collection.*

18 Ibid.

19 Ibid.

20 Ibid.

21 Ibid.

22 Ibid

23 John 19:33–34.

24 M.A.S. Abdel Haleem (trans.), *The Qur'an* (Oxford, 2004), 5:110.

25 Ibid., 4:157–158.

26 Meyer, *Judas: The Definitive Collection.*

27 Ibid.

28 Ibid.

29 Ibid.

30 Mark 15:43.

31 Meyer, *Judas: The Definitive Collection.*

32 Ibid.

33 Jacobus de Voragine, *The Golden Legend*, trans. Christopher Stace (London, 1998).

34 Genesis 4:15.

35 Hyam Maccoby, *Judas Iscariot and the Myth of Jewish Evil* (London, 1991).

36 Paul Franklin Baum, 'The English Ballad of Judas Iscariot', *PMLA* (the journal of the Modern Languages Association of America), 1916.

Chapter Seven

1 C.L. Halligan and W.A. McFadzean, 'The Judas Needle', *Anaesthesia*, 68/7 (2013), 782–83.

2 Dante Alighieri, *The Divine Comedy Volume One: Inferno*, trans. Mark Musa (Indiana, 1971).

3 See L.F. Salzman, 'English Trade in the Middle Ages', *Spectrum* 7/1 (January 1932).

4 Justinian I between 535 and 554.

5 Dante Alighieri, *The Divine Comedy Volume One: Inferno*, trans. Mark Musa (Indiana, 1971).

6 Like Cerberus, the three-headed 'hellhound' of Greek mythology.

7 See Susan Gubar, *Judas: A Biography* (New York, 2009).

8 Enrique Lamadrid and Michael Thomas, 'The Masks of Judas: Folk and Elite Holy Week Tricksters in Michocan', *Studies in Latin American Popular Culture*, 9 (1990), 191.

9 As captured in Diego Rivera's 1920s mural, *Burning Judases*.

10 Reported in *The Tablet*, 1 June 1850.

Chapter Eight

1 *Bonaventure: Classics of Western Spirituality*, ed. Ewert Cousins (New Jersey, 1978).

2 http://ferrabra.deviantart.com.

3 Ernest Zitser, *The Transfigured Kingdom: Sacred Parody and Charismatic Authority at the Court of Peter the Great* (Cornell, 2004).

4 Jesus drives the moneylenders out of the Temple (Mark 11:15–19) saying they have turned it into a 'robbers' den'.

5 Exodus 22:24.

6 M.A.S. Abdel Haleem (trans.), *The Qur'an* (Oxford, 2004), 2:275–278.

7 Janet Robson, 'Envisaging Sin', ch. 3 of her PhD thesis, given to the author.

8   Ibid.

9   Janet Robson, 'Judas and the Franciscans: Perfidy Pictured in Lorenzetti's Passion Cycle at Assisi', *Art Bulletin*, 86/1 (March 2004), 31.

10 Acts 2:20.

11 H. Martin: 'The Judas Iscariot Curse', *American Journal of Philology*, 37 (1916), 434–451.

12 Kim Paffenroth, *Judas: Images of the Lost Disciple* (Louisville, 2001).

13 Adrian House, *Francis of Assisi* (London, 2000).

14 Robson, 'Envisaging Sin'.

15 Saint Bonaventura, *The Breviloquium* (New York, 2005).

16 Robson, 'Envisaging Sin'.

17 Robson, 'Judas and the Franciscans'.

18 The origins of this superstition may lie in the Old Testament, in the Book of Proverbs 28:22, where it is warned: 'He chases after wealth, the man of greedy eye, not knowing that want is overtaking him.'

19 Now in the Toledo Museum of Art.

20 Paul Franklin Baum, 'The English Ballad of Judas Iscariot', *PMLA* (the journal of the Modern Languages Association of America), 1916.

21 Hyam Maccoby, *Judas Iscariot and the Myth of Jewish Evil* (London, 1991).

22 Robert Michael, *A History of Catholic Anti-Semitism* (New York, 2008).

23 Annette Weber, 'The Hanged Judas of Freiburg Cathedral', in Eva Frojmovic (ed.), *Imagining The Self, Imagining Others: Visual Representation and Jewish-Christian Dynamics in the Middle Ages and Early Modern Period* (Boston, 2002).

24 Jeffrey Khan, *Judas Iscariot: A Vehicle of Medieval Didacticism* (Utah, 1976).

25 John 13:30.

26 Robert Held, *Inquisition: A Guide to the Exhibition of Torture Instruments from The Middle Ages* (Dorset, 1987).

Chapter Nine

1 Exodus 16:13; Numbers 11:31–34.
2 *The Tablet*, 21 February 1891.
3 J.S. Purvis (ed.), *York Cycle of Mystery Plays* (New York, 1957).
4 'Very flat, Norfolk', says Amanda in Noël Coward, *Private Lives* (1930).
5 Luke 22:44.
6 Harley 4012 in London's British Library.
7 M.R. James, *Saint William of Norwich* (Cambridge, 1896).
8 David Nirenberg (trans.), *Communities of Violence: Persecution of Minorities in the Middle Ages* (Princeton, 1996).
9 Though not unprecedented – it was the same in the porch of Freiburg Minster.

Chapter Ten

1 Quoted in Alexander Murray, *Suicide in the Middle Ages*, vols 1 and 2 (Oxford, 1998).
2 Peter Dronke, *Forms and Imaginings: From Antiquity to the Fifteenth Century* (Rome, 2007).
3 *Collected Works of Erasmus: Colloquies* (Toronto, 1997).
4 Desiderius Erasmus, *Enchiridion Militis Christiani*, ed. A. O'Donnell (London, 1981).
5 Roelof van den Brock, *Pseudo-Cyril of Jerusalem 'On the Life and the Passion of Christ'* (Boston, 2012).
6 See Susan Gubar, *Judas: A Biography* (New York, 2009).
7 See Richard Marius, *Martin Luther: The Christian Between God and Death* (Harvard, 1999).
8 Martin Luther, *Sermons on the Passion of Christ* (Michigan, 2009).
9 Helmut Lehmann and Jaroslav Pelikan (eds), *Luther's Works* (Saint Louis, 1958).
10 Ibid.
11 Gerhard Falk, *The Jew in Christian Theology* (Jefferson, 1992).

12 See Marius, *Martin Luther*.

13 Joseph Haroutunian and Louise Pettibone Smith (trans.), *Calvin's Commentaries* (Philadelphia, 1958).

14 Ibid.

15 Hyam Maccoby, *Judas Iscariot and the Myth of Jewish Evil* (London, 1991).

16 Ibid.

17 Leon Poliakov, *The History of Anti-Semitism from Voltaire to Wagner* (Pennsylvania, 2003).

18 Robert Buchanan, *The Poetical Works* (Boston, 1874).

19 Jonathan Swift, *The Complete Poems*, ed. Pat Rogers (New Haven, 1983).

20 In an exchange with Edmund Burke, detailed in Jerome Christensen's *Lord Byron's Strength: Romantic Writing and Commercial Society* (Baltimore, 1993).

21 George H. Evans (ed.), *The Theological Works of Thomas Paine* (Montana, 2012).

22 David Mason (ed.), *The Collected Writings of Thomas De Quincey* (London, 1897).

23 Ibid.

Chapter Eleven

1   The Irish poet, Brendan Kennelly, produced a bestseller with his 1991 *The Book of Judas*, a 400-page epic.

2   Hyam Maccoby, *Judas Iscariot and the Myth of Jewish Evil* (London, 1991).

3   See Piers Paul Reid, *The Dreyfus Affair* (London, 2012).

4   Ibid.

5   Sara Reynolds, 'One Traitor or Another: The Dreyfus–Judas Connection During the Dreyfus Affair', *University of Florida Journal of Research*, 13/1 (autumn 2011), 1–5.

6   Ibid.

7   Pierre Birnbaum, *The Anti-Semitic Moment: A Tour of France in 1898* (Chicago, 2011).

8 Reid, *The Dreyfus Affair.*

9 Maccoby, *Judas Iscariot.*

10 'Elgar and Religion', broadcast on BBC Radio 3 on 5 June 2007.

11 In sleeve notes for the 2012 recording of *The Apostles* by the Halle Orchestra.

12 Robinson Jeffers, *Dear Judas and Other Poems* (New York, 1977).

13 Included in the Afterword to Jeffers, *Dear Judas,* by Robert Brophy.

14 See Robert Wistrich, *Hitler and the Holocaust* (New York, 2001).

15 Mary Mills, 'Propaganda and Children during the Hitler Years' (Jewish Virtual Library, 2014).

16 See Susan Gubar, *Judas: A Biography* (New York, 2009).

17 Ibid.

18 See Kennelly, *The Book of Judas.*

19 John 13:30.

20 George Steiner, *No Passion Spent* (London, 1996).

21 David Kertzer, *The Pope & Mussolini: The Secret History of Pius XI and the Rise of Fascism in Europe* (London, 2013).

22 Maz Reinhart (ed.), *Infinite Boundaries: Order, Disorder and Reorder in Early Modern German Culture* (Truman, 1998).

23 See Kim Paffenroth, *Judas: Images of the Lost Disciple* (Louisville, 2001).

24 Helen Waddy, *Oberammergau in The Nazi Era* (Oxford, 2010).

25 Ibid.

26 Reinhart, *Infinite Boundaries.*

27 Paffenroth, *Judas.*

28 Karl Barth, *Church Dogmatics, the Doctrine of God: vol. 2* (London, 2004).

Chapter Twelve

1 As part of the collection, *Ficciones,* published in Spanish in 1944 and in English translation in 1962.

2 Jorge Luis Borges, *Labyrinths,* ed. Donald Yeats and James Irby (New York, 1964).

3   John 1:14.
4   John 13:27.
5   Nicos Kazantzakis, *The Last Temptation of Christ* (New York, 1960).
6   Shūsaku Endō, *Silence*, trans. W. Johnston (London, 1976).
7   Reported in an editorial in *America* magazine, April 1971.
8   Reported in *The Tablet*, 19 May 2007.
9   Reported in *The Times*, 12 January 2006.
10 Ibid.
11 Pope Benedict XVI: *Jesus of Nazareth: From the Baptism in the Jordan to the Transfiguration* (London, 2007).
12 Ibid.
13 Reported in *The Tablet*, 26 April 2014.
14 John Allen: *Boston Globe*, 19 April 2014.
15 *Sunday Telegraph*, 8 April 2012.
16 Iona and Peter Opie, *The Lore and Language of Schoolchildren* (Oxford, 1959).
17 Carole Sexton, *Confessions of a Judas Burner* (Liverpool, 1992).
18 Reported in *The Tablet*, 27 March 1948.
19 C.K. Stead, *My Name Was Judas* (London, 2006).
20 Jeffrey Archer and Father Francis Moloney, *The Gospel According to Judas by Benjamin Iscariot* (London, 2007).

Chapter Thirteen

1   Hyam Maccoby, *Judas Iscariot and the Myth of Jewish Evil* (London, 1991).
2   See Peter Stanford, *The Devil: A Biography* (London, 1996).
3   See *Daily Telegraph*, obituary, 6 March 2014.
4   R.J.L. Kingsford, *The Publishers' Association 1896–1946* (Cambridge, 1970).
5   Adam Phillips, 'Judas for Now', collected in *One Way and Another* (London, 2013).
6   *Rolling Stone* magazine, 18 September 2012.
7   Sid Lowe, *Fear and Loathing in La Liga* (London, 2013).

8   April DeConick, *The Thirteenth Apostle: What the Gospel of Judas Really Says* (New York, 2009).

9   Phillips, 'Judas for Now'.

Epilogue

1   John 20:15.

Index

Page numbers in *italics* refer to figures.

Picture Acknowledgements

© De Agostini/Getty Images: pages 139, 170, 195.

© Getty Images: page 200.

© Genevra Kornbluth: page 158.

Princeton University Art Museum, Museum Purchase, Fowler McCormick, Class of 1921 Fund. Photo Bruce M. White © 2014/ Princeton University Art Museum/ Art Resource NY/Scala, Florence: page 200.

By permission of the Master and Fellows of St John's College, Cambridge, UK, MS K.21, folios 47v, 48r, 50r: page187.

Staatsgalerie Stuttgart (Inv.Nr: 523 a-e), Jerg Ratgeb *Herrenberger Alter* 1519, (detail) photo © Staatsgalerie Stuttgart: page 171.

© Kit Stanford: pages 12, 67, 136, 177.

Toledo Museum of Art, Gift of Edward Drummond Libbey (1923.3154A-B), Valentin Lendenstreich *Wing of the Wüllersleben Triptych* 1503 (detail): page 165.

Württembergische Landesbibliothek Stuttgart, Stuttgart Psalter Cod.Bibl.Fol.23, fol 53r: page 163.

© Phil Yeomans/BNPS (Bournemouth News and Picture Service UK): page 277.